PEARSON   ALWAYS LEARNING

Critical Approaches to Writing about Film

Third Edition

John E. Moscowitz
Broward College

Cover image courtesy of the Everett Collection.

Pearson Learning Solutions, 501 Boylston Street, Suite 900,
Boston, MA 02116
A Pearson Education Company
www.pearsoned.com

Printed in the United States of America

000200010271670050

TS/TB

ISBN 10: 1-256-92185-8
ISBN 13: 978-1-256-92185-1

Copyright Acknowledgments

Dedication

This book is dedicated to my wife Kathy, who not only had to put up with my months of preoccupation about the book as well as its writing, but also endless discussions and questions at supper about it. Unlike the first and second editions, she was additionally enlisted to carefully edit the manuscript. For all of this, I offer my sincerest appreciation and thanks.

Acknowledgments

I would like to thank Trish Joyce for the hours we spent discussing the Learning Community concept and its manifestations in linking our two separate courses together—Film as Literature and Short Fiction—under its aegis. We have linked our two classes together the last three years and thought it would be appropriate to mention the experience at length in an appendix.

Donna Samet has been most helpful in guiding me on how to incorporate my course Film as Literature and its text into a linked Learning Community course. Since to make this a smoothly functioning reality, it involves more than just the two instructors and their students, her advice and help was invaluable.

Jeff Nasse, my Dean and head of our English department, quickly approved my application and did all he could to make sure my sabbatical leave was uncomplicated. He did so that I could get to work on the third edition expeditiously.

A substantial portion of the book was based on submissions by some outstanding students that I have had in my Film as Literature classes over the years. Past contributors from the Second Edition include Mary Beth Hofstein, Casey Cook, Holly Griffith, and J. David Bright. Present contributors whom I have had the pleasure of knowing more recently are Andres Benatar, Harrison S. Barrus, and Candice F. Woolcock.

I would be remiss if I didn't mention the guidance and help I received from Pearson's Acquisitions Editor, Deborah Schmidt. During those leisurely days back in May when I first undertook this edition through some stress-filled times in October, getting the book ready for print, she was there. Thank you, Deborah.

Finally, there are the professional journalists whose copy written reviews I borrowed with permission to use in this text.

CONTENTS

Appendices

PREFACE

It has been about seven years since *Critical Approaches to Writing about Film—Second Edition* was published. Since that time, besides a bevy of new movies that have emerged, significant changes in documentation practices and formats have occurred that must be incorporated when writing critically about motion pictures. Any new edition of *Critical Approaches to Writing about Film* must reflect such innovations. The *Third Edition* builds upon its predecessors in exploring different approaches to writing critically about the cinema.

The book is targeted for such courses as Introduction to Film, Introduction to Cinema Studies, and Film as Literature which are taught at numerous community colleges and four-year institutions. Film as Literature—which originates in English departments, often for writing credit—especially needs different models of varied approaches, formats, and lengths inherent in written discussion of film. To that end, this text furnishes theory, discussion, and examples of written reviews, critiques, comparative analyses, and documented research projects about the cinema. Techniques used to create movies are integrated into numerous instructional paragraphs and sample papers.

The text considers those writing approaches best suited for analyzing a cinematic source in the college classroom. To do so, the student explores how to

- Choose a particular perspective when reviewing a film,
- Write reviews of the same film but of varying lengths,
- Adopt a fitting tone when critiquing a movie,
- Enhance English writing skills,
- Select methods for writing comparative analyses,

- Adopt and adapt printed sources—from short stories, novels, and plays—into movies, and
- Research and then create a documented essay on a motion picture.

Critical Approaches to Writing about Film—Third Edition employs various strategies, presentations, and conventions when considering these and other procedures and topics suggested by the title. Samples of written pieces examining both classic and more contemporary cinema encompass

- Demonstrations by the author of techniques used and perspectives taken to writing film reviews, critiques, comparative analyses, and documented research papers,
- Student-written essays of various lengths, formats, and approaches to specific films, including pieces submitted as "learning community" (discussed on page vi.) projects,
- Sample published pieces by professional reviewers and film critics, and
- Analytical critiques by academic colleagues.

Numerous conventions are incorporated into writing reviews or other critical pieces on film. They help to give all well-written reviews a unity in format as to what key elements must be included. Thus, the well-written and complete review should

- Contain lead-ins, plot overviews, and obligatory credits,
- Take subjective stances and make evaluations,
- Present precursory and contemporary parallels and/or influences,
- Introduce and develop points of emphasis, and
- Create effective concluding remarks.

To illustrate such concepts and their variations, sample passages or complete essays immediately follow the text. The length of any given sample can vary greatly, as will be demonstrated in many of the chapters.

Comparative analysis is often used as a teaching tool. An entire chapter (5) is devoted to this writing approach. The comparative format has been helpful in

- Demonstrating multiple writing options on the same film,
- Illustrating how film adopts—and adapts—its literary source, and
- Portraying remakes of film classics and showing how they differ from the original in their treatment of the material in order to appeal to new audiences.

Demonstration of proficiency in research techniques and forms are the norm in many higher education courses. Those that study the various aspects of cinema are no different. Using Modern Language Association (MLA) format, this text shows in its final chapter (6) how to

- Select researchable topics,
- Employ proper means of organization for an individualized paper, including the outline,
- Consider and use varied relevant written and electronic sources,
- Gather and cull data,
- Streamline the documentation process through photocopying or screen printouts and color coding,
- Incorporate in-text (parenthetical) citations and Works Cited pages,
- Create "Documentation Packets" of secondary sources used in the body of the research paper as in-text citations, and
- Prepare both the initial and final drafts.

Since the publication of the first edition in 2000, additional audiences have been considered for possible adaptation of *Critical Approaches to Writing about Film as* a supplementary text. It has already been incorporated into First Year Experience programs, such as Composition I (English 101), and even Composition II (English 102) courses. Since most of these beginning English courses teach the research paper and documentation practices, as well as incorporate the various modes of expository writing, this text can be considered quite helpful. Its ample chapters on the review, the analytical critique, the comparative critique, and the research paper can be used in concert with any handbook or multi-sectioned rhetoric. The only difference here is that the research topics would originate from the world of the cinema rather than from a myriad of subjects within other disciplines.

The book is divided into six chapters and three appendixes, which are the following:

Chapter 1: Preparation for and the Process of Film Criticism
Chapter 2: Style and Structure in Film Criticism
Chapter 3: Types of Film Criticism: The Review
Chapter 4: Types of Film Criticism: The Analytical Critique
Chapter 5: Types of Film Criticism: The Comparative Critique (Analysis)
Chapter 6: Types of Film Criticism: The Documented Research Paper

Appendix A: Documentation of Primary and Secondary Sources of Works Cited

Appendix B: Glossary of Cinematic Terms

Appendix C: Film as Literature and the Learning Community

As can be expected, each chapter builds on material from previously presented chapters. Appendix A documents all written or film material referred to in the text from primary sources (the movies themselves and, in some cases, their literary precursors) and the secondary critical sources about them. Appendix B provides a glossary of cinematic terms as a helpful reference, including a number that have come into use since the *Second Edition*. Appendix C explores how Film as Literature can be smoothly integrated into a collaborative Learning Community construct.

Appendix C is NEW! For the first time, *Critical Approaches to Writing about Film* introduces and discusses a rediscovered approach in higher education: the Learning Community. The Learning Community concept goes well beyond "team teaching" in the same classroom to the intentional integration of curricular components (themes, historical framework, plot, mood, characterization, setting, etc.) from different genres and disciplines. Appendix C links Film as Literature to the use of this text in the Learning Community construct. Some sample applications would link Film as Literature with one of several possible Learning Community cohorts:

- Centered around a specific literary source, such as the short story, the play, or the novel;
- Based on one of the creative arts, such as Art Appreciation or Music Appreciation;
- Focused on seminal figures from courses in history, politics, or science;
- Concerned with the world of business, such as Business Law, Business Ethics, and Introduction to Management; and
- Related to social equity issues within the American criminal justice system.

Commentary follows the enhancements to Chapter 6, which focuses on creating the research paper and those documentation practices integral to its production. Aspects of such commentary and instructions would provide

- Updating MLA changes influencing in-text citations,
- Incorporating MLA Works Cited models for primary and secondary sources,

- Integrating reprinted critical literary sources and their inherent "double citations" into Works Cited pages,
- Navigating the credibility minefield of blogs and other on-line critical resources,
- Creating "Documentation Packets": rationale, features, and functioning.

Finally, *Critical Approaches to Writing about Film—Third Edition* is intended to be used as either a primary or supplementary text. This would likely be determined by how much emphasis is placed on the concepts of critical expression and the number of written assignments given as such.

It should be noted that all *unsigned* articles and excerpts can be attributed to John E. Moscowitz, author of this text.

1

PREPARATION FOR AND
THE PROCESS OF FILM CRITICISM

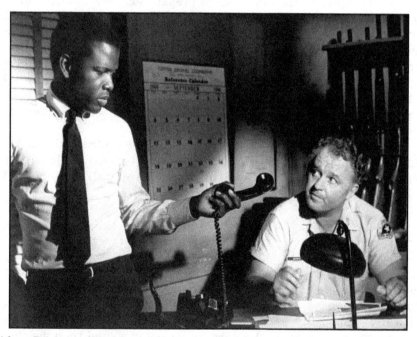

Sidney Poitier and Rod Steiger in Norman Jewison's In the Heat of the Night
(1967). United Artists. Courtesy of The Kobal Collection at Art Resource, NY.

Film has been provoking reaction via the written word ever since its earliest versions flickered hesitantly on the makeshift screens of the 19th century. Over the years, writing about film has become a cottage industry. Journalists write reviews and critical features about current and past movies. Authors pen popular books about cinema's history, its movers and shakers, and those whose faces have been projected larger-than-life before millions. Academics produce scholarly papers and theoretical monographs about the motion picture. Students labor to present their viewpoints in the form of reviews, critiques, comparative analyses, and research papers. Lately, because of the indiscriminant growth of the Internet, anyone can voice an opinion that is instantly read by millions through blogs, tweets, and such. In fact, such mass interconnectivity has proven problematic when judging the seriousness, validity, and expertise of those voicing opinions or such views presented as "facts."

This chapter offers a methodical preparation for film criticism and suggests different procedures to employ while within that process. The mindset adopted during the actual critiquing is important since one must distinguish between the objective and subjective components of film criticism and judge when one perspective is more appropriate at the expense of the other. Various types of written cinematic criticism will be introduced, including an awareness of the different audiences, approaches, styles, and lengths for reviews, critiques, comparative analyses, and documented research studies.

When writing about film, one should be acquainted with and willing to use appropriate cinematic terms. Consequently, this edition's expanded **Glossary of Cinematic Terms (Appendix B)** should be most helpful to the reader.

Preparation

In the main, we watch movies either for entertainment and/or information. Yet, if we are going to seriously understand and analyze a film, we must be prepared to watch it *critically*, not passively. To watch a film critically—especially with the intention of eventually writing about it—we need to first know the purpose for doing so and then develop a plan for executing it.

Having a Purpose

Why does one take the time and effort to critique a movie? The reasons vary, yet are similar to those for critiquing a musical work, a play, a novel, or a nonfiction book; or, for that matter, critiquing an automobile, an airline service, a college course, a restaurant, and so on. Besides informing and then persuading us as to what decisions to make regarding the worth of the object being analyzed critically, the writer must consider that entity or concept objectively. How so?

- By amassing data,
- Organizing it,
- Analyzing its meaning, and
- Making a series of evaluative judgments that lead to its ultimate appraisal.

Thus, writing the critique essentially documents the analytical/evaluative process on paper or electronically. In most critical analyses, there is also some subjectivity; yet, a skilled critic will be able to distinguish between what is objective (factual and non-opinionated) and what is subjective (intuitive and reflecting one's personal tastes) and when to use one or the other appropriately.

Why are critical papers assigned in college courses? Doing so eventually leads to tangible proof of critical reading and/or critical viewing, followed by critical thinking and organizing, then, finally, critical writing. Whereas merely relating what happened, when, and to whom in their proper order is no more than factual recounting. However, *why* and *how* something occurred and if it works for the reader/viewer, is *critical evaluation*. It is this critical perspective in its various written formats that is the objective of many college courses, including those in literature and the arts, of which film is very much a member.

But why write a critical piece on a movie? Isn't film just an expression of mass culture for a mass audience—at its lowest common denominator—that is churned out indiscriminately? Or, as some have been heard to disparagingly comment, "Y'know, it's only a movie . . ." True, many poorly conceived, shoddily crafted, and exploitive films have been foisted on the public. But they should be and have been branded as such by critics and reviewers. Excellent motion pictures have also been produced; such fine work also, therefore, should be assessed then identified as well. One must be reminded that a work being printed on paper and bound in cloth is no guarantee of quality. Like everything else creative, some efforts are inferior, many are average, and some are exceptional. Be reminded that the writing and editing of a book often involves only a handful of individuals, whereas the making of a motion picture employs hundreds—sometimes thousands—of people. They, in turn, must labor together under the relentless pressures of time, budget, and, in some instances, grueling geographic locations and sound stage environments.

There is another reason for analyzing and discussing any work of art or literature, and especially film. In many instances, a movie is a fairly accurate portrayal of life: of how the human condition is at present, was in the past, or, perhaps, can be in the future.

But if movies show life, does the cinema always portray life accurately? Neutrally? Apolitically? Fairly? Of course not! Therefore, critical discussion, either oral or written, tries to distinguish accuracy from exaggeration, evenhandedness from bias, the real from the imaginary, and fact from opinion, and even ferret out the purpose of the film (if other than to earn a profit and garner plaudits). In looking at a moving picture critically, we not only make more sense of the film but, perhaps, more sense of ourselves, the relationships that we have with others, and the multifaceted world at large.

Developing a Plan

Before watching a new film prior to writing its review, or before organizing your thoughts preceding the critiquing of a cinema classic, you must be aware of your intended *audience*. Is the review intended as a formal essay for your professor? Is it anticipated as an article in the campus newspaper? Is it perhaps envisioned as an informal verbal account for the film club? How long should it be? How knowledgeable is your audience? These and similar questions must be answered *before* you can proceed with the development of a plan. Obviously, the longer the project, the more detailed the planning must be. It might involve seeing the movie once or twice or renting the digital video disc (DVD) and taking notes. When working with older films, it may involve conducting library or Internet research for previously written critical material. Since any given film can be reviewed or critiqued from dozens of perspectives, a fresh, honest, and personal perception can still be made even after performing research.

The Tools and the Process

Once a plan of execution is decided upon, serious data gathering begins. First we will consider the materials and technology involved. If in a theater, you need the obvious: a pencil with an eraser, a notepad, and a penlight. However, if the screening takes place in the comfort of your home, a battery-powered laptop computer would be a worthy substitute for the aforementioned materials when viewing a video on a videocassette recorder (VCR) or a disc on a DVD player (with a remote control device strongly recommended).

Before we progress any further, we must first distinguish the *film review* from the other forms of written critical expression on cinema. The review makes an important distinction from the rest: it assumes that the reader may *not* be familiar with the movie in question and definitely has *not* seen it. For the other types of critical expression, the assumption is the opposite: namely, that the reader *is* somewhat familiar with the motion picture in question and *has* seen it. The review, therefore, immediately poses some restrictions on the writer. The reviewer must not retell the entire plot and not divulge the outcome of the climax and its denouement. There are times when these restrictions can be violated without integrally harming the review—as when evaluating some farces—but, in most cases, details of the climax and the ending must be avoided. (Other aspects of the written movie review will be discussed at length in Chapter 3.)

Taking Notes in the Cineplex

Critical viewing of a film is quite different from attending the local movie house with a box of popcorn in one hand, an enormous cup of soda in the other, and then kicking back in your stadium seating, over-upholstered chair to enjoy mindlessly two hours of entertainment. That is casual movie viewing and what you are left with afterwards are some random impressions and emotional reactions. Many of the subtleties have been missed because the watching has been passive rather than active. *Active watching*, however, is a crucial component of *critical viewing*. The process is analogous to reading for pleasure versus reading critically, such as to prepare for an exam. Before the viewing can take place, you must have already asked yourself questions about your expectations of the film. These expectations could be determined by your familiarity with the following:

- The director's style, biases, preferred subject matter, and/or body of work;
- The actors and whether they are well established stars, an ensemble of character players, or a cast of virtual unknowns; and
- The genre's pronounced stylistic qualities—such as those found in the western, the comedy, or the action adventure (with its increasing dependency on special effects).

It may be that the movie is a "small" or "indie" film with a low budget, an unrecognizable cast and director, and a title which gives no indication of its genre or theme. Certainly, the context of your expectations and prior knowledge would differ for such a film compared to "The Rock's" latest action blockbuster.

For the initial viewing of a film at a local theater, it is best to go when the audience is scanty. Matinees and twilight shows offer the best times, and the rates for admission are also lower than at later evening showings. Even before you seek that preferred middle aisle center seat, get all the important credits written down before the film actually begins running. The poster advertising the film in the lobby or near the outdoor box office has information as to the stars, the director, producer, screenwriter, and other major contributors to the film. Even better would be the complete list of credits furnished on the Internet Movie Database (Imdb.com). Additional information can be obtained either before or after the showing from recent reviews in the local newspaper or from such nationally circulated newspapers as *The New York Times* and *USA Today*, which are often available at your local public or college library.

First, find a seat away from others so that their rustlings or whispers won't distract you, and your penlight and jottings won't annoy them. As the credits begin scrolling, make sure the list of actors is separate from the other credits since, eventually, you will be filling in the names of the characters that the cast plays. As the movie unfolds, try to discern the setting. Sometimes, it is obvious: such as a seedy section in a wintry, contemporary San Francisco; or a tree-lined residential street with single family homes during summer in the 1950s. (Automobiles and their license plates as well as clothing help fix the era.) In many films that are set in exotic locales or historical periods, either a voice-over or information appearing across the screen announces the setting, such as "German East Africa, September 1915" (from John Huston's *The African Queen* made in 1951).

Next, try to identify the tone of the film, e.g., humorous, suspenseful, exciting, or realistic. Once determined, this then helps you decide the genre: whether it is a comedy, mystery, thriller, or drama. Of course, through word-of-mouth, television trailers, or other forms of advertising, you may already know the genre and tone. The music accompanying a movie often strongly suggests its tone.

As you scrutinize a film, you are absorbing and processing information and events as they unfurl on the screen while simultaneously silently questioning yourself about what you see. These would include inquiries about the relationship of the characters to each other as they are introduced or the significance of certain events as they occur. You would also be aware of numerous visual and symbolic clues and try to comprehend their impact upon the plot or theme.

As an example, let's look at the opening scene in Rob Reiner's 1989 romantic comedy classic, *When Harry Met Sally*. The dialogue between them is snappy, intelligent, with an edge of sarcasm. Because of the theme of their conversation—the impossibility of platonic friendships between single men and women—sexual tension is precipitated. Because Harry and Sally are packing a car, they are preparing for a long trip from Chicago to New York City. Already you have the elements of a screwball comedy and a "road" film with all the expectations of what these two forms of cinema imply.

During other films' first half hour, however, you may not yet have an idea of where the film is going and thus what you are going to emphasize in your critical paper.

An example could be the first reel of Norman Jewison's *In the Heat of the Night* (1967). We see a well-dressed African American man (Sidney Poitier) suddenly accosted by a sheriff's deputy in an empty, small Mississippi town's railroad station, and then jostled into a police car, under suspicion for first degree murder. By the second half hour, not only is he freed but we discover that he is a police detective himself—working in Philadelphia, Pennsylvania—and has begrudgingly agreed to stay there to help investigate the killing. So the film has now morphed into a police procedural.

Each review or critique, besides including the standard relevant information already mentioned on the credits and such (called *boilerplate*), emphasizes a few other points and develops them. Such positions will come gradually as you perceive patterns evolving in the film or become interested in particular aspects of it. These are the attributes that will make your review or critique different from someone else's piece. You may want to emphasize the theme of mistaken identity as the suspect keeps changing in Jewison's film. Or you may focus on the ever-changing relationship between Sheriff Gillespie (Rod Steiger) and Mr. Tibbs (Sidney Poitier). Or you may concentrate on the film's socio-historical context, given the time and place of the setting.

Throughout the movie, you will want to take notes and jot down words of anything that may be useful to you later. Do not worry about organization at this juncture. At the movie's finale, you can still glean much useful information as the credits scroll by before the theater's houselights come up, such as memorable song titles or locations where the film was shot. It is best to see the film again, either later that day or the next. If seeing a film once more is not possible, then within twelve hours of the initial screening—while the film's images, insights, and the connections between them are still vivid—study your notes carefully, re-organize them, and then write the rough draft.

Let me give another example, this time not of a review but a critique of a motion picture screened in the classroom. The class is assigned to write individual papers on *Double Indemnity* (1944). Everyone would probably furnish similar boilerplate. Each would mention the setting (Los Angeles, California, in the 1940s). Included would be mention of Billy Wilder, the director who also wrote the screenplay adapted from the James M. Cain novel. The names of the major cast members and the characters they play obviously would be listed in the students' papers. Very likely, a short paragraph would summarize much of the film's plot. (In fact, this would probably closely resemble what is typically written on the plastic jackets of movie DVDs.) But from this point on, the writers move in divergent directions. One student might concentrate on this black-and-white film's creation of atmosphere and mood, mentioning the deliberate play of light and shadows in the interior sets and the exterior scenes shot at night. Another might expound on the major building blocks of *film noir*—a subgenre of the mystery film—and how *Double Indemnify* exemplifies it. Yet another class member may explore the motifs of lust and greed of Walter Neff (Fred MacMurray) and Phyllis Dietrichson (Barbara Stanwyck) and how they lead ultimately to murder. Someone else might analyze how the title specifically relates to one of the intricate clauses of life insurance policies; then show how this normally mundane world of actuarial tables and survivors' benefits furnishes the fabric from which this gripping movie originates. Finally, one can discuss how the skillful employment of the voice-over and clever dialogue can incisively develop the characters.

I have just skimmed the surface of topics that could be written about this highly acclaimed motion picture. The differing approaches will become clearer when the different types of cinematic critical writing are presented in greater detail in succeeding chapters.

In summary, the process for viewing a film critically in a theater follows these chronological steps:

1. Attend a performance at a time when crowds are smallest, i.e., weekday matinees or twilight showings.
2. Copy any useful information on your notepad from the movie poster of your film or off the Internet prior to arrival at the cineplex.
3. Jot down useful information on a notepad from the opening credits using a penlight and pencil.
4. Discern the setting, tone, and genre as soon as possible.
5. Comprehend the interplay of the characters and their relationships to each other and the plot.
6. Focus on one or two aspects of the film that you could develop.
7. Write down anything you find important during the film, including memorable quotes.
8. Glean information from the closing credits.
9. See the film again within 24 hours. If not possible, within 12 hours read and re-organize your notes and then write your first draft.

Using the VCR or DVD Player

The videocassette recorder and now the digital video disc player have revolutionized how we see movies on television. No longer need viewers be victimized by network censors and their arbitrary edits; no longer need film enthusiasts be bombarded indiscriminately by mind-numbing advertisements coming at increasing intervals as the movie rolls toward the climax; no longer need movie fans be chained to their easy chairs and couches, daring not to leave for two minutes and miss an important segment. In fact, the preferred technology for a review or any other critical essay would be the VCR or DVD player. Using such a device, you can stop the film wherever and whenever you want, freeze a frame, or use the rewind and play buttons either to view some piece of action again or catch the exact wording of an important exchange of dialogue. You can observe a passage repeatedly to search for any subtleties in characterization, theme, or symbolism that may have eluded you previously.

Since the video of a film has been made and released after both the first- and second-run theatrical engagements, and since there is already a wealth of information available in periodicals and on the Internet, you can use such technology for not only writing a review but any other critical assignment. Writing a review is an exercise in a type of format and really is not contingent on the release date. In fact, you may be assigned to write a review on *Gone with the Wind*, even though it made the first of its many runs back in 1939.

The methodology that you use for writing a review by viewing a video or DVD is similar to that which you use when watching a film critically in the movie house. The suggestion, again, is to do preliminary research to obtain all the necessary information involving the cast and credits beforehand. Of course, you may opt to rewind and freeze-frame a few times to glean that data from the introductory and final credits. Again, as the video unfurls, you want to discern the setting, the tone, and the genre of the feature. In time, a number of aspects of the film will intrigue you so that you follow and then develop them into the main thrusts of your review or other critical piece.

The attitude that you take during a critical VCR viewing (or in a theater, for that matter) should be interrogatory. You must keep questioning the meaning of what you see and jot down these conjectures. They can always be answered after the showing has ended, when you review your notes. From the opening moments to the final credits, you need to be generating questions about such typical aspects of a film as the:

- Movie's title and its significance,
- Format of the opening credits—whether there is static background behind them or action is transpiring—and its effect,
- Purpose of the film's opening minutes regarding establishment of setting, theme, mood, characterization, and/or tone,
- References to other films,
- Patterns indicative of the director's style,
- Impact of lighting, music, sound, special effects, camera shots, costuming, and set design on the film and importance of verisimilitude,

- Strengths and weaknesses in casting,
- Lapses, if any, in continuity,
- Sloppiness, complexity, or tightness of plot, and
- Effectiveness and validity of the final scene and ending shot.

It is always best to write the rough draft while the film is still fresh in your mind. If you own the video or have borrowed it for a considerable length of time, the immediacy for writing the first draft is lessened considerably—you may not even want to write a draft until you have seen the work an additional time or two. However, if it is rented from the local video mart or through Netflix, you probably will choose to view it again within 24 hours and then write the initial version.

For writing a lengthy critical paper, you will want to see the video a few times and then integrate your critical viewing notes with your other research. This would consist of copies of reviews, plot summaries, excerpts from articles, books, and the like from the library since you will want to combine your impressions and insights with those of other critics, reviewers, and scholars. Make sure to give credit when appropriate and employ standard documentation practices such as in-text citations and a works cited page.

In summary, the process for viewing a film critically on a VCR or DVD player follows these chronological steps:

1. Gather and make available other reviews, plot summaries, lists of credits and the like.
2. Start the video. On your notepad, jot down any useful information that adds to what you already have. Especially important would be what you can gather about setting, tone, and genre.
3. Note the interplay of the characters and their relationships to each other and the plot.
4. Focus on one or two aspects of the film that you could develop.
5. If doing a comparative study, note the parallels as they unfold.
6. As you watch, jot down anything else that you could conceivably use later on in your paper. Do not hesitate to use the rewind, play, and freeze-frame functions of your VCR for quoting purposes and discerning cinematic subtleties to incorporate later in your first draft.
7. Glean information from the closing credits.
8. See the video again within 24 hours. If you own it, see it another time or two before writing the first draft. (Note that DVDs have additional features pertinent to the film that could prove valuable.)
9. Integrate and document additional source material with your notes and insights as you compose your first draft.
10. Proofread, edit, and write your final draft on your computer.

2

STYLE AND STRUCTURE
IN FILM CRITICISM

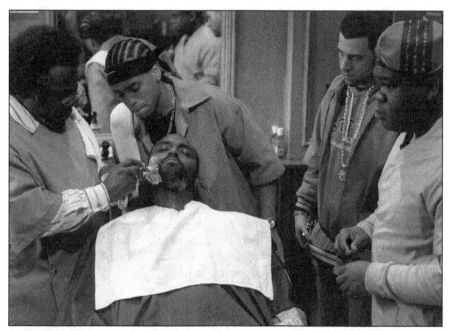

Cedric the Entertainer, Michael Ealy, DeRay Davis, Troy Garity, and Anthony Anderson in Tim Story's Barbershop *(2002). MGM.* Courtesy of The Kobal Collection at Art Resource, NY.

Once the preliminary fieldwork has been done—completed the research, amassed the data, and screened the film (either at the theater or at home on a VCR or DVD) you are ready to write. For a shorter piece of 300 words or less, an outline (which is strongly suggested for a longer paper) is optional. In almost whatever type of critical paper on the cinema that you write, *boilerplate* will be included, such as the following:

- Title of the film
- Genre
- Date of release
- Director and perhaps additional contributors
- Literary source if not an original screenplay
- Leading cast members
- Main theme (basically, what the film is about)

The main thrust of your paper will state some insights and develop them fully about the movie in question. During the course of the essay, you will probably make some evaluative judgments about the film in general, or some specific aspects of it, or both. Subjectivity is part of any film criticism because so much of this form of writing has to deal with one's personal interpretations and preferences.

———————————— **The Subjective Attitude** ————————————

Subjectivity is an essential element of the review and, to only a slightly lesser degree, any other type of critical essay: thus, it should be incorporated into your piece. By definition, any of the four types of critical work—review, critique, comparative analysis, or documented research paper—must do more than merely summarize the plot. All four types of critical papers mentioned above and covered in detail by this book in Chapters 3 through 6 *analyze* aspects of a film.

Objectivity Coexisting with Subjectivity

Comprehending the difference between the objective viewpoint and the subjective viewpoint is a key issue. Any critical piece has both to varying degrees. Subjectivity is more than just a declarative judgment; subjectivity expresses an opinion, suggests an impression. Objectivity, however, is based on incontrovertible fact. Much of the following statement is obviously subjective and judgmental; those words that make it so are in bold print.

Schindler's List, made by Steven Spielberg in 1993, **was not only one of the most important films of that year but will prove to be a landmark in the history of modern filmmaking.**

Compare it with following short paragraph below which is entirely objective:

Director Steven Spielberg's *Schindler's List*, released in 1993, won a number of Academy Awards and other cinematic honors for that year. It garnered Oscars for Best Picture, Best Director, and Best Actor (Liam Neeson) among others.

Add the following bold print phrase after "among others" in the last sentence above, and the otherwise objective paragraph ends on a subjective note:

. . . among others, **making it the most important film of that year, and, because of its subject matter, one of the most significant motion pictures of any year.**

The use of adjectives, adjective phrases, adverbs as well as nouns can change an objective statement into one that is subjective. Specific word choice is most important since the connotative weight that certain words convey adds subjectivity. (This concept will be expanded upon in the next major section of this chapter, *Word Choice and Sentence Mix*). Those words below in bold print are subjective: remove them and the short paragraph becomes objective.

In 1993, Steven Spielberg's **most significant effort to date**, *Schindler's List* told the **unlikely but true** story of a German industrialist who risked his life to save his **doomed but dedicated Jewish** employees, and, simultaneously, **effectively** subverted **the juggernaut of** the Nazis' **war machine**.

Making Judgments

Evaluative (subjective) statements and words can be made anytime or anyplace within your paper. Since the reader should be able to recognize by the context of the sentence and your word choice when you are making a subjective statement, you should avoid such comments as: "I think," "in my opinion," "I believe," and the like, except for emphasis. It should be already understood by the reader that what you are expressing is what you think or believe or is your opinion.

In comparing the following two paragraphs, the second is stronger because the subjective opinion is clearly understood. However, in the first example, statements of the "I/my" phrases (in boldface) are too numerous and unnecessary.

I didn't know that much about classical music, much less Mozart's body of musical work, yet I was able to recognize is genius in Milos Foreman's *Amadeus* (1983). **My musical naiveté proved no impediment to enjoying** his masterful melodies and orchestrations. From his earliest compositions and performances to those written just before his untimely death, **I was amazed** at the volume, richness, and breadth of Mozart's musical accomplishments— **despite my being so untutored in classical music.**

In the paragraph above, the "I/my" phrases weaken the impact of the flow of words and make the whole paragraph more tentative and more conditional than it need be. It also unwittingly shifts the emphasis away from the material being discussed—namely, Mozart's talents—to the insufficiencies of the writer.

The paragraph below, although admitting the writer's ignorance of classical music (but without using an I/my phrase), focuses less on the critic's shortcomings and more on the genius of the title subject of the film.

Unfamiliarity with much of the music of Mozart poses no impediment to the appreciation of the genius of the man and his work. *Amadeus* (1983), the excellent Milos Foreman rendering of what drove Wolfgang Amadeus Mozart from his formative years as a child prodigy— displaying his unique talents as both composer and performer—until his premature death, is an enthralling cinematic experience. Despite a lack of fundamental knowledge of classical music, one could still appreciate and be astounded by the richness and breadth of his melodic and orchestral accomplishments. That they were made within such a relatively short lifetime makes him even more remarkable.

Important as evaluative proclamations may be, evidence to support such claims is even more so. You may be expressing an opinion, but backing it up with instances from the film or elsewhere makes your piece more compelling and complete. Such evidence supporting your judgments need not be in the same paragraph as long as they eventually appear in your paper.

As an example, the following few paragraphs, although not a complete review, nevertheless, make some subjective statements that are supported with enough evidence from the film to give credence to those claims.

Barry Levinson is a director known for his occasional motion picture journeys to the city of his roots, Baltimore, Maryland —especially the Baltimore of his past. *Diner* (1982), *Tin Men* (1987), and *Avalon* (1990) are all bittersweet reminiscences of former times experienced by Levinson himself or his family in that city. Even the former television series *Homicide*, which Levinson produced, was set and shot on location in his home town. However, it is *Diner* that best captures the nostalgia and the wistfulness of a middle-aged moviemaker towards the failed dreams of youth.

The title is very apropos since the action begins, ends, and constantly returns to the meeting place of the main male characters of this ensemble film. The setting is December, 1959, and Levinson has faithfully recreated the ambience of the "Silent Generation" of the 1950s. The tight skirts, snug pants, tab collar shirts, and thin ties along with either young men's short hair or swept back "wet" hairstyles, specific rock n' roll tunes, and large-finned automobiles—so redolent of those times—are all accurately in evidence. More important than these material representations are the thoughts, biases, philosophies, and dreams bandied about over hamburgers, french fries with gravy, slices of pie and mugs of coffee.

The fellows are in their early twenties, and all, to varying degrees, either are drifting or uncomfortable with the choices that they have made or are about to make. Eddie (Steve Guttenberg) is to be married in a few weeks and, being a secret virgin, is scared stiff of the wedding night; Shrevie (Daniel Stern) is already married to Beth (Ellen Barkin), and both are finding that they have little in common; and Boogie (Mickey Rourke) is a hairdresser by day, sometime law student by night, and compulsive womanizer and gambler all the time in between. The other characters are searching for that ineffable something to give direction, stability, and maturity to their existences. Yet, there is a sense that life is slipping by them and their best years are past.

Their precious friendship is the connection to those better times. Their almost nightly meetings at the Fells Point Diner and talks about football, rock n' roll, and sex provides the glue that keeps their friendship together.

Notice how the second and third paragraphs develop the assertions made in the first paragraph. Highlighting an incident or two and then concluding remarks would complete this review. It should be mentioned, however, that the first paragraph could serve as a launching pad for a comparative analysis where the two other Levinson films that are mentioned would be discussed, showing the common elements of all three motion pictures. (More on the comparative analysis paper will be covered in Chapter 5.)

How Much to Retell

One of the problems that many students have—regardless of the type of critical writing project—is knowing when to turn off the faucet of plot summarizing. Size of the piece should determine the amount of plot summation. All of the four critical forms discussed in this book—movie review, critique (critical analysis), comparative analysis, and documented research paper—use plot summaries, but only the *précis* or *synopsis* summarizes the entire plot in detail. A critical work is not synonymous with the précis. A précis explains what has transpired, not why. On the other hand, the four critical forms, since they are analytical, definitely address themselves as to the "why and how" as well as to the "what."

No matter which of the four forms you use, before writing the first draft, you must decide what you are going to say about a film. What is the point(s) of your critical essay? Although you should mention a certain amount of boilerplate—including, among others: production and cast credits, genre, literary source, plot summary—one of these should be expanded and emphasized. The same can be said of one of the other more literary aspects of film: setting, characterization, theme, or tone. One example of such focus could be comparative in nature, involving **producers and directors**: *How the physical comedy of Charlie Chaplin in 1914–15 influenced the slapstick comedies of Mack Sennett and Hal Roach a decade later.* Another could be centered upon **setting**: *The psychological effects of the Vietnamese jungle upon the soldiers in Oliver Stone's* Platoon (*1986*).

The review that follows of *Glengarry Glen Ross* (1992) provides the necessary boilerplate but also identifies its main thrust in the opening paragraph. It further develops the theme in the second paragraph. Every subsequent paragraph is still tied to the paper's emphasis, even though one section will focus on the plot, another on the actors, and a third on the setting. Yet, they all reinforce the focus of the review, namely, this film's portrayal of hell. Both the piece's title and its conclusion also buttress the point that this review is making.

Hell, Version of: America in the Nineties

Director John Foley opens *Glengarry Glen Ross* with a rainy night in a dingy section of Brooklyn, immediately establishing a somber disquieting mood for the film. The camera pans across a seedy commercial street framed by elevated train tracks and moves into a shabby real estate office. Its inhabitants—a number of middle-aged to elderly burned-out salesmen—are soon given one of the profanest and most memorable tongue lashings in recent screen history by Blake (played most effectively by Alec Baldwin), a hotshot sales executive from the head office, downtown. They are threatened with consignment to hell and its ultimate torment: being fired. In reality, though, they are already there and have been for years.

Dante Alighieri wrote *The Inferno* at a time when Europe was emerging from the Dark Ages and perceived his concentric-circled hell as a netherworld swarming with demons, furies, and other vengeful denizens. Inflicting continuous torture upon those souls eternally damned, these supernatural oppressors seemed credible enough to the medieval mind. Centuries later, Jean Paul Sartre saw no need to venture below the crust of planet Earth for his vision of the infernal regions. His play, *No Exit*, portrays hell to be already well-established right here on the surface and peopled entirely with other humans. David Mamet's drama and subsequent film script of *Glengarry Glen Ross* sees a portion of hell in a sleazy branch real estate office circa today [1992]. The damned and their hellhounds share the same occupation: real estate sales.

Sinners, no doubt, but, nonetheless, hardworking professionals, they are all clawing to survive in a business where deceit elbows out truth, survival tramples collegiality, and "What-have-you-SOLD-for-us-lately?" is calculated in nanoseconds. The characters are skillfully played by a cast that should garner more than its fair share of Oscar nominations. There is Moss (Ed Harris): envious, hot-headed, a no-crap-taking guy but not much of a closer, yet desperate enough to plan a burglary of his own office to steal and sell prime real estate leads. Aaronow (Alan Arkin): who has neither few original thoughts nor the guts to be the heist's co-perpetrator. Levene (Jack Lemmon): smarmy, desperately inventive, pathetic, at times the Lomanesque old timer who, nevertheless, goes for the jugular when backed into a corner. Finally, there is Roma (Al Pacino): a seemingly world-weary philosopher who subtly transforms into a shark whenever the blood scent of a sale enters his waters.

All of these men do show flashes of humanity and camaraderie, especially in their contempt for (and fear of) the main office. But uniting against a common enemy gets short shrift when numero uno in sales for the month will get a new Cadillac; the man in second place, a set of steak knives; and the rest, pink slips. Mention must be made of the fine performance of Kevin Spacey as the office manager who is the lightning rod for the threats from headquarters above and the derision of his salesmen below.

The climax is electrifying; with most of the principals giving an acting tour de force that demonstrates numerous mood swings in just a few minutes. Most turn on each other when the enemy no longer is the company but their fellow salesmen. They struggle frantically: some to keep their jobs, others to keep out of prison.

Materialism, greed, betrayal, corruption, fraud, and mendacity parade across the screen in the stirring finale. The actual burglar is found out, but none of them really profits from the discovery. Instead, they all will suffer, being even more entrenched in the hell of their own making.

In the review of *Glengarry Glen Ross* above, the theme is that the real estate agency is a glimpse of contemporary hell and that the agents and their manager are both sufferers and tormentors in it. The title of the review, *Hell, Version of: America in the Nineties*, suggests the theme. Although the climax and ending of *Glengarry Glen Ross* are alluded to, the statements are generalized enough so as not to diminish the impact on anyone who sees the movie for the first time after reading the review. Both the climax and the denouement are mentioned, but only to the degree that they connect to the theme of the review.

To further help you make the decision when to stop plot summarization and begin analysis, the following is a précis of Ridley Scott's *Thelma and Louise* (1991). Notice how no analysis or personal opinion interferes with the narrative. This synopsis, if presented as a critique, would be unacceptable because of its lack of analysis and focus. It would fall short as a review because it does not make any evaluation of the movie, goes into too much detail about each adventure and its respective climax, and then gives away the denouement.

Girlfriends on the Road . . . and on the Lam: A Summary of *Thelma and Louise*

In Ridley Scott's *Thelma and Louise*, two friends, waitress Louise Sawyer (Susan Sarandon) and housewife Thelma Dickenson (Geena Davis) from Little Rock, Arkansas, decide to take a weekend getaway without their respective boyfriend and husband. Neither informs her man of her intentions. Louise in her Thunderbird convertible picks up Thelma and comments that her friend is carrying far more luggage than is needed for their holiday. When Louise learns that Thelma has also brought her husband's pistol, she confiscates it for safekeeping from Thelma—who does not even know how to fire it. Louise is the older and more knowledgeable of the pair, while Thelma is more naïve.

After driving all afternoon and into the evening, they stop at a roadside honky-tonk for some food, drinks, and fun. Thelma starts conversing with a man she meets at the bar, Harlan Puckett (Timothy Carhart). He buys her a few drinks and eventually pulls her out on the dance floor. He makes a number of passes. She refuses, explaining she is married. Tipsy, she stumbles away from him into the parking lot, searching for Louise's car. Puckett follows Thelma, grabs her, and tries to force his way upon her amidst the parked cars and pickups. Louise has been looking for her friend, finds Thelma, sees the assault in progress, retrieves the gun, and waves it at Puckett. He backs off Thelma, but in releasing her, hurls an insult at Louise who reacts by pulling the trigger, wounding him, perhaps mortally. Both women rush to the car and leave the parking lot, tires squealing. In an instant, they've perpetrated a serious crime and are on the run.

Both agree that any claims of self-defense would be a non-issue since Puckett had no weapon at any time and offered no resistance once threatened with the gun. They don't expect fair treatment from the justice system. They stop at a diner to plan their next moves, finally deciding to flee to Mexico. They realize that a major problem, however, is lack of enough money.

Meanwhile, the investigation of the killing has begun. Hal Slocum (Harvey Keitel), a detective of the Arkansas State Police, interviews witnesses, especially one of the waitresses.

Louise telephones her boyfriend Jimmy (Michael Madsen) about the crisis but gives him few specifics. She then instructs him to withdraw her money and wire it to her at the Vagabond Motel in Oklahoma City. By now there is an APB sent out for the apprehension of the two women.

From an outdoor phone booth, Thelma calls her husband Darryl (Christopher McDonald). They quickly get into a heated argument; she mouths a profanity, and hangs up. Right outside the toll phone is a handsome young drifter, J.D. (Brad Pitt), who tries to hitch a ride. Thelma seems agreeable but Louise refuses.

Thelma and Louise head for Oklahoma City; for unspecified reasons, Louise refuses to route their escape through Texas to Mexico, which is the shortest distance. While on the road, they notice J.D. hitching; but this time they give him a lift.

Back in Arkansas, Detective Slocum and the other investigators confront Darryl and pepper him with questions about his wife and their relationship. The women are now suspects.

When they arrive at the Vagabond Motel, Jimmy is there to meet them. He and Louise get a separate room, leaving Thelma alone in the other room. The couple discuss Louise's trouble, their relationship, argue, and then he proposes marriage, giving her a ring. J.D. knocks on Thelma's door, pleading to come in from the rain. She agrees and they talk. He eventually confesses that he's on parole for robbery—mainly gas stations and convenience stores—and even gives details on his modus operandi (M.O.). Sex follows.

The next morning, Louise and Jimmy have breakfast in the motel café. After Louise promises to get back to him when her crisis ends, Jimmy leaves to catch a taxi for the airport. Thelma then rejoins Louise, boasts that she spent the night with J.D., whom she has left showering in her room. The women rush back there only to find both the man and the money gone.

Desperate for cash, Louise is crushed and breaks down. The roles of the women now change. Thelma takes charge. Meanwhile, Slocum and the other agents return to Darryl's house to tap all his phones and set up a call location identification system.

Thelma enters a roadside market and per J.D.'s instructions, robs its cash register. They have money but both women are now outlaws. The robbery has been videotaped by the store's security system which gives the police an idea where the two are. The police have also interviewed Jimmy upon his return to Little Rock. They soon apprehend J.D. and bring him into custody. He divulges where he got the money. During his interrogation, it is obvious that Hal is sympathetic to the women's plight.

Louise suggests that Thelma call Darryl to determine if the police are there, tapping the phone. She does so. By his reaction, she knows the law is in her home and hangs up. Then Louise calls Darryl again, asking asks to be connected to the detectives. A brief dialogue between Louise and Hal ensues. She finds out that they know about J.D., the market robbery, and their final destination, Mexico. As a consequence, the women decide to change course and follow a more circuitous route. As they pass through beautiful desert scenery, they both admit to enjoying greater freedom—and fun—than they have had in quite a while.

They see a huge oil tanker truck, which they had passed before, and again receive a burst of verbal obscenities and gestures. Thelma guesses that Louise was raped in Texas but Louise refuses to elaborate on the experience. Suddenly, they are tailed by a Nevada state trooper who signals them to pull over. He informs them they have been speeding at more than 100 miles an hour and orders Louise, the driver, to enter his vehicle. Before he can arrest her, Thelma saunters over and puts her pistol to his temple and demands that he get out of the car. He begins blubbering as Louise removes his automatic revolver and ammunition. They wreck both his radios and shoot holes in his trunk. Then they force him into the enclosed, perforated area, lock it, and toss the keys away.

Eventually, Louise calls Detective Slocum again and states that she might not turn herself in. He then divulges that he knows what happened in Texas, is very sympathetic, and worries that the women will get shot. When Louise hangs up, Thelma is fearful that Louise will make a deal but she is assured that Jimmy isn't an option, and they will remain desperadoes, facing a murder charge, and continue their flight to Mexico.

Once more they pass that tanker truck, but this time tell him to follow them. They stop off the road. He leaves his truck and approaches them mouthing his sexually explicit proposals. However, they lambaste him verbally about all his derogatory remarks to them. He seems dumbfounded. They demand he apologize. When he refuses, they shoot up his truck, inevitably blowing up the tanker. They leave him fuming and cursing but do have a souvenir, his cap, which Thelma now wears.

Thelma and Louise spy a horde of police cars heading in the opposite direction and immediately pull off the road, speeding across the desert. The police follow them in hot pursuit. During the car chase, they crash through roadblocks, cause mayhem, and, temporarily, escape the lawmen.

While driving across a high mesa, Louise suddenly hits the brakes, coming to a screeching halt. A front wheel is dangling over the edge of a deep canyon: the Grand Canyon. A helicopter emerges up in front of them from below, while police cruisers hem them in from behind. The police rush out of their vehicles, take defensive positions, and train their loaded weapons on the Thunderbird. The helicopter lands and Hal bursts out of it, pleading with them to surrender.

The women look at each other, hug, and express their mutual love. Then the car is put into gear, the accelerator is gunned, and they fly over the edge of the Grand Canyon. A freeze frame captures them encircled by blue sky as the credits roll.

In summary, the précis (also known as an overview) is quite different from the review or the critical analysis (critique). The précis above introduces the characters sequentially and provides the plotline for the film. Yet, the précis doesn't touch upon the theme, the mood, and the tone and furnishes few if any analytical remarks. The writer doesn't conjecture what prompts the two principals' decisions and the consequent actions that result from them.

The following is the transcript of a review of *Thelma and Louise* delivered by Linda Lopez McAlister for *The Women's Show*, on WMNF-FM in Tampa, Florida on December 21, 1998. It definitely goes beyond a précis in its analysis of the film.

Thelma and Louise

Feminists! If you don't go see another film all year, you're going to want to see "Thelma and Louise." It is, wonder of wonders, a genuine Hollywood feminist film. Don't be fooled as I was, by the previews into expecting a mindless car chase comedy—a sort of Burt Reynolds buddy film with women instead of men. "Thelma and Louise" is a very female buddy film; it is one long car chase, and it does have delicious moments of humor, but it's much more than that. It's also a philosophical film, one that existentialist feminist Simone de Beauvoir would love, for it depicts two ordinary women living under patriarchal domination in small-town Arkansas who actually succeed in achieving their liberation. I don't know anything about screenwriter Callie Khouri but she and director Ridley Scott have created a remarkable existentialist feminist film from, of all places, Metro-Goldwyn-Mayer.

That this is not just a mindless comedy becomes very clear early in the film. On their way to a weekend in the mountains, Thelma, a middle-class housewife and Louise, her waitress friend, stop at a Western bar to have a little fun. Thelma is nearly raped and Louise, in rescuing her, shoots and kills the man who did it. Instinctively, they run while they try to comprehend what happened and figure out what to do. One of the things they know they can't do is turn themselves in and expect fair treatment from the criminal justice system, since Thelma has been flirting and dancing with the guy all evening. They know that nearly everyone would say that what happened to her is her own fault. Even Louise is tempted to think that for a minute, but she thinks about it and she knows better. One of the many glories of this film is the skill with which both Susan Sarandon who plays Louise and Geena Davis who plays Thelma hone in unerringly on the emotional truth of these women. Both characters are fully realized, totally believable human beings with all the weaknesses and quirks and strengths and beauty they embody.

As their situation vis-à-vis the law gets progressively worse and their plans for getting money and crossing the Mexican border go awry, both women, but especially Thelma, undergo enormous change. As they become outlaws they are outside not only the civil laws but the Laws of the Father as well and they begin to discover and express their own potential, their own feelings, their own strength, and to appreciate and support one another. Thelma has a fling with another cowboy (this time consensual) and she discovers real sexual pleasure for the first time. She also discovers she has a knack for armed robbery and she does a nifty job of locking a policeman in his trunk (thoughtfully having Louise shoot out the radio and shoot in a few air holes so he can breathe).

When they have nothing left to lose, when they realize that they not only cannot but do not want to go back to their earlier lives, they are freed to speak with their own voices. Several times in the film they encounter a trucker who plagues them with gross gestures and obscene comments. Finally they decide to confront him. Every woman who has ever had to endure such treatment (and what woman hasn't?) will simply love Louise and Thelma's revenge on this pig.

Can such flaunting of patriarchal values be tolerated in a Hollywood film? Will they be allowed to live happily ever after in Mexico? No, but to have done so would have been to trivialize the characters and the film. What happens is even more extraordinary for a mainstream American film. These two ordinary women who have turned out to be so very remarkable achieve liberation of a more profound sort. They achieve what the existentialist philosophers call transcendence. Having once experienced what it is to make their own choices, speak with their own voices, and take responsibility for their own actions, they are unwilling to relinquish that freedom. And they choose freely and with full awareness of the meaning of their choice not to relinquish it. It is an extraordinary resolution that ennobles Thelma and Louise—the characters and the film. And it is a stinging indictment of this society that the choice they make is the sane and reasonable one.

For the WMNF *Women's Show* this is Linda Lopez McAlister on "Women and Film."

Although her piece is much shorter, Linda Lopez McAlister's commentary above goes well beyond the précis appearing before it. You will notice that unlike the first example, it does not slavishly follow every twist, turn, and eddy of the plot. Its theme—that the movie makes some important feminist and even existentialist statements—is announced in the first paragraph and is supported throughout. The commentator voices opinions, provides explanations, and cites examples which go deeper than the straight chronological divulgence of events that one finds in the précis.

Adopting a Tone

The tone you adopt in a critical paper already is a subjective element of the critique and, especially, the review. Often in reviewing a comedy, the tone the reviewer adopts is light, even humorous. In fact, reviews are usually slightly more informal in word choice and tone than critiques or other critical forms. Perhaps, the most serious, no-nonsense tones are reserved for the documented research paper. *Tone*, as we are using it here, means the critic's or writer's voice. Make sure that the tone you adopt for a critical piece is appropriate for the subject of the film, the tone of the film, and your reaction to and evaluation of the film. Notice in the following opening sentence, the jaunty, sarcastic (and completely inappropriate) tone employed for the troubling and provocative motion picture Sophie's Choice (1982):

> Watch Meryl Streep as she reaches into her bag of ethno-imitative tricks and takes a stab at a Polish accent . . . in the midst of a WW2 concentration camp no less!

The Alan J. Pakula film with its extensive flashbacks by Sophie (Meryl Streep) to her torturous life in a Nazi concentration camp, would not be fitting for such a jocular tone—even if the critic feels her performance, for example, is greatly wanting. The intent and texture of the film militate against such a casual tone for the following reasons:

- The tone of the novel by William Styron from which the movie is based is serious;
- The tone of the film itself is serious; and
- The tone of the performances of Meryl Streep and Kevin Kline, its principal characters, is serious.

Therefore, the review could be expected to be no less so—even if the critic sees the end product as flawed.

The use of irony and sarcasm is a double-edged sword. On one hand, it can make for an effective and entertaining review; on the other, it may betray some deep biases of the critic about the subject matter, the type of film subgenre, or the personnel involved—especially the director and actors. Irony, parody, and sarcasm can be compelling—especially when a film is being panned. But again, if the use of these tonal elements is excessive or unfair and the evidence provided is unconvincing, employing such a tone can backfire. Pretentious words and lengthy, torturously structured sentences are also inappropriate. Your main objective is to communicate your opinion and to justify it clearly and convincingly. However, using jargon, obfuscating ideas, and selecting sophisticated, multisyllabic words to impress your readers will not accomplish your original intended goals.

The review presented below of Danish director Lone Scherfig's *One Day* (2011) is deeply flawed. It is riddled with errors in tone, organization, and voice. It reveals key information about the climax and ending that is poor form, especially for this genre, the romantic drama. Its language is excessive in panning the film: obviously the critic does not like it—which is the reviewer's prerogative—but the phrases get too personal and sarcastic in condemning its principal players. Even the title is a bit too snarky. The words, phrases and sentences in **Bold** throughout the piece below need to be revised. If they were to be, the review—although negatively critical—would, at least, be more fair and credible. Ironically, in actuality, the motion picture received mixed reviews—some of them glowing from nationally recognized critics—and also had some success at the box office and DVD rental market thereafter. Thus, by now it should be recognized that film reviews are very subjective and personal.

One Day . . . Why Should I Care?

This **Flick** can be reviewed in one **sentence: A** waste of talent, a waste of good looks, a waste of time!

Anne Hathaway in most of her films is a **fine** actress with **drop dead gorgeous**, beguiling charm, and solid acting acumen. All three were **M.I.A.** in this film. Jim Sturgess, her male romantic counterpart, lacks leading **guy LOOKS (but then, what is "leading guy looks" these days?)**, totally **lacks** charisma, and even less **acting chops in evidence.** Getting back to **Anne, she does not emerge unscathed in the portrayal of her character.** She portrays Emma Morley, **a recent college graduate, up from the working middle class class unconvincingly. Anne** is overly staid, serious-minded, seemingly prudish, high strung, **tightly wound**, and **as an American actress** drifts annoyingly in and out of her Yorkshire accent.

So what about Jim Sturgess? **What about him?** His character is forgettable **and so is Jim** of an unduly privileged, rich, lazy, self-centered, irresponsible, untalented, dull, **and not kind.**

What about plot? So what about it? Just because Emma suddenly dies on her bike (hit by a speeding truck while darting through a cross-cutting alley) as she heads for climactic closure, is that supposed to make it a worthy film? Just because Dexter seems to become a mensch, does that

excuse his otherwise yawn-provoking performance previous to the last 10 minutes of the film? And the film's structure?

Okay, so we visit the "couple" every year on July 15th: so what? Other than that being the anniversary of their first meeting, what does that prove? A string of random, unrelated incidents over the next 22 years? Okay, they go through many changes but so does everybody, right? She, despite her intellect and degree, slings Mexi-hash (of the ingestible not inhalable variety) at some Anglo-Mexican variation of the cuisine in some beanery, keeps on writing though—can't give up on her dream, can she?—then moves on to some other forgettable position—whatever that was and finally writes a kiddie book that is a great success (without having any kiddies of her own). During the interim, Dexter does, however (have kiddies, I mean), get married and then divorced. He still drinks and does drugs, loses his job as a TV emcee-type (they call them "presenters" in sunny, olde, England) becomes rudderless washed up has-been, lost in the wilderness—you get the picture—, but nevertheless, a "loving father" to his kiddies.

I guess what I don't like about this flicker is that it is seriously adrift, it is never anchored nor does it move in a direction for satisfying character development and closure. It's like a whole bunch of unrelated phrases strung together that are supposed to make up a complete paragraph, you know? A bunch of unrelated scenes that are supposed to make a complete movie?

But what do I find is the big mystery here? What do I think keeps the two characters going in maintaining their quasi-romantic friendship all this time? What new law of chemistry have they created that keeps that annual glue going and even strengthening? Why do they kill her off when it seems that things are finally going to get resolved? Just to show he kind of always loved her?

I don't think so.

As you can see, the review above is extremely flawed. It is too biased and doesn't provide convincing evidence or examples for its opinions. It is jumbled and disjointed in how it is presented. It complains about the lack of a clear structure and smooth flow in the film yet is written in a manner that is redolent with the same flaws of choppiness and discontinuity. Some of the word choice shows poor taste and the tone, at times, becomes too conversational and casual. Its main points are hard to recognize and are disorganized without clear-cut movement from introductory remarks to development of main points to concluding comments. The author uses the first person too often and quite annoyingly. Most of the interrogatory statements are unnecessary and quickly become distracting.

What follows is a revised review of *One Day,* which although still remains a pan of the film, nevertheless, presents its views fairly and clearly, developing its opinions cogently. Notice that the title has also been modified to reflect a less snarky attitude.

One Day . . . To Be Forgotten

Lone Scherfig's *One Day* (2011) is a motion picture that can be reviewed in one statement: a waste of talent, a waste of good looks, a waste of time!

Anne Hathaway in most of her films shows solid acting acumen by her talent for nuance when developing her characters. The fact that she can be glamorously attractive, radiating a beguiling charm has also stood her in good stead. However, all three of these qualities—looks, charm, and acting ability—are sadly missing in action in this disappointing adaptation of the David Nicholls' best-selling novel. Jim Sturgess, her male romantic counterpart, evidences few leading man qualities since he both lacks the charisma and acting chops to maintain his end. Getting back to Ms. Hathaway, she portrays Emma Morley, a young woman with working/middle class roots, who has just graduated from the University of Edinburgh. Emma is overly staid, serious-minded, seemingly prudish, high strung, and—via Hathaway's Americanized vocalizations—annoyingly inexact in her attempts at a Yorkshire accent.

And what about actor Jim Sturgess? His character, Dexter Mayhew, is forgettable as is Sturgess' rendering of him. Dexter, basically, is an unduly privileged, rich, lazy, self-centered, irresponsible, untalented, dull, and unkind young man.

The plot structure focuses on the annual return of the two principal characters the same day (July 15th) most years from 1988 to 2011. Somehow those days' events relate to their individual pasts as well as times together, and also give hints to their future. Such a framework is supposed to provide the continuity on which to build the story. Unfortunately, instead of serving as a vital link that through the years strengthens the characterizations and tightens the plot, you have an anniversary of their first meeting that leads to a string of random, unrelated incidents over the next 22 years. Admittedly, they experience a number of personal events—either relating to their careers or personal relationships with others—that alter them somewhat but not enough to consume the viewer. She, despite her intellect and degree, begins waiting tables at a Mexican restaurant and continues doing so for a few years. Admittedly, she does not give up her dream but keeps on writing and submitting. She then moves on to some other forgettable position. During this time, she completes a volume directed at the adolescent/young adult market with considerable success. Her personal life also undergoes some permutations. She meets a would-be comedian, whose career as a funny-man never leaves the ground. They begin a relationship, move in together, in time marry, and then break-up.

During the interim, Dexter gets married to another, has some children, but, in time, gets divorced. His shortcomings of excessive drinking, drugs and self-absorption continue over the years. He eventually loses his job as a television emcee (called a "presenter" in the British Isles). He becomes a depressed, rudderless has-been at a relatively young age. However, during this period of personal decline, he continues to be loving, affectionate father to his offspring.

The main conceit of the film, that annual reunion on July 15th continues, giving the audience the opportunity to look in on their strange friendship. It is obvious that Emma has strong feelings for Dexter beyond the platonic—exactly why is never that clear. He too has developed a strong co-dependency on keeping not only the yearly meeting going, but strengthening their friendship as well. Perhaps if Dexter can get past his self-absorbed/self-destructive phases, he can fully acknowledge and express his incipient passion for Emma.

There is a distracting then disturbing image of Emma riding her bicycle through the busy city streets which appears periodically throughout the film. Her facial expression seems troubled or perhaps vacant; her body language suggests physical exhaustion. We have a sense of foreboding. Ultimately, its meaning is borne out at the movie's climactic ending.

Unfortunately, *One Day* is seriously adrift, never moving in a direction for satisfying character development and closure. The rationale for the two principals enduring and ever-mutating relationship is unsatisfying. Given, it is a story supposedly of a great friendship and more, but given the lack of any observable chemistry between Emma Morley and Dexter Mayhew, the answer to the question "Why?" is never fully resolved.

Without surrendering any particulars, the ending is startling. But, nevertheless, it seems contrived and unnecessary. One certainly doesn't leave the experience with a sense of loose ends neatly tied.

The re-written review immediately above does away with *ad hominem* (personal) attacks of the actors and avoids sarcasm. The film is cast in negative light but the critic attempts to justify that judgment. The premise of the work is flawed with reasons demonstrated for its shortcomings. Comments about the film's conclusion are deliberately generalized so as not to give away its plot details.

Following, in contrast, is a glowing review of Christopher Guest's *Best in Show* (2000). Note that the tone employed is breezy as it pokes fun at some aspects of the film. After reading the piece, you should be left with the impression that the reviewer liked the movie, taking liberties with it affectionately.

It's Not Only about the Dogs . . .

Christopher Guest and his troupe of multi-talented comedic actors and writers have done it again with *Best in Show* . . . and better than ever! Through Guest's "mockumentary" style, we explore the demimonde of nationally competitive pedigreed dog shows: the dogs, the owners, the handlers, the impresarios—the whole shtick.

The mockumentary in Guest and company's hands initially seems like a legitimate documentary. Individuals within the context of their normal day-to-day lives talk to an unseen interviewer. What is remarkable about this film is how the audience gets sucked in and then manipulated by the players and script. Our first laughs are really snickers—and somewhat guilty at that—because the movie seems so much like a legitimate, mainstream documentary: you know, talking heads narrating incidents, explaining esoterica. And yet, we can't help but feel that something about each character is a little off. As the film draws to its hilarious climax and epilog, we fully realize what has been going on as the incongruousness of the situations and looneyness of each owner or handler increases. Guffaws and belly laughs replace smirks and chortles.

The first reel of the film introduces us to the different dog owners and their canine charges. It visits them at their respective homes all over the country. Harlan Pepper (Guest) owns a bait and tackle shop in rural North Carolina. He lauds his championship caliber bloodhound and believes the dog, although young, can go all the way to capture the "best in show" ribbon. Then there are the Flecks from Florida whose entry is an adorable Norwich terrier, a breed, incidentally, that although very cute, nevertheless, looks like a mongrel. The Flecks are an unusual couple—to say the least! (In fact, all the "couples" are rather unusual.) Gerry Fleck (Eugene Levy) was literally born with two left feet and his wife Cookie (Catherine O'Hara) had such an active premarital sexual life that she is constantly running into men who "knew her when . . ." Gerry's reaction to all of these revelations is a surprised bemusement. Then there are the Swans, Meg (Parker Posey) and Hamilton (Michael Hitchcock). Initially, we meet this Yuppie pair at their psychiatrist's office, sporting matching braces on their teeth. The analyst actually doubles as their canine shrink, since their Weimaraner is even more neurotic than they are. Let's not forget the trio composed of the Cabots and their dog trainer Christy Cummings (Jane Lynch). Sherri Ann Ward Cabot (Jennifer Coolidge) is the female half of a June-last-day-of-December marriage to silent octogenarian Leslie (Patrick Cranshaw) but her life really revolves around her prize-winning poodle and, to an increasing degree, Christy. Last but not least are those flamboyant interior decorators and proud Shih Tzu owners, Stefan Vanderhoof (Michael McKean) and his significant other Scott Donlon (John Michael Higgins).

After meeting the driven dog owners at their respective homes, we move to Philadelphia, site of the Mayflower Kennel Club's annual pageant. We meet the organizers of this canine equivalent to the Oscars, the hosting hotel's manager, and others involved in the event.

The pomp and circumstance of the dog show itself—with its pretentiousness and gravity—is deflated by the wacky sports commentary of Buck Laughlin (Fred Willard, who comes very close to stealing the show). As the ill-informed color guy, Buck is totally out of his league in the rarefied world of pedigreed dogdom. If ignorance is bliss, his ignorance leads to a cornucopia of outrageous non sequiturs, double entendres, and the like, which puncture the contrived seriousness of the proceedings.

The finale of *Best in Show* is tense, intense, and, ultimately, quite humorous. The epilog finds those qualities and/or issues introduced at the outset being drawn to their logical conclusions. Life goes on after the Mayflower, apparently quite successfully so, even for the losers.

The tone in the review above is consistent with the subject matter, namely, a quick-paced comedy. Note that the title not only gives an indication of some of the movie's features but hints at the reviewer's tone as well. Also notice that specifics about the climax and conclusion are not mentioned—usual for most reviews.

—————————— Word Choice and Sentence Mix ——————————

In all forms of writing, the words chosen and the sentence syntax (flow) determine effective writing: it is not only what you say (substance) but how you say it (style). To put together well-written sentences, paragraphs, and papers means being able to:

- Recognize the differences between the denotative and connotative meanings of words;
- Select the most specific (concrete) word to convey your intended interpretation;
- Avoid using clichéd phrases; and
- Vary both sentence length and structure to avoid repetitiveness in sentence patterns.

Denotation and Connotation

The **denotative** meaning of a word is its dictionary and more inclusive definition. Thus, such words as *actor, player, trouper, thespian, performer, entertainer, impersonator, mime,* and *mummer* are all synonyms in their denotative meanings. However, **connotative** meanings refer to the associations that words carry and are actually more restrictive. Each of the denotative synonyms for "actor" listed above have entirely different associations from each other and thus different connotations (connotative meanings):

- *player:* one who acts in a movie or play;
- *trouper:* one who is a member of a cast of a play or movie;
- *thespian:* now a somewhat pretentious word for a stage actor;
- *performer:* one who takes part in any type of public performance be it on stage, in a nightclub, on film; he/she can be an actor, dancer, singer, comic, impressionist, musician, or professional athlete for that matter;
- *entertainer:* one who entertains; especially, a popular singer or comedian;
- *impersonator:* one who imitates someone else—such as an another performer, politician, or celebrity—often for comical effect;
- *mime:* one who silently imitates certain human acts, gestures, expressions, and characteristics;
- *mummer:* now one of a group of people in similar elaborate costumes who march in parades often playing instruments.

Misuse of words connotatively can be quite embarrassing and unintentionally funny. Imagine someone saying in praise of the following actor's comedic talents, "My favorite *mummer* of the last decade or so is Will Ferrell: he really makes me laugh." Or someone marveling at the classical acting skills of Sir Laurence Olivier: "His abilities as a Shakespearean *impersonator* were unrivaled in his prime."

It is important to use synonyms to make your writing more interesting to the reader. However, the connotative accuracy of your choices is equally vital. Therefore, when you consult a thesaurus to find a synonym or that "perfect" word for your intended meaning, make sure that you select a word that you are familiar with from your reading and have used before in your writing.

Specific Wording

Overdependence on generalized terms makes for inferior writing. In everything you write—not only film critiques—you want to be as concrete as possible. Concreteness usually leads to accuracy, whereas overgeneralization not only makes for dull reading but may also contribute to misinterpretation. In the following introductory paragraph of a critique, those words that are too broad and need to be more specific are boldfaced; the title of the film is italicized.

> *Gone with the Wind*, **a memorable endeavor made some decades ago about Americans at war, was highly acclaimed. Derived from the bestseller, it contains all that the audience can desire. It has been faithfully produced from its source and has had top notch direction, writing, acting, and such. No wonder it has been such a cinematic favorite!**

As can be clearly seen, this opening paragraph is too vague and broad. The only concrete features are the production's name; we are not even told that it is a motion picture. The following paragraph, however, converts every vague statement above into one far more specific. Now it is the **concrete words and phrases** that are in boldface.

> The **David O. Selznick production** of *Gone with the Wind* **(1939)**—that **sprawling epic** of the **American Civil War**—to **many movie-goers is still the greatest American movie of all time.** No wonder! **Based on the Margaret Mitchell runaway bestseller of the same name, it contains all of the elements of the historical romance novel—a great love story, opulent settings, events of historic importance, the gamut of human emotions, set pieces typical of the era**—here translated so

well **into cinema. Its faithfulness to the novel's plot, characters, setting, tone, and themes, has not gone unnoticed and
unrewarded. It has amassed a total of no less than nine
Academy Awards. The winners include Victor Flemming:
direction; Sidney Howard: screenplay; Vivien Leigh (as
Scarlet O'Hara): best actress; Hattie McDaniel (playing
Mammy): best supporting actress; Ernest Haller and Ray
Rennahan: cinematography; Hal C. Kern and James E. New-
com: editing; William Cameron Menzies: production design;
and, finally, Lyle Wheeler: art direction.**

Cliché Avoidance

All good writing avoids clichés, trite expressions, and unoriginal figura-
tive language. This is especially so if the paper is trying to adopt a serious, more formal tone. Film clichés include, among others:

a cast of thousands	silver screen
movie mogul	boffo
blockbuster	a film the whole family will enjoy
sex symbol	heartwarming saga
action-packed	whodunit
movie (film) siren	film (screen) starlet
girl (boy) crazy	riding off into the sunset
Tinsel town	hooker with the heart of gold
blazing six-guns	oat burner
shocker	on the edge of your seat
chills and thrills	box office hit
two thumbs up	boulevard of broken dreams
rogue cop	the lovely [person's name]
sidekick	meanwhile, back at the ranch
bloodlust	blood curdling scream
damsel in distress	hot number
bobbysoxers	the "heat"

And these are just the "tip of the iceberg" (another cliché). Just to
show how prevalent clichés are, below is a partial list of clichés that
have become film titles:

a dog's life	life at the top
a face in the crowd	no strings attached
against all odds	not a pretty picture

all that jazz	odd man out
battle of the sexes	one from the heart
born yesterday	on the town
catch-22	over the edge
do the right thing	shadow of a doubt
duck soup	shoot the moon
fair game	side effects
forbidden fruit	something borrowed
friends with benefits	take the money and run
game change	the best years of our lives
going places	the company man
going the distance	the other woman
good hair	the right stuff
ides of March	the way of the world
it's a wonderful life	this is it
just go with it	till the end of time
just looking	up in the air
kiss of death	win win
larger than life	you can't take it with you
life as we know it	you don't know jack

Variance of Sentence Length and Structure

A well-written paragraph will contain sentences of varied lengths and structures. Sentences that follow the same predictable pattern of structure and/or length eventually make the piece boring. Sentences that are long with complicated structures, if continued, will make the paragraph ponderous and unwieldy. Sentences that are short which follow the same sentence pattern make the paragraph choppy and juvenile.

Substantively, the three paragraphs below say the same thing. Each, however, varies greatly from the others in sentence length and sentence structure.

#1

Although not a blockbuster at local cinema complexes and, in fact, not enjoying widespread distribution, *Zoot Suit* (1981), nonetheless, has had a great artistic impact upon the professional film critic community as well as the discriminating movie going public at large. Hollywood has rarely seen the likes of this film that meshes dancing and music in what must be regarded as an alternative if skewed take on the traditional American musical genre, playing for savvy Southern California audiences rather than the sophisticated mavens of Broadway. This neo-theatrical experience is the brainchild of Luis Valdez, who not only wrote the screenplay (based on his eponymous stage play) but also masterfully directed the production of a story of racism and intolerance—based on an actual incident—against the setting of Los Angeles during the turbulent era of World War II. Here, the ethnic victims are not the disenfranchised African Americans in their backwater quasi-feudal communities of the Deep South nor the marginalized immigrant Jews in their teeming Lower East Side of Manhattan ghetto but instead the focus is upon the hardscrabble but hard-working Mexican Americans of the East Los Angeles barrio.

This first paragraph, with its lengthy sentences (at least 40 words each) and complicated structure makes for laborious reading. The language is also overblown and confusing.

#2

Zoot Suit (1981) has not been a smash hit with movie audiences. It has not had wide theatrical distribution. Discriminating viewers and critics, though, have given it acclaim. This is an unusual film for Hollywood. It has music and dancing but is not the standard studio fare. Luis Valdez wrote the screenplay from his own stage play of the same name. He also directed the movie. It is about racism and intolerance. It is based on an actual incident. The play takes place in Los Angeles during World War II. It is not about black people in he South. It is not about Jews in a New York ghetto. It is instead about Mexican Americans in East L. A.

The second paragraph becomes boring because of the uniformity of its declarative statements and structural predictability (subject-verbobject pattern). Its language is very dry and, at times, repetitive with a marked absence of vivid adjectives and phrases.

#3

Not all significant and critically acclaimed films are blockbusters or are even subject to wide theater distribution. *Zoot Suit* (1981), written and directed by Luis Valdez—who adapted it from his own stage script—has greatly impacted many who saw it. It is an unusual hybrid, mixing the dancing and songs of the musical with the strident political themes of the social commentary drama. Based on an actual incident in World War II era Los Angeles, it focuses on the racism and intolerance of those times. The players here, though, are mainly Mexican Americans rather than the Southern blacks or immigrant Jews of earlier social dramas. The colorful, working class milieu that composed the East Los Angeles barrio life of the early 1940s is presented in this striking albeit disquieting production.

The third paragraph is similar in essence to the other two in content but presents it in a manner that is more readable. Notice that its sentences vary both in length and structure. The language, while being richer, is still accessible to the reader.

Main Components of the Critical Essay

A critical work on the cinema—be it short review or lengthy research paper—will be organized to contain the standard components of the essay. To capture the reader and introduce the primary emphasis or direction of the paper is the function of the *lead-in sentence(s)*. The lead-in is so closely connected to the *introduction* of the piece that we will look at them together. The *topic sentence* is the focal point of any paragraph. Since it is the keystone sentence of the paragraph, all other sentences either derive from, lead to, or elaborate upon the topic sentence. The topic sentence is common to all paragraphs of the essay and, therefore, will be discussed in this subsection. Eventually, either in the introductory paragraph or soon thereafter, the *main point* or *thesis* of the entire essay is made. Once the thesis is stated, the *subordinate points* or *minor inferences* about it are presented to support and strengthen its assertion(s). Just as your paper needs lead-ins and the introduction at the outset, it also requires a *conclusion (concluding remarks)* at its completion. These can take many forms, just as with introductory statements.

The Lead-In/Introduction

Both writing and film share yet another element in common: the use of lead-ins and introductions. Whether it is an essay, short story, novel, or play, the reader/audience must be "hooked" early. In a movie, during the first ten to fifteen minutes, we should be getting engrossed; if not, the director and scriptwriter are in danger of losing us. In a critical essay, there is no excuse for a factual but dull opening paragraph. Even if the writer feels the need to serve the boilerplate immediately to get it out of the way, somewhere in that initial paragraph should be a statement that is enticing, challenging, fascinating, disturbing, entertaining, or funny, building a bridge to the main concern of the essay. There is no set format to follow, only common objectives. In each sample paragraph or two below, the lead-in both captures the reader's interest and moves arterially toward the heart of the paper.

There are a number of tactics ("lead-ins") the writer can employ to entice the reader. Below are a number that have been influenced by Jean Wyrick's *Steps to Writing Well with Additional Readings*:

- probing question
- provocative statement
- arousing statistic

- relevant anecdote
- applicable allusion
- moving description
- arresting fact
- relevant example(s)
- nettlesome problem/misconception
- evocative personal experience
- intriguing contrast
- apropos comparison/analogy (75–76)

The first sample of a lead-in paragraph looks at *Mother and Child* (2009), a film which centers on the lives of three women and their varied but strong feelings about bringing a child into the world and raising it.

> A naïve, fourteen-year-old girl in the throes of her first love is in the process of losing her virginity. Flash forward 35 years to that same person, Karen, now a 50 year-old nurse (Annette Bening). Then we meet that grown child, Elizabeth, presently a practicing attorney (Naomi Watts), coming to grips with a dilemma in which she unexpectedly finds herself. Finally, there is Lucy, a successful entrepreneur (Kerry Washington), who is married but childless and desperately wants to adopt a child. How the concept of motherhood inextricably binds them together makes writer/director Rodrigo Garcia's *Mother and Child* such a poignant and powerful work.

The introductory paragraph initially announces an event that has been shared by millions of women over the centuries but is no less significant. We then move on to broach its consequences decades later. This first paragraph also provides some important *boilerplate* (film credits and factual information) about the writer/director as well as the movie's three female principals. Finally, it identifies the central theme that concerns this motion picture.

The next example of a lead-in is an excerpt of the review by *New York Times* critic Bosley Crowther of the 1959 French/Brazilian film, *Black Orpheus*. Crowther captures the reader's interest in this short paragraph by juxtaposing the frantic gaiety of Rio during carnival—with all its music, colors, and action—with a "melancholy" plot. Nevertheless, he also provides important boilerplate of the movie by including the film title and the director's name and nationality.

> All tangled up in the madness of a Rio de Janeiro carnival, full of intoxicating samba music, frenzied dancing and violent costumes, the Frenchman Marcel Camus presents us a melancholy tale in his color film, "Black Orpheus" ("Orfeu Negro") . . . (3163–64).

The following lead-in introduces director Martin Scorsese's recreation of a New York City 125 years ago in his film *The Age of Innocence* (1993).

With the opening shots, we are immediately transported into an older, seemingly gentler New York: a city without skyscrapers, where carriages and surreys traverse the streets rather than taxis and buses; where the pace of life is perceptively slower and more orderly, and where the social classes are separated by gulfs wider and more rigid than they are today.

Once again, director Martin Scorsese has chosen Manhattan for his film's setting. However, this time he does not present the urban underbelly of life in the 1970s, as he did in *Mean Streets* (1973) and *Taxi Driver* (1976) but instead examines the genteel mores and customs of Gotham's blue-blooded aristocracy more than a century before. This is the world that Edith Wharton portrayed in her novel *The Age of Innocence* (1920) which now Scorsese faithfully evokes to the smallest detail in his rendering of her romantic story of manners.

Besides establishing the setting—a source of some of Scorsese's earlier named films—the introduction mentions the sub-genre of this motion picture. These two introductory paragraphs include such subjective remarks as "seemingly gentler," "pace of life is perceptively slower," and "faithfully evokes to the smallest detail." These statements furnish some early judgments of the movie. Also identified is Edith Wharton's source of the film which has been rendered true to her original.

The Topic Sentence

The topic sentence can be found anyplace in a paragraph. In the subsequent paragraphs, the topic sentence is in bold print. Note that the topic sentence although found in a different position in each paragraph has all the other sentences of the paragraph relating to it.

The first example makes reference to Cecil B. De Mille's *The Ten Commandments*. The topic sentence clearly appears at the outset of the paragraph in bold print. The rest of the paragraph, printed in regular text, supports and elaborates upon that topic sentence.

The Ten Commandments, **released in 1956—perhaps the most grandiose achievement of his career—illustrates why Cecil B. De Mille was considered the master of the Hollywood Biblical spectacle.** All the elements of such a sub-genre were in place. The cast of thousands were living flesh and blood extras, not computer-generated cyber creations. The movie (actually a re-make of his own 1923 effort) was shot in glorious Technicolor, mandatory for any Biblical extravaganza. The special effects for their day were cutting edge: including the construction sequences of a new city on site, manifestations of the Ten Plagues, and the parting of the Red Sea. In addition, most of the epic was filmed on location in Egypt and the Sinai Desert. The exorbitant production costs rivaled anything Hollywood moguls had spent previously. The motion picture received six Academy Award nominations.

The second example looks at *Body Heat*. Here, not only does the topic sentence appear towards the end of the paragraph, but the piece also, whimsically, adopts and maintains an extended metaphor throughout.

Begin with a healthy dollop of sweltering summertime South Florida. Next, mix beach surf and venetian blinds with multiple quantities of iced tea. Then garnish with leafy palm fronds and the play of their shadows to reinforce the setting and intensify the mood. To this, add a beguiling femme fatale (Kathleen Turner) matched with a handsome but incompetent lawyer (William Hurt), who both conspire to murder her unsuspecting but shadowy husband (Richard Crenna). Shake it all vigorously. **You now have *Body Heat*: Laurence Kasdan's film noir cocktail, Florida style**. His 1981 directorial debut blends the semi-tropical drink rather well in this two-hour version of his own screenplay.

The Main Point (Thesis)

Some critical essays on film begin the introductory paragraph by announcing the standard *COMPLETE THESIS STATEMENT (CTS)*. This is composed of the **Subject + Complete Predicate + Minor Inferences**. In this pattern, the *Simple Thesis* (ST—*subject plus complete predicate/verb phrase,* i.e., what is being said about it) are then immediately followed by the *Minor Inferences* (MI—secondary or supporting points). All occur within the same sentence. Another variation of this formula, has the minor inferences coming quickly on the heels of the simple thesis in the next sentence. In many comparative papers and research studies, however, the CTS may not be introduced so obviously at the very beginning of the essay. In the movie review, with so much important boilerplate to be presented, the actual CTS could be considered as that personal insight or those few points that the writer wants to develop. Often the review's title—if it is not solely the same as the motion picture's name—will allude to this primary focus of the review.

To summarize, there are two versions of the CTS:

- The first has all three major components in ONE SENTENCE: **Subject + Complete Predicate + Minor Inferences.**
- The second version has the FIRST SENTENCE as the **Simple Thesis** and the SECOND SENTENCE are its **Minor Inference.**

In the review of *Glengarry Glen Ross* (appearing earlier in this chapter), the CTS states that the real estate agency offers a glimpse of contemporary hell, with the minor inferences showing how all the agents and their manager build this horrible environment where they are both the sufferers and the tormentors in it. The title of the review, "Hell, Version of: America in the Nineties," points to that theme and can be considered the simple thesis.

Each of the four paragraphs below contains a complete thesis statement about John Hancock's wonderful motion picture of 1974, *Bang the Drum Slowly*. All four examples use the orthodox CTS pattern with three of the versions having the supporting points incorporated into the same sentence. However, the fourth example has the minor inferences following immediately in the next sentence. The simple thesis (ST) itself is capitalized while the minor inferences (MI) or supporting points are in bold print.

#1
John Hancock's 1974 film *BANG THE DRUM SLOWLY* IS ABOUT FRIENDSHIP, BASEBALL, AND MORTALITY all looked at with **humor, poignance,** and **understatement.**

#2
BANG THE DRUM SLOWLY, a small 1974 film by John Hancock, is **funny, poignant, and understated** as it LOOKS AT FRIEND-SHIP AND MORTALITY IN THE WORLD OF PROFESSIONAL BASEBALL.

#3
The motifs of FRIENDSHIP AND MORTALITY DOMINATE JOHN HANCOCK'S *BANG THE DRUM SLOWLY* (1974), the **under-stated, poignant, yet funny** little film set in the world of MAJOR LEAGUE BASEBALL.

#4
Taken from the Mark Harris book of the same name, *BANG THE DRUM SLOWLY* is director John Hancock's 1974 film that REVOLVES AROUND BASEBALL, FRIENDSHIP, AND MORTAL-ITY. It does so with **humor, poignancy, and understatement.**

The following paragraph below, on the same movie, puts the simple thesis in one sentence with the minor inferences in the next. Both are placed within the larger context of an introductory paragraph.

When we think of Major League Baseball today, not only do superbly gifted athletes come to mind but also a world ruled by multi-year, multi-million dollar contracts, product endorsements, and increasing alienation from the fans. Almost forty years ago, professional baseball players focused more on the team and on the game, and on their contributions to the first and their performances in the second, respectively. Released in 1974, *Bang the Drum Slowly* is a small film by John Hancock which looks at the game from that earlier perspective. THE FILM, essentially, DELVES INTO THE MOTIFS OF FRIEND-SHIP AND MORTALITY IN A BASEBALL SETTING. It does so in a manner that is both **funny,** yet **poignant,** and always **understated.**

The first three sentences are used as lead-ins to the central idea, namely, of the film's focusing upon the motifs of friendship and mortality in the world of professional baseball. However, the minor inferences concentrate on the tones of understatement, humor, and poignancy in developing those motifs.

Subordinate Points and Examples

Minor Inferences (known also as *Subordinate* or *Secondary Points)* elaborate on the thesis. They do so by using scenes or incidents of the movie as *concrete examples* of these points. Since the examples derive from or refer back to the subordinate points, they should be seen as clearly connected to the thesis statement.

The following paragraphs build upon the introductory paragraph previously presented for *Bang the Drum Slowly* and expand the subordinate points of the simple thesis. Through anecdote and example, they concern themselves with the humor, poignancy, and understatement (minor inferences) that run throughout the film and characterize it.

The friendship between Henry Wiggens (Michael Moriarty) and Bruce Pearson (Robert De Niro) seems quite unlikely, incongruous, even comical at first. Henry is the urbane, ace pitcher from New York City. Bruce, on the other hand, comes from a small town in Georgia and perennially has to fight for a place on the roster as a catcher. Physically, they are like Mutt and Jeff: Henry, is tall and rangy; Bruce is average in height and slight in build. Yet there is a bond between them and it is introduced during the opening credits as we see them jogging around the perimeter of the ball field during a team practice. This bond strengthens between the two men as the movie progresses.

The film opens on a note of pathos which is curiously restrained. In fact, throughout the film, humor, poignancy, and understatement are interwoven like a three-stranded rope. Henry and Bruce are leaving the Mayo Clinic in Rochester, Minnesota. Bruce has been diagnosed with Hodgkin's disease, a form of cancer. They are driving on a road silently flanked by fields flecked with snow. Bruce is impassive while Henry glances at him occasionally. Henry's voice-over declares:

"Actually, he got over it fairly quick. You might not think so, but it's true. You're drivin' along with a man who's been told he's dyin', yet everything keeps goin' along. I mean, it's been hard enough roomin' with him when he's well. He chews this disgustin' tobacco; he's pissed in the sink; and, as a catcher, he's a million dollars' worth of promise with two cents on delivery. Most people didn't even know he was with the club. He was almost too dumb to play a joke on and now he'd been played the biggest joke of all."

They arrive at Bruce's parents' house and their son declares he's fine. Later, though, while fishing with Henry, he confesses that he is confounded at how earlier as a kid he almost drowned, then avoided death in Vietnam, and narrowly missed getting killed by a truck. But now, without taking risks, he's got a fatal disease. He laconically sums up his condition: "I been handed a shit deal, boy. I'm doomed." He mispronounces "doomed" as if it has two syllables. That night, he is seen burning his clippings in a bonfire.

The Conclusion

There are many approaches for writing a convincing concluding paragraph or section. Too often, students restate the thesis, which makes for a humdrum and repetitious ending since so much of the paper already has been devoted to stating then justifying or proving the simple thesis and its minor inferences. Actually, the options one has for writing a conclusion are as varied as those of the introduction, especially when writing about film.

With the conclusion too, you can employ a number of approaches other than the obvious and repetitive restatement of the thesis (which should only be used for longer papers of more than 10 pages). Below are summarizing methods for consideration (again based on the previously mentioned book by Jean Wyrick):

- mentioning broader implications of the essay
- calling for action to be taken
- warning provoked by the essay
- providing a quotation that summarizes the essay's thrust
- witticism that emphasizes the essay's substance
- submitting an image/description for greater perspective

- asking a rhetorical question suggested by the essay
- telling a story or joke inspired to add closure to the essay (78–79)

A series of excerpts from some professional reviews best illustrate the different ways one can handle an ending. Note as you read the reviews, how often there is a connection between the opening remarks and the concluding statements. This is not at all repetition but, rather, coming full circle.

Bosley Crowther, in his review, decidedly did not like Jean-Luc Godard's *Breathless* (1960). His opening paragraphs castigate the film and his final opinions reaffirm many of his earlier views.

As sordid as is the French film, "Breathless," . . .—and sordid is really a mild word for the pile-up of gross indecencies—it is withal a fascinating communication of the savage ways and moods of some of the rootless young people of Europe (and America) today.

Made by Jean-Luc Godard, one of the newest and youngest of the "new wave" directors who seem to have taken over the cinema in France, it goes at its unattractive subject in an eccentric photographic style that sharply conveys the nervous tempo and the emotional erraticalness of the story it tells. And through the American actress, Jean Seberg, and a hypnotically ugly new young man by the name of Jean-Paul Belmondo, it projects two downright fearsome characters. (3239)

Now for Crowther's conclusion:

All of this, and its sickening implications, M. Godard has got into this film, which progresses in a style of disconnected cutting that might be described as "pictorial cacophony." A musical score of erratic tonal qualities emphasizes the eccentric moods. And in M. Belmondo we see an actor who is the most effective cigarette-mouther and thumb-to-lip rubber since time began.

Say this, in sum, for "Breathless": it is certainly no cliché, in any area or sense of the word. It is more a chunk of raw drama, graphically and artfully torn with appropriately ragged edges out of the tough underbelly of modern metropolitan life. (3239)

The concluding remarks of a review for Elia Kazan's 1954 classic *On the Waterfront* provides some additional points to consider for the full appreciation of this film.

On the Waterfront is more than deserving of the eight Academy Awards that it received. It is rare that Hollywood is able to make a film about a social/labor issue right off the newspaper headlines that is not a sensationalistic, one-dimensional piece but rather a sober, multi-textured endeavor. A work that not only brings to light a societal problem but renders it with such in-depth character development, excellent technical execution, and sensitive writing. The Oscars, which cover areas so varied as acting, direction. screenwriting, production (best picture) and the technical areas of cinematography, editing, and art direction attest to its achievement.

When it reached Broadway, Richard Rodgers' and Oscar Hammerstein's *Oklahoma!* redefined the American stage musical. Writer Leslie Donaldson, in the final paragraph of his overview of the screen production of *Oklahoma!* (1955), says its impact on the Hollywood movie musical was just as influential.

> The score for *Oklahoma!* includes many Rodgers and Hammerstein classics. All of the most familiar songs were included in the film, among them "O, What a Beautiful Morning," "Surry with the Fringe on Top," "People Will Say We're in Love," "I Cain't Say No," "All Er Nothin'" and, of course, the title song "Oklahoma!" Jud, however, unlike his counterpart in the stage version, in the film sings only one song , "Poor Jud's Daid." *Oklahoma!* was Rogers' and Hammerstein's first musical, and it continues to prove extremely durable in frequent revival productions. It was a landmark production for the American musical theater and had effects on movie musicals that followed far greater than its producers could have imagined. (1248)

What follows is a complete critique of John Ford's *Cheyenne Autumn*. It is written under the assumption that the reader is familiar with the film—released in 1964—and much of the filmography of its renowned director. In this piece, the movie's breach of geographic integrity, tone, and storyline and their combined impact on the film are discussed in full as the main thrust of the essay. The conclusion refers back to the introduction and major focus of the piece while making a few final observations and speculations. Some important additional aspects of this critique should be noted, including the

- functional aspects of the title, including the film's name,
- lead-in passages of the introduction,
- thesis statement at the end of the introductory section,
- plot summary within the body,
- development of the minor inferences (subordinate points) of the thesis statement,
- integration of credits (boilerplate) and evaluative remarks throughout, and
- concluding comments in reference back to the main thrust of the essay.

Cheyenne Autumn: Too Many Stories Wedged into One

John Ford began his directing career in 1917, during the silent movie era, with *The Tornado*, not surprisingly, a western. He made the transition into sound in 1928 and made his last film *7 Women*, a drama, in 1966 to end a film career of 50 years. All told, he was involved in some form of directing activity in 139 projects. During that time, he amassed four Academy Awards as Best Director for *The Informer* (1935), *The Grapes of Wrath* (1940), *How Green Was My Valley* (1941), and *The Quiet Man* (1952). He received a fifth directorial Oscar nomination for his work in *Stagecoach* (1939), the only western of the quintet.

In some of Ford's later works, he showed a greater maturation and sensitivity towards the treatment of his traditional subject matter. In *The Man Who Shot Liberty Valance* (1962), the romantic view of the gunfighter Ford turned on its head as the gunslinger was suddenly seen as killer for hire, operating on less than pure motives. John Ford also put a different take on the "noble" U.S. cavalry versus the "bloodthirsty Indians" in *Cheyenne Autumn*, released two years later, where he portrayed Native Americans much more sympathetically. This theme, incidentally, was more successfully developed almost thirty years later by Kevin Costner's Oscar-winning epic *Dances with Wolves* (1990).

Despite all of Ford's acclaim—he has been called America's foremost director—this last western, *Cheyenne Autumn*, proved to be a disappointment rather than the capstone of his work in the genre. It did not measure up to some of his great westerns of the past, including *Stagecoach* (1939), *Fort Apache* (1948), *The Searchers* (1956) *Sergeant Rutledge* (1960) and the aforementioned *The Man Who Shot Liberty Valance*. It showed some shortcomings in its casting, and greater flaws in its choice of geographic location continuity, tone, and, especially, storyline.

The least of *Cheyenne Autumn's* deficiencies had to do with some of the casting decisions. It was a mixed bag. On the positive side, the performance by Richard Widmark as Captain Thomas Archer, a cavalry officer morally conflicted by following orders versus following his conscience was strong. The same could be said of Edward G. Robinson's solid performance as the highly principled Secretary of the Interior. Carroll Baker played Deborah Wright, the Quaker schoolmarm as both sensitive and credible. However, all the major Cheyenne roles were played by non-Native Americans, including Ricardo Montalban, Gilbert Roland, Delores Del Rio, and an unconvincing Sal Mineo.

More disturbing was the location continuity—especially in terms of geographic accuracy—that was taken by Ford. Historically, the 1500 mile trek began from the dry scrub prairie of Oklahoma to the more lush, high plains and mountains of Wyoming and Montana, the Northern Cheyenne ancestral lands. However, the director decided on his all but trademarked location of Monument Valley in the Southwest where Arizona, New Mexico, Colorado, and Utah meet at the Four Corners.

Ford intended this to be primarily a serious even tragic work; however, the tone of the Dodge City interlude was anything but. It played as broad comedy even farce. It had very little to do with such events as the forced march that the Cheyenne imposed upon themselves back to their origins. Their decision to leave their Oklahoma reservation came after being lied to once too often by the U.S. government officials. After their tribal numbers had been decimated almost two-thirds by disease and inability to adjust to the barren land foisted upon them by Washington, the remnants of the tribe decided to break their treaty. They began their arduous journey back to the territory of their forefathers. But when Ford suddenly shifted the focus to Dodge City, Kansas, the main concern now seemed to become the gambling and saloon women rather than the plight of the Cheyenne. The likes of Marshal Wyatt Earp (James Stewart), Doc Holliday (Arthur Kennedy), and a local cardsharp (John Carradine) all took their licks doing comedic turns. The tone of the film totally collapsed, the mood was broken, and at this point, the film lost itself.

This, of course, also diverted us from the main plot development, namely, the desperate Cheyenne attempt to escape both starvation and retribution by the cavalry, who are chasing them. Another sub-plot was also imposed on the movie. Back in Washington, D.C., a sympathetic Secretary of the Interior (Robinson) found himself entangled in politics before he could leave the city, head west on the transcontinental railroad, and intervene directly on the Indians' behalf, thus settling the conflict right there on the Great Plains.

If the location scenes could have been more faithful to the geographical terrain of the historic events—Oklahoma has nothing comparable to the red sandstone mesas and breathtaking vistas of Monument Valley; if the tone of desperation at the tribe's flight had been maintained by removing the diversion of the Dodge City sequence; and if the sympathetic Cabinet member's role had been re-written so as to fit more smoothly into the plot, then this film could have indeed been one of John Ford's best.

The title of the critique, *"Cheyenne Autumn: Too Many Stories Wedged into One,"* relates to two conflicting elements that ensnare the film. But before this issue is presented and developed, a lead-in passage furnishes background material on the enormous cinematic achievements of John Ford. At the outset, however, of the third paragraph of the introduction, the direction changes radically with the word "Despite." From this point on some serious mistakes made by Ford while undertaking this project are pointed out. By paragraph's end we are presented with the complete thesis statement on why this potentially great film missed the mark.

Since the reader is supposedly quite familiar with this motion picture, the storyline is loosely alluded to rather than detailed, since one of the main points made is that the film has too many subplots that distract us from the main thrust of the work. Other aspects that contribute to the weakening of the movie are discussed as well. Throughout this main section of the essay (the body) boilerplate and evaluative comments are interwoven when fitting.

In the final paragraph, concluding remarks refer back to the film's major stumbles. It suggests if each could have been mitigated or avoided totally, the end result would have been a crowning success for its director.

Revision Techniques

Every rough draft has initially to be converted into a first draft and then proofread, edited, re-written, honed, and polished before it can be submitted to a professor or a publisher. Such revision techniques can be broken down into two component areas: proofreading and self-editing. The differences between them are not so much in kind as they are to degree; of the two, however, self-editing is the far more time-consuming, disciplined undertaking.

Proofreading

Proofreading basically is a one-step process. In a way, it is the mirror image of brainstorming. In brainstorming, you write down a number of ideas and keywords about a topic before organizing them into a recognizable pattern or outline prior to creating the rough draft. With proofreading, you make a first pass at rereading the draft and correcting mistakes as you go along. In this procedure, typographical errors and missteps in spelling, capitalization, punctuation, and other mechanical miscues are discovered and rectified. If using a hard copy, errors are underlined or circled and corrected as nearby as possible, using a pen or pencil in a color other than black. If working on a computer, corrections are made on the spot, leaving no evidence of the previous miscues.

An effective method of proofreading is to do so at the sentence level—not the paragraph level—to isolate and catch the maximum number of mechanical slips. Although you have already read each sentence from its first word to its last, this method of proofreading *has you start from the last sentence of the paper and work your way back to the first, sentence by sentence.* This method works because it breaks the continuity between sentences, insuring that each sentence is separated from the rest. It is in trying to correct sentences for mechanical errors that the contexts of the other sentences before and immediately after actually get in the way. If you were to read normally while looking for errors—that is, from the beginning of your essay straight through to its conclusion—your eyes would occasionally trick you into perceiving something as correct (because you expect it to be) when, in actuality, it is wrong. Remember, proofing for mechanical errors is not the same as rereading for content flaws, which will be discussed in the next subsection on *self-editing.*

The sample paragraph below is a complete but short critique of Robert Rossen's *All the King's Men* which got the Academy Award for Best Picture in 1949. The selection is rife with errors.

Robert Penn Warren successful novel *All The Kings Men,* loosely based on the life of Louisiana political legend Huey King Fish Long have been transformed into an engaging cinema classic of the same name. The film (1949) does so by transposing the excellent characterization of the book by excellent casting of the film. This is especially evident by it's choice of Broderick Crawford, to play Willie Stark, Oscar winner for best actor. And by the supporting cast of Mercedes McCambridge, also an Oscar winner and John Ireland. The motion picture is not only the story of a overly ambitious, slick-tongued politico whose also a pick em up by the bootstraps hill billy Who will not stop at nothing. to get what he wants. We've heard that one before. But here we have the story of the rise a man who has nothing but his drive, courage, and a sense of the people—his people—downtrodden though they may be— and the heartfelt desire to right their wrong. To get for them what they truly deserve and what they have earned. But the story doesn't end well. But this is also the story of his fall. He betrays his friends, his honesty becomes corrupted, his noble goals becoming blind megalomania. Finally, what he has become leads directly to his death by assasination, before his good traits can emerge to save him. And the title? It's signicance is that like the nursery rhyme, by the end of his life run, all the kings horses and all the kings men could put Humpty Dumpty (read Willy Stark) back together again.

Below we see what happens to the paragraph after a quick proofreading. All the necessary corrections have been incorporated into the original's text below and appear in bold print. You will also note that the single paragraph has been expanded into four and a title has been added.

All the King's Men: Faithfully Reproduced on the Screen

Robert Penn Warren's successful novel *All the King's Men*, loosely based on the life of Louisiana political legend Huey **"Kingfish"** Long has been transformed into an engaging cinema classic of the same name. The film (1949), **directed by Robert Rossen,** does so **by** transposing the **book's** excellent characterizations **through the film's remarkable** casting. This is especially evident by **its** choice of Broderick Crawford **to play Willie Stark, winning an Oscar as Best Actor for it.** And by its selection of a **top-notch** supporting cast, **namely,** Merced McCambridge **as Sadie Burke (Academy Award for Best Supporting Actress),** and John Ireland, **for his sensitive portrayal of Jack Burden.**

The motion picture is not only the story of **an** overly ambitious, slick-tongued politico, **who's** also a pick- **'em-up-by-the-boot-straps hillbilly, and who** will not stop at **anything** to get what he wants. We've **seen** that one before. But here we have **an account** of the rise a man who has nothing but his drive, courage, and a sense of **justice for** the people—his people—downtrodden though they may **be,** and the heartfelt desire to right their wrongs. He aims to get for them what they truly deserve and what they have earned.

However, the **tale** doesn't end well. **For** this is also the **saga** of his fall: **how** he betrays his friends; **how he lets others corrupt his honesty; and how he permits** his noble goals to **mutate into** blind megalomania. Finally, what he has become leads directly to his death by **assassination,** before his good traits can **re-**emerge to save him.

And **what of significance of** the film's title? **It harks back to** that **old** nursery rhyme. **For by** the end of his life's run: "All the king's horses and all the king's men couldn't put Humpty Dumpty (read **Willie Stark**) back together again."

Self-Editing

Self-editing (rewriting) is a more time-consuming, deliberate procedure than proofreading. Rewriting involves heavy revision: where not only are random errors discovered and corrected, but numerous words are changed, various sentences are restructured, certain ideas are deleted or added, and the document as a whole is scrutinized for possible major reorganization. One brief read-through is not sufficient. Each rereading can have specific and limited objectives, among them:

- conformity of margins and spacing
- consistency of typographical fonts and print conventions
- consistency of theme and emphasis
- accuracy of details and statistics
- correction of errors in spelling, punctuation, grammar, capitalization, usage, subject verb agreement, and tense agreement
- completeness and balance of the whole
- conformity of style and tone
- lack of confusion between objective/subjective elements
- clarity at the sentence and paragraph levels
- admixture of sentence lengths and structures

With this in mind, we turn to a relatively short review of the 2002 comedy *Barbershop* directed by Tim Story with screenplay credits going to Mark Brown. We will first look at the initial draft of the review with its accompanying handwritten corrections and edits and then note the changes made in the rewritten final version.

MORE THAN JUST AN HAIRCUT AND A SHAVE

One of the *more* common businesses in most~~ly~~ ~~any~~ neighborhood*s* *is* *the* ~~^~~ barbershop~~s~~. This usually is a place where somebody can get ~~their~~ *his* hair cut, with or without a shampoo, ~~or~~ *have it* styled, even ~~get~~ *enjoy* a shave.

But in African American neighborhoods, specially in the older inner cities, the barbershop ~~is~~ *serves as* much more. One can say, it is a vital institution for ~~dissemenation of~~ *disseminating* information, ~~you can~~ air*ing* opinions, ~~or to~~ *and* tak*ing* the ~~communities~~ *community's* pulse on issues of mutual concern. In Tim Story's film ~~of~~ Barbershop ~~that seems to be~~ *[italics]* the main point *is* that for black men especially ~~it is~~ *such* an *establishment is an* essential community institution that far exceeds its ~~tonsatorial~~ *tonsorial* services.

Calvin Palmer (Ice Cube) ~~who~~ is the fiscally beleaguered proprietor who inherited this business from his father. He does not at all have the calling for cutting hair and would rather

51   *Style and Structure in Film Criticism*

sellout for a healthy profit and dable into something more profitable and more quick too]. In fact, this is precisely what he
has done. we learn. But this isn't so easy or simple since others
are involved: his family, his employees (seven of them and all
barbers), and the diverse denizens of the beauty salon come
exclusive mens club. Yet now, on the enterprise's last day under
his ownership, Calvin has strong second thoughts. Obviously, the
précis of the movie is whether he can reverse the deal (which he
made with Lester, the local hoodlum). But before the audience
learns of the outcome, theres a whole lotta laughter to
wade through experience.

What makes the movie is not the storyline or conflict but
rather the rich banter that run richly throughout the film by
the talented ensemble cast. A bref introduction of the players
should be helpful. First and foremost is Cedric the Entertainer
as Eddie, the elderly haircutter with years of experience and an
empty chair. But that's awright. Eddie can't be bothered by clipping, combing, and shaping since there are too many topics that
he pontificates on. His opinions are iconoclastic, be they on
notables or events. His bits on Rosa Parks, O.J.Simpson, and Rodney King maybe unsettling but, nevertheless, hilarious. His performance steals the show.

Keith David as Lester Wallace is both sinister and slick,
and being the consummate character actor that he is, inhibits
this roll comfortably. Then there's Leonard Howze as Dinka, a
Nigerian emigrant who hopes his constant conversations with customers and fellow workers in the shop will help him loose his
accent. The rapper Eve does an acting turn as the sassy, sharp-
tongued Terri, whose therapeutic bottle of "apple juice" always

has less remaining ~~then~~ than when she last left it. Let's not forget

Troy Garity (expertly portrayed by Isaac Rosenberg), the white

hip-hop-speaking, soul brother wannabe. Michael Ealy is Ricky

Nash, an ex-con desperately trying to stay on the straight and

narrow by trimming hair. And, of course, there is Sean Patrick Thomas as Jimmy

James—the college boy "working his way ~~thru~~ through"—who is far less

knowledgeable than he thinks. Rounding out the cast ~~is~~ are Anthony

Anderson as J.D. and Lahmard Tate as Billy: two incompetent

thieves who steal a ATM machine and then don't know what to do

with it in the subplot of the film.

The main ~~plot~~ storyline may be trite and the subplot is decidedly far-

fetched, yet ~~through~~ via the funny, outrageous, but insightful dia-

logue, the viewer gets a sense that this barbershop is a special

place: Within ~~the~~ its impoverished, dilapidated Southside of Chicago

neighborhood, ~~a place~~ it is the barbershop that helps foster and strengthen the bonds

of the community.

Now we look at the self-edited, revised, re-written version. The
changes run the gamut from marginal adjustments to typographical
errors to restructuring sentences to augmenting the original with additional material. The end product is tighter and smoother flowing as well
as cleaned of its mechanical errors.

MORE THAN JUST A HAIRCUT AND A SHAVE

One of the more common businesses in most neighborhoods is the

barbershop. This usually is a place where somebody can get his

hair cut (with or without a shampoo), have it styled, or even

enjoy a shave. But in African American neighborhoods, especially

in the older inner cities, the barbershop serves as much more.

One can say it is a vital institution for disseminating information, airing opinions, and taking the community's pulse on issues of mutual concern. In Tim Story's film *Barbershop* the main point is that for black men especially, such an establishment is an essential institution that far exceeds its tonsorial services.

Calvin Palmer (Ice Cube) is the fiscally beleaguered proprietor who inherited the business from his father. He does not at all have the calling for cutting hair and would rather sell it for a healthy profit, investing the proceeds into a more quickly lucrative enterprise. In fact, we learn this is precisely what he has done. But this isn't so simple since others are involved: his family, his employees (seven, and all barbers), and the diverse denizens of the hair salon cum exclusive men's club. Yet now, on the enterprise's last day under his ownership, Calvin has strong second thoughts. Obviously, the plot of the movie centers upon whether he can reverse the deal made with Lester, the local hoodlum. But before the audience learns of the outcome, there's a torrent of laughter to wade through.

What makes Tim Story's *Barbershop* is not the storyline or central conflict but rather the rich banter that runs consistently throughout the film by its talented ensemble cast. A brief introduction of the players should be helpful. First and foremost is Cedric the Entertainer as Eddie, the elderly haircutter with years of experience and an empty chair. But that's all right. Eddie can't be bothered by clipping, combing, and shaping hair since there are too many topics that he must pontificate upon. His opinions are iconoclastic be they on notables or events. His bits on Rosa Parks, O. J. Simpson, and Rodney King may be unsettling but are, nevertheless, hilarious. His performance steals the show.

Keith David as Lester Wallace is both sinister and slick, and being the consummate character actor that he is, inhabits this role comfortably. Then there's Leonard Howze as Dinka, a Nigerian immigrant who hopes his conversations with customers and colleagues will help him lose his accent. The rapper Eve does an acting turn as the sassy, sharp-tongued Terri Jones whose therapeutic bottle of "apple juice" always has less remaining than when she last left it. Let's not forget Troy Garity (expertly portrayed by Isaac Rosenberg), the white hip-hop-speaking, soul brother wannabe. Michael Ealy is Ricky Nash, an ex-con desperately trying to stay on the straight and narrow by trimming hair. And, of course, there is Sean Patrick Thomas as Jimmy James—the college boy "working his way through"—who is far less knowledgeable than he thinks. Rounding out the cast are Anthony Anderson as J.D. and Lahmard Tate as Billy: two incompetent thieves who, in the subplot of the film, steal an ATM machine and then don't know what to do with it.

The main storyline may be trite and the subplot is decidedly farfetched, yet via the funny, outrageous, but insightful dialogue, the viewer gets a sense that this barbershop is a special place. Within its impoverished, dilapidated Southside of Chicago neighborhood, it is the barbershop that helps foster and strengthens the bonds of the community.

This chapter has looked at the styles and structures employed in writing film criticism. It first explored the different attitudes adopted in critical writing. Numerous excerpts and full-length examples illustrated such concerns as objectivity and subjectivity, judgment, plot summary (the précis), and tone. Word choice was deemed important especially in the areas of denotation and connotation, concreteness, and cliché avoidance. Also discussed was sentence variation in structure and length. The chapter then considered the main components of any critical paper including the lead-in sentence (or section) and the part it plays in the introduction. Then broached were the topic sentence, the thesis statement, its subordinate points, and the conclusion. All of these were liberally peppered with examples. The last major element mentioned were revision techniques, namely, proofreading and self-editing.

If we look ahead, Chapters 3 through 6 look at specific types of film criticism. These include the review, the critical analysis (analytical critique), the comparative analysis, and the documented research paper respectively. Finally, we have the three Appendixes (A through C) and the Index which ends the text.

3

TYPES OF FILM CRITICISM: THE REVIEW

Bradley Cooper, Ed Helms, and Zach Galifianakis in Todd Phillips' The Hangover, Part II *(2011). Warner Bros.* Courtesy of The Kobal Collection at Art Resource, NY.

The second chapter mentions that there are four modes of critical written expression about film that this text explores: the *review*, the *critical analysis* (also known as the *analytical critique*), the *comparative analysis*, and the *documented research paper*.

The *review* is the most popularized form of film criticism. We see examples of the review in student newspapers, the daily press, popular magazines, television, and on Internet blogs, among others. The two most typical functions of a review are to *provide an overview* and to *make an evaluation* of a movie, usually in release at either first or second run local theaters or directly released to DVD. Since the review is a type of critical format, it can be applied to any film regardless of release date. The review also makes an important assumption: that the reader has NOT seen the movie in question.

─────────────── **Audience and Format** ───────────────

Recognizing your audience is the first hurdle to jump when writing a review. Knowing your readership will help determine the tone, style, vocabulary level, and length of the critical piece. What you say and how you say it will differ, depending on whether you direct the review, let's say, toward sixth graders, the general adult public, or your college professor.

As previously stated, the reviewer has the obligation to both briefly overview and evaluate the film. In so doing, the reviewer furnishes the necessary *boilerplate* (credits and more) including: title, year of release, genre, director, literary source (if there is one), other technical staff, and major cast members. In addition, a partial plot synopsis gives the reader some idea as to what to expect in the film. *However, the critic must be sure to avoid detailing the climax and ending,* especially in a thriller, suspense drama, or mystery. The reviewer is then expected to develop one or two aspects of the film that have made a particular impact on him or her. All of these elements are considered part of the overview section—a major responsibility of the critic.

Without some subjective evaluation, however, the reviewer is basically dispensing a plot summary with screen credits and a few insights but little else. The readership expects more: Was it a decent film worthy of investing seven, eight, ten, or even twelve dollars per head? If so, why? If not, how come? Judgment is a requisite of the review. Such an evaluation and, perhaps, a recommendation must be made in a logical manner supported by convincing arguments and facts. In summary, the review should include these components:

- boilerplate—title, release year, genre, director, literary source, other technical staff, cast members

- partial plot synopsis
- point(s) for development
- evaluation/recommendation

In the last chapter, you saw numerous samples of complete movie reviews. All contained the aforementioned major components and all were directed to a college-level audience. Following, however, are three sample introductory paragraphs that review Sydney Pollack's 1982 hit *Tootsie*. The content differs somewhat in each, since it is determined by the maturity level and background knowledge of the audience to which it is directed. The first example is meant for sixth graders; the second is intended for a general adult public; and the third is addressed to a professor of film studies. All three reviews are written as if the movie were playing at local theaters.

#1 (SIXTH GRADERS)
Michael Dorsey, played by Dustin Hoffman, has been an actor—on and off—in New York City for twenty years. Unemployed again, he is really eager to work on the stage or in front of a camera. To get a role in a television soap opera, Michael has no choice but to become Dorothy Michaels. First, he shaves his face, arms, and legs. After that, he puts on makeup and a wig. Finally, slipping into women's clothing and high heels, Michael leaves for the tryout. When he gets the job soon after, the fun really begins in *Tootsie*, the zany comedy directed by Sydney Pollack.

#2 (GENERAL ADULT)
"Method" actor Michael Dorsey (Dustin Hoffman) once again is walking the New York City streets, looking for work and haunting the unemployment office. He knows he is talented and devoted to his craft; yet, after twenty years, Dorsey has been more off the stage than on it and been behind in his rent more often than in front of an audience. Desperate for acting work, he auditions for a soap opera as Dorothy Michaels—easily his most demanding acting stretch ever. We watch, fascinated, as Michael Dorsey transforms himself into Dorothy Michaels in *Tootsie*, the delightful Sydney Pollack comedy. Dorsey shaves his appendages and face, plucks strategic hairs, applies cosmetics skillfully, sets the wig in place, and squeezes into undergarments, clothes, and high heels. When his convincing performance nets him the role, the fun not only begins but we also gain some subtle insights into what it is like for a man to live the role he has created as a woman.

#3 (PROFESSOR OF FILM STUDIES)
The concept is not new: the ancient Greeks and the Elizabethans employed it. Earlier comedies of the twentieth century milked it for

laughs. Thus, when director Sydney Pollack puts Dustin Hoffman in drag, we might expect yet another guffaw-filled, pratfall-laden, slapstick farce. Not so. We should expect more from Messrs. Hoffman and Pollack in *Tootsie* and we get it. The tired premise has a few unique twists that make it fresh. Hoffman as Michael Dorsey is an unemployed New York City actor. A fanatical proponent of the "Method" school, he is almost unemployable as he questions every line and assails every director and playwright with his own interpretations of the script. However, for him to end his twenty-year stint in thespian purgatory calls for radical measures: he commits to audition for a television soap opera as Dorothy Michaels—a decidedly desperate stretch. Yet, professional that he is, Dorsey skillfully transforms himself into Dorothy, reads his lines during the casting call, and wins the role. Not only does the fun now really begin, but so do inquiries into sexual identity reversal and what it entails.

Notice how the introductory paragraph focusing upon sixth graders uses very direct language. Michael Dorsey's background and current problem are stated in the first two sentences. What he does to prepare for the audition takes up the bulk of the paragraph, but the last sentence serves as a segue to the rest of the review.

In the introductory paragraph aimed at an adult audience, the structural development is the same: we meet Michael Dorsey, learn of his chronic problem, witness the lengths that he goes to for the audition, and then prepare to proceed with the rest of the review. But here, more details are given, using more mature language and more sophisticated sentence formation.

Finally, the third sample immediately adopts a scholarly tone, alluding to the theater of the ancient Greeks and the Elizabethans for historical comparisons. Eventually, Dorsey is psychologically dissected with examples of his extreme behavior which contribute to his chronic unemployablility. Despite additional concepts that are broached, the structure of the paragraph still resembles that of the other two.

———————— Tone, Style, and Word Choice ————————

A review, besides sketching an overview of the plot and furnishing boilerplate information on a movie, also gives some personal insights on the film and makes evaluative commentary on it. By so doing, it adopts an attitude towards that motion picture. This can be solemn, playful, sarcastic, scathing, and reverential, among others. The style of language can be informal or formal. In the informal review, slang expressions and some liberties with sentence structure are more likely to be taken. This will also be reflected in the word choice and vocabulary level of the language used. The formal review is more restrictive, eliminating use of slang and colloquialisms, and most, if not all, non-standard English terminology.

The Serious Review

A serious tone in a review is just that: sarcasm, double entendres, irony, overly clever word play and a surfeit of slang should be in short supply. Notice in the following introductory remarks how the critic sets an earnest, straightforward tone in the review of *Il Postino (The Postman)* the Italian language film made by British director Michael Radford in 1994.

> It is 1953 in a poverty-ridden fishing village off the Italian mainland. Mario Ruoppolo, a dreamer, has been temporarily hired as a postman. Pablo Neruda, the world famous Chilean poet, has just been exiled by his homeland because of his Communist leanings to this remote island. Realizing the extraordinary demands about to be made on his tiny postal system, the local postmaster chooses Mario, who possesses a bicycle needed to deliver the volume of mail to Neruda in his mountaintop villa. Mario, meanwhile, has fallen in love with the local beauty but realizes that a mastery of words—expressed poetically—is necessary to win her. What develops eventually is a touching relationship between a sophisticated man of letters and a simple rustic united in the pursuit of love through poetry.

Although the film *Il Postino* does contain humorous segments, the paragraph above directs us towards the unlikely friendship between two men who are worlds apart culturally. Yet what they have in common—a love for women and poetic verses that voice such romantic feelings—bridges the gap between them.

Another film that receives a serious treatment from the opening paragraph and, indeed, throughout the rest of the review, is Mike Nichols' troubling 1971 effort, *Carnal Knowledge*.

> Mike Nichols is no stranger to controversy: he created an uproar following his adaption of Edward Albee's play *Who's Afraid of Virginia Woolf* (1967); he broke new ground with *The Graduate* (1968), and he ruffled many feathers with his adaptation of the Robert Heller novel *Catch-22* (1970). But nothing was comparable to the uproar that greeted him after the initial screenings of *Carnal Knowledge*. His searing opus on the extremes of contemporary American sexual mores shocked many even though the "Sexual Revolution" had been proceeding for more than five years. The film covers a span of more

than 20 years, from the 1940s through the late 1960s. It focuses on two college roommates—Jonathan (Jack Nicholson) and Sandy (Art Garfunkel) and the women in their lives, mainly, Bobbie (Ann-Margaret) and Susan (Candice Bergman) during the course of that time. With this motion picture, director Mike Nichols and his screenwriter, Jules Feiffer, take a very frank look at the drives that impel sex and romantic love and the differing perceptions of each, depending on gender.

The Humorous Review

Humor is a tone that is frequently used in reviews. Its purpose can be to ridicule (as in a "pan") or to fondly poke fun at in a more positive assessment. Often a humorous or light tone accompanies the critical remarks about a comedy or another genre movie with significant comical undertones. Such is the case in this introduction to a review of Tony Richardson's 1963 Oscar-winning smash *Tom Jones*.

> *Tom Jones*—such a plain name for a character of such wonderful excesses—is a motion picture about the larger than life eponymous rogue set in 18th Century England. Adapted from the sprawling classic novel by Henry Fielding, written more than two centuries ago, this fast-paced film is filled with a bawdy spirit that mirrors the picaresque protagonist's lust for life. Lust, a more than appropriate word to describe a major quality of young Jones in this comedic masterpiece since it depicts Jones' (Albert Finney) lust for women, food, drink, adventure (read: trouble) and fun. We avidly follow his escapades—be they through the idyllic English countryside or teeming streets of London—as Tom flouts authority at all levels and in all ways. The scene where Tom gorges himself on oysters and other decadent delicacies followed by a romp in bed with a willing lass has become a classic set piece.

The Pan

A reviewer is not always going to enjoy what he/she sees or believe it has many redeeming qualities. Some movies are poorly written or poorly directed; others exhibit inferior acting. The public has a right to be warned about those films regarded as "turkeys," "bombs," and "flops." Below is an unsympathetic review of the sequel to *The Hangover* (2009). Made in 2011, it is simply entitled *The Hangover Part II*. It is followed by Renata Adler's pan of Sergio Leone's *The Good, the Bad, and the Ugly* (1966) which appeared in the *New York Times*.

The Hangover Part II: Box Office First—So Do Quality and Originality Even Matter?

You would think that the original aesthetic objectives for *The Hangover, Part II* would be modest enough: make a decent sequel and the people will come . . . in droves. Apparently, the producers did away with "decent" and thus ignored any pretensions of even modest quality and originality. Not only is the second film rigidly formulaic but because it goes over so much of the same ground, really isn't that funny.

The original, directed by Todd Phillips, surprised everybody: first, it was bawdy (expected, given the title and premise) but also clever (unexpected). Second, it had an original twist—a film that although centered around a bachelor party is actually about the consequences of it the morning after rather than the actual soirée itself. Finally, it proceeded not via the expected chronological time-line leading up to the big event and its excesses, but instead furnished a series of flashbacks more common to a detective mystery where the characters and the audience try to find out what the hell happened? And it really worked. Despite being obviously produced for mass commercial appeal, it was carried off so successfully that it received critical acclaim as well as a high ca-ching return ($485 million). The primary cast was another of the comedy's strong points: Bradley Cooper played Phil, a married teacher although an unapologetic party guy; Ed Helms was Stu, a dentist, also in a committed relationship although less happily so; and Alan, portrayed by the irrepressible Zach Galifianakis, the brother of the bride, not yet chewing upon the fruits of employment. Finally, the setting— Las Vegas with all its vagaries—also aided the production. Thus, *The Hangover* was a hit and deserved to be.

But this review is not about the initial foray but about the one that has followed. As with any sequel, the question we are immediately compelled to ask is whether the second offering matches or— rarest of achievements—even surpasses the first? The answer, unequivocally and quite tersely: NOT AT ALL! This is so despite the fact that the main and some of the supporting cast have been reassembled and given their original roles. The location, however, has moved far away across the Pacific to Bangkok, Thailand, and its environs—both seedy and luxurious.

Although Todd Phillips also directed this second go-round, the same cannot be said of the writing team—Phillips, Craig Mazin, and Scot Armstrong—and it shows. The plot structure of *Part II* slavishly follows the first. Instead of a bachelor party gone awry, here calamity strikes at a supposedly innocent, beach bonfire near the resort where the wedding party are all staying. The groom who went missing in *The Hangover* now safely stays back at the hotel; however, here it is the 16-year-old prospective brother-in-law cum genius level Stanford pre-med who is missing the next morning. And again no one remembers what happened at the beach the night before. Not only that, Instead of awakening to various stages of disarray and incapacity at a Vegas Strip $4,000 per night luxury suite, the boys grope towards consciousness in a seedy Bangkok dive, miles away from the resort. More and more parallels abound—both major and minor. What is not consistent, however, are the mingling of laughs and cleverness. Here, though, only the original's raunchiness is one-upped while the line of bad taste is crossed with impunity.

Much is asked of the audience in the suspension of disbelief department. Some of the shock and violence seems truly gratuitous. One example: when proof of the missing brother-in-law is given, we see a Stanford class ring tightly wrapped around his severed finger—when the ring alone would have been enough. Even the happy ending totally begs our credibility: how could the kid-genius' family be so forgiving and welcoming to the groom and his entourage who were charged with protecting their precious son? (We learn early on that he is a concert-level violinist as well as being a young surgeon-in-training.) How could the loss of a crucial finger be accepted so graciously (even in a farce)?

Sure, *The Hangover Part II* has made a profit hand over fist at the theater and now in DVD rentals and sales. But it is sad that the makers of this film have so easily accepted the sequel's "tough act to follow" rule of thumb by adding their own sobriquet: "So why even try?"

Notice at the outset, the title of the review hints at the tone of this critical piece and its evaluation of the film. The second paragraph introduces the general problem of any sequel—the tough act to follow—by crowing about the positive qualities of the predecessor. The third paragraph begins to identify the why and how of this sequel's shortcomings. Each succeeding paragraph identifies additional defects or excesses that hurt the film. Along the way, the general premise, the plot, and the players are mentioned. Finally, in the last sentence, the movie is condemned for having taken a formulaic easy way out to make huge profit and abandoned any honest effort to make a more creative albeit humorous sequel.

It should be noted that because a full paragraph was written to discuss the merits of the original, some would claim this comes close to being a Comparative Analysis essay (which is discussed fully in Chapter 4) rather than a Review. However, because there is so much evaluation in this piece and the parallels of the two films are generalized rather than very detailed, this definitely leans towards being more of a review than a comparative critique.

Pans are not confined to comedies that are excessive or just fall short of expectations. Critic Renata Adler loathed Sergio Leone's "spaghetti western" *The Good, the Bad, and the Ugly* and states her opinion forthrightly in her review of January 1968.

The Good, the Bad, and the Ugly

"The Burn, the Gouge, and the Mangle" (its screen name is simply inappropriate) must be the most expensive, pious and repellent movie in the history of its peculiar genre. If 42d Street is lined with little pushcarts of sadism, this film, which opened yesterday at the Trans-Lux 85th Street and the DeMille, is an entire supermarket.

The plot—and in their eagerness to mutilate someone, the writers continually lose track of it—seems to run as follows: A man whose pseudonym is Bill Carson, and who owns a clam-shaped snuffbox, knows the whereabouts of $200,000. Three characters, Burn (Clint Eastwood), Gouge (Lee Van Cleef), and the Mexican, Mangle (Eli Wallach)—whose names in the film are Joe, Setenza, and Tuco, respectively—are anxious to get hold of it. Ultimately, Clint Eastwood gets it. The action takes place in the West during the Civil War. That is all. It lasts two and a half slow hours.

The movie entitled "The Good, the Bad, and the Ugly" forgets all about Bill Carson for an hour. Then, he makes a brief appearance, rolling his one eye (any number of characters in the movie have lost an eye, or an arm, or a leg, or two legs), and dies, covered with blood and flies and making rasping noises, in incredible agony. Before expiring, he divulges the location of the cemetery in which the money is buried to Mangle, and the gravesite to Burn.

The sole purpose of the snuffbox is to enable Gouge to jam Mangle's fingers quite painfully in it. Gouge himself is missing a joint of a finger in his gun hand. The camera dwells on this detail lovingly.

Eli Wallach, as the Mexican, has a wound over his left eye, which heals and reopens throughout the film for no apparent reason. He is throttled three times, sun-scorched, and once so severely beaten by Van Cleef that anyone who would voluntarily remain in the theater beyond this scene (while he might be a mild, sweet person in his private life) is not someone I should care to meet, in any capacity, ever.

Wallach rolls his eyes, makes hideous gastro-intestinal noises to convey shades of emotion, and laughs incessantly. Among his feldspar teeth, there is one capped with what looks like a molten paper clip. He also forgets, from time to time, what sort of ethnic part he is playing; and particularly when he is called to shout, his Mexican is laced with Riverdale.

Van Cleef's acting consists of displaying a stubble of beard and narrowing his eyes. Aside from various other shootings and beatings he administers, he shoots one man through a salad bowl (although most of the movie takes place in arid country, there are an awful lot of salads and vegetables) and another through a pillow. In the end, he is shot. There is scarcely a moment of respite from the pain. Most of the scars and wounds are administered about the face, and even Eastwood, as the hero, spends a good part of the movie with his face blistered. His face and voice are expressionless throughout.

The film is the third of a trilogy ("A Fistful of Dollars" and "For A Few Dollars More" preceded it.) There are immortal lines in the special context. One, just when it appears there is going to be a nonviolent moment in the film, from an officer who is preaching against brutality: "Sergeant," he begins, "gangrene is eating my leg away. Also my eye." Another, when Eastwood surprises Wallach in the bathtub: "Put your drawers on and take your gun off," he says. (33:1)

Renata Adler's critical jabs at *The Good, the Bad, and the Ugly* run rampant throughout her review. Her initial sentence pillories the movie by renaming it "The Burn, the Gouge, and the Mangle." She calls it "repellent" because of its excessive sadism. After a brief synopsis of the plot, she identifies those set pieces that exhibit the gratuitous violence that she condemns so strongly. She also castigates the acting of some of its principals—namely, Eli Wallach, Lee Van Cleef, and Clint Eastwood—in the interpretations of their roles. The fact that the supporting cast and all the extras are Italian and have their words dubbed she perceives as further weakening the film.

The Rave

The rave review is one that applauds a movie on multiple fronts. The screenplay, the direction, the acting, the set design, the music score all seem exceptional. Films that get raves—especially those from the distinguished critics of the big newspapers, magazines, and trade journals—get nominated and win Academy Awards and other prestigious cinematic honors. Most reviews, as can be guessed, however, land somewhere on the spectrum between the pan and the rave. Two examples of rave reviews—one full length the other a capsule—on the same film follow. The first is Bosley Crowther's review of *The Best Years of Our Lives* (1946) and the second—on the same motion picture—is short, unsigned, and shows that a glowing review can be written in about 160 words or so. Then we have an additional full length rave review by Roger Ebert on *The Color Purple* (1985).

William Wyler's *The Best Years of Our Lives* has quite a pedigree: screenplay by Pulitzer Prize-winning playwright Robert E. Sherwood, based on the novel *Glory for Me* by celebrated author MacKinlay Kantor, and produced by Samuel Goldwyn who pulled out all the stops to assemble a cast of some of Hollywood's premier talents. This review by the venerable Bosley Crowther appeared in the *New York Times*.

The Best Years of Our Lives

It is seldom that there comes a motion picture which can be wholly and enthusiastically endorsed not only as superlative entertainment but as food for quiet and humanizing thought. Yet such a one opened at the Astor last evening. It is "The Best Years of Our Lives."

Having to do with a subject of large moment—the veteran home from the war—and cut, as it were, from the heart-wood of contemporary American life, this film from the Samuel Goldwyn studio does a great deal more, even, than the above. It gives off a warm glow of affection for every day, down-to-earth folks.

These are some fancy recommendations to be tossing boldly forth about a film which runs close to three hours and covers a lot of humanity in that time. Films of such bulky proportions usually turn out the other way. But this one is plainly a labor not only of understanding but of love from three men who put their hearts into it—and from several others who gave it their best work. William Wyler, who directed, was surely drawing upon the wells of his richest talent and experience with men of the Air Forces during the war. And Robert E. Sherwood, who wrote the screen play from a story by MacKinlay Kantor, called "Glory for Me," was certainly given genuine reflection to his observations as a public pulse-feeler these last six years. Likewise, Mr. Goldwyn, who produced, must have seen this film to be the fulfillment of high responsibility. All their efforts are rewarded eminently.

For "The Best Years of Our Lives" catches the drama of veterans returning home from war as no film—or play or novel that we've yet heard of—has managed to do. In telling the stories of three veterans who come back to the same home town—one a middle-aged sergeant, one an air officer, and one a sailor who has lost both hands—it fully reflects the delicate tensions, the deep anxieties, and the gnawing despairs that surely have been experienced by most such fellows who have been through the same routine. It visions the overflowing humors and the curious pathos of such returns, and it honestly and sensitively images the terrible loneliness of the man who has been hurt—hurt not only physically but in the recesses of his self-esteem.

Not alone in such accurate little touches as the first words of the sergeant's joyful wife when he arrives home unexpectedly, "I look terrible!" or the uncontrollable sob of the sailor's mother when she first sees her son's mechanical "hands" is this picture irresistibly affecting and eloquent of truth. It is in its deeper and broader understanding of the mutual embarrassment between the veteran and his well-intentioned loved ones that the film throws its real dramatic power.

Especially in the readjustments of the sailor who uses prosthetic "hooks" and the airman who faces deflation from bombardier to soda-jerker is the drama intense. The middle-aged sergeant finds adjustment fairly simple, with a wife, two grown-up kids and a good job, but the younger and more disrupted fellows are the ones who really get it in the teeth. In working out their solutions Mr. Sherwood and Mr. Wyler have achieved some of the most beautiful and inspiring demonstrations of human fortitude that we have had in films.

And by demonstrating frankly and openly the psychological blocks and the physical realities that go with prosthetic devices they have done a noble public service of great need. It is wholly impossible—and unnecessary—to single out any one of the performers for special mention. Frederic March is magnificent as the sergeant who breaks the ice with his family by taking his wife and daughter on a titanic binge. His humor is sweeping yet subtle, his irony is as keen as a knife and he is altogether genuine. This is the best acting job he has done. Dana Andrews is likewise incisive as the Air Forces captain who goes through a grueling mill, and a newcomer, Harold Russell, is incredibly fine as the sailor who has lost his hands. Mr. Russell, who actually did lose his hands in the service and does use "hooks," has responded to the tactful and restrained direction of Mr. Wyler in a most sensitive style.

As the wife of the sergeant, Myrna Loy is charmingly reticent and Teresa Wright gives a lovely, quiet performance as their daughter who falls in love with the airman. Virginia Mayo is brassy and brutal as the latter's two-timing wife and Cathy O'Donnell, a new, young actress plays the sailor's fiancée tenderly. Hoagy Carmichael, Roman Bohnen, and Ray Collins will have to do with a warm nod. For everyone gives a "best" performance in this best film this year from Hollywood. (27)

From the first sentence on it is clear that we are reading a rave review. The rest of the fairly lengthy piece supports this claim with superlatives about the acting, the direction, and the script of this exceptional motion picture. The article applauds the film for exposing a very timely issue of that era: the problems of the returning World War II veteran. That this motion picture does so with such humanity and realism, enabling it to reach the audience at once and keep it engrossed for the entire three hours running time is especially remarkable.

The capsule review of *The Best Years of Our Lives* that follows the Crowther article was written in 2012 and besides being a glowing review—though far less detailed—also puts the film in a unique historical perspective (66 years later). Unlike the Crowther review, which was quite lengthy, this review makes its salient points in less than 200 words, including its title.

The Best Years of Our Lives: Still Relevant Today

Besides the excellence of its cast, story, and direction, *The Best Years of Our Lives* has remarkable relevance for today's audiences. The film centers around the lives of three veterans, who upon their return home after hostilities have ended find difficulties—expected and unforeseen—adjusting to civilian life. Their stories have been handled with great sensitivity and credibility by director William Wyler and his crew.

What makes this classic so meaningful today is that over the course of the last eight years this country has been involved in two wars overseas. And in each of these years, too many of our discharged military have been ill-equipped to adjust to the peacetime rhythms and demands of life back in the United States. This has led especially to a host of psychiatric and psychological disorders as well as physical disabilities that are not being addressed sufficiently today.

What the Wyler film did so many years ago is look at some of these readjustment problems with the hopes that our government and people would confront these issues more openly and fully. The same holds true today.

One of the challenges of any filmmaker is to successfully convert one medium to another: a short story or novel into cinema, or a stage drama into a motion picture. Roger Ebert's highly laudatory review of director Steven Spielberg's conversion of the Alice Walker novel *The Color Purple* mentions that a director often cannot be 100% faithful to every aspect of the original source.

The Color Purple

* * * *

Date of Publication: 12/20/1985

There is a moment in Steven Spielberg's "The Color Purple" when a woman named Celie smiles and smiles and smiles. That was the moment when I knew this movie was going to be as good as it seemed, was going to keep the promise it made by daring to tell Celie's story. It is not a story that would seem easily suited to the movies.

Celie is a black woman who grows up in the rural South in the early decades of this century, in a world that surrounds her with cruelty. When we first see her, she is a child, running through fields of purple flowers with her sister. But then she comes into clear view, and we see that she is pregnant, and we learn that her father has made her pregnant, and will give away the child as he had done with a previous baby.

By the time Celie is married—to a cruel, distant charmer she calls only "Mister"—she will have lost both her children and the ability to bear children, will have been separated from the sister who is the only person on Earth who loves her, and will be living in servitude to a man who flaunts his love for another woman.

And yet this woman will endure, and in the end she will prevail. "The Color Purple" is not the story of her suffering but of her victory, and by the end of her story this film had moved me and lifted me up as few films have. It is a real, warm, hard, unforgiving, triumphant movie, and there is not a scene that does not shine with the love of the people who made it.

The film is based on a novel by Alice Walker, who told Celie's story through a series of letters, some never sent, many never received, most addressed to God. The letters are her way of maintaining sanity in a world where few others ever cared to listen to her. The turning point in the book, and in the movie, comes after Celie's husband brings home the fancy woman he has been crazy about for years—a pathetic, alcoholic juke-joint singer named Shug Avery, who has been ravaged by life yet still has an indestructible beauty.

Shug's first words to Celie are: "You as ugly as sin." But as Shug moves into the house and Celie obediently caters to her husband's lover, Shug begins to see the beauty in Celie, and there is a scene where they kiss and Celie learns for the first time that sex can include tenderness, that she can dare to love herself. A little later, Celie looks in Shug's eyes and allows herself to smile, and we know that Celie didn't think she had a pretty smile until Shug told her so. That is the central moment in the movie.

The relationship between Shug and Celie is a good deal toned down from the book, which deals in great detail with sexual matters. Steven Spielberg, who made the movie, is more concerned with the whole world of Celie's life than he is with her erotic education. We meet many members of the rural black community that surrounds Celie. We meet a few of the local whites, too, but they are bit players in this drama.

Much more important are people like Sofia (Oprah Winfrey), an indomitable force of nature who is determined to marry Harpo, Mister's son by a first marriage. When we first see Sofia, hurrying down the road with everyone trying to keep up, she looks like someone who could never be stopped. But she is stopped, after she tells the local white mayor to go to hell, and the saddest story in the movie is the way her spirit is forever dampened by the beating and the jailing she receives. Sofia is counterpoint to Celie: She is wounded by life, Celie is healed.

Shug Avery is another fascinating character, played by Margaret Avery as a sweet-faced, weary woman who sings a little like Billie Holiday and has long since lost all of her illusions about men and everything else. Her contact with Celie redeems her; by giving her somebody to be nice to, it allows her to get in touch with what is still nice inside herself.

Mister, whose real name is Albert, is played by Danny Glover, who was the field hand in "Places in the Heart." He is an evil man, his evil tempered to some extent by his ignorance; perhaps he does not fully understand how cruel he is to Celie. Certainly he seems outwardly pleasant. He smiles and jokes and sings, and then hurts

Celie to the quick—not so much with his physical blows as when he refuses to let her see the letters she hopes are coming from her long-lost sister.

And then, at the center of the movie, Celie is played by Whoopi Goldberg in one of the most amazing debut performances in movie history. Here is this year's winner of the Academy Award for best actress. Goldberg has a fearsomely difficult job to do, enlisting our sympathy for a woman who is rarely allowed to speak, to dream, to interact with the lives around her. Spielberg breaks down the wall of silence around her, however, by giving her narrative monologues in which she talks about her life and reads the letters she composes.

The wonderful performances in this movie are contained in a screenplay that may take some of the shocking edges off Walker's novel, but keeps all the depth and dimension. The world of Celie and the others is created so forcibly in this movie that their corner of the South becomes one of those movie places—like Oz, like Tara, like Casablanca—that lay claim to their own geography in our imaginations. The affirmation at the end of the film is so joyous that this is one of the few movies in a long time that inspires tears of happiness, and earns them. "The Color Purple" is the year's best film.

What critic Roger Ebert in his review most importantly mentions is that the film *The Color Purple* is quite a faithful adaptation of the Alice Walker novel. Director Steven Spielberg demonstrated this fidelity to the text in terms of "depth and dimension." He regards the film as an inspiring work of art which he recommends as the best movie of the year.

Comedies—even zany ones—can get rave reviews. As an illustration, we have John Waters' *Hairspray* (1988). The film takes place during the early 1960s in the auteur's beloved city of Baltimore, Maryland. He often lampoons this town and its denizens in many of his other—and far more controversial—works. In fact, this film is decidedly a departure for Waters and shows, if he chooses, he can produce work that appeals to a wider audience. It should be noted that this film inspired a Broadway musical and a Hollywood remake in 2007.

The following review by Desson Howe of the *Washington Post* praises just about every aspect of this nostalgic and surprisingly insightful movie. With the large amount of ensemble dancing to a cavalcade of rock 'n roll and soul music hits, this could be more accurately categorized as a musical comedy.

Hairspray (PG)

Desson Howe
February 26, 1988

BALTIMORE, 1963. TUBBY housewife Edna Turnblad, polyester frock stretched taut over her body (picture Ralph Kramden in drag) tries to explain to her husband Wilbur why her daughter Tracy (picture a teen-age Ralph Kramden in drag) likes to do the mash potato on the local TV dance show.

"Wilbur," she says, "it's the times. They are a-changin'. Somethin's blowin' in the wind. Fetch me my diet pills, would you Hon?"

It's just a taste—or whiff—of John Waters' hilarious trash blanche comedy "Hairspray," the latest from the guy who gave us cult hits "Pink Flamingos," "Mondo Trasho," "Desperate Living" and "Polyester."

Shot in Waters' hometown, with cult faves (renowned transvestite Divine as Edna, blond-on-blond regular Mink Stole) and kitschmongering household names (Sonny Bono, Pia Zadora, ex-Blondie Debbie Harry), "Hairspray" is a gleeful wallow in the 1960s gook of beehive 'dos and Leslie Gore music—with a positive desegregation message besides.

White teenagers do the Madison, the Pony, and the Roach to black music on "The Corny Collins Show" while their black contemporaries watch from home. Their onscreen dancing is restricted to "Negro Day," the last Thursday of the month.

The issue divides Waters' crazy-quilt world. Schoolgirl Tracy (Ricki Lake) leads the positive integrationists, with fast-talkin' black deejay Motormouth Maybell (Ruth Brown). The opposition's led by TV station chief Arvin Hodgepile (Divine, in men's clothing) and the blond 'n' weaselly Von Tussle family—Tracy's personal rival Amber (Colleen Fitzpatrick) and parents Velma (Debbie Harry, with Connie Stevens-meets-Mommie Dearest relish) and Franklin (Bono at his all-time nasal best).

Waters writes warmth into his caricatures, lifting "Hairspray" above cartoon cult. You love 'em all, whether it's Divine squeezed into a tight, groovy little number she picked off the rack at the "Hefty Hideaway" shop, or Zadora's Beatnik, who thinks she is Odetta, or the demented Dr. Frederickson (Waters himself, a psychoanalyst who assails Tracy with a psychedelic pinwheel and a sort of fluorescent electric cattle prod for teens. It seems inappropriate to call ick noir auteur Waters a breath of fresh air. But amid the stale odor of our man-made, musty, Muzaked lives; he's a welcome gust of Renuzit.

Same Film: Differing Opinions

Not all raves are universally shared. Some pictures are highly controversial and elicit strong feelings both pro and con. One such film is Neil LaBute's *Your Friends and Neighbors* (1998). Condemned by some in the strongest terms, it is lauded by others as evidenced in the following review by *Chicago Sun-Times* columnist and PBS film commentator Roger Ebert.

Your Friends and Neighbors

* * * * (R)
Cary: Jason Patric
Man: Ben Stiller
His Partner: Catherine Keener
Man: Aaron Eckhart
His Wife: Amy Brenneman
Artist's Rep: Nastassja Kinski
Written and directed by Neil LaBute.
Running time: 100 minutes.
Classified R (for explicit dialogue).

Neil LaBute's "Your Friends and Neighbors" is a film about monstrous selfishness—about people whose minds are focused exclusively on their own needs. They use the language of sharing and caring when it suits them, but only to their own ends. Here is the most revealing exchange in the film:
    Are you, like, a good person?
    Hey! I'm eating lunch!
    The movie looks at sexual behavior with a sharp, unforgiving, cynicism. And yet it's not really about sex. It's about power, about forcing your will on another, about having what you want when you want it. Sex is only the medium of exchange. LaBute is merciless. His previous film, "In the Company of Men," was about two men who played a cruel trick on a woman. In this film, the trick is played on all the characters, by the society that raised and sur-

rounded them. They've been emotionally short-changed and will never hear a lot of notes on the human piano.

LaBute's "Your Friends and Neighbors" is to "In the Company of Men" as Quentin Tarantino's "Pulp Fiction" was to "Reservoir Dogs." In both cases, the second film reveals the full scope of the talent, and the director, given greater resources, paints what he earlier sketched. In LaBute's world, the characters are deeply wounded and resentful, they are locked onto their own egos, they are like infants for which everything is either me! Or mine! Sometimes this can be very funny—for the audience, not for them.

Of course they have fashionable exteriors. They live in good "spaces," they have good jobs, they eat in trendy restaurants and are well-dressed. They look good. They know that. And yet there is some kind of wall closing them off from one another. Early in the film, the character played by Aaron Eckhart frankly confesses he is his own favorite sexual partner. A character played by Catherine Keener can't stand it when her partner (Ben Stiller) talks during sex, and later, after sex with Nastassja Kinski, when she's asked, "What did you like best?" she replies, "I liked the silence best."

Ben Stiller and Keener are a couple; Eckhart and Amy Brenneman are a couple. In addition to Kinski, who works as an artist's assistant, there is another single character, played by Jason Patric. During the course of the movie these people will cheat on and with one another in various ways.

A plot summary, describing who does what and with whom, would be pointless. The underlying truth is that no one cares for or about anybody else very much, and all of the fooling around is just an exercise in selfishness.

The other day I spent a long time looking at the penguins in the Shedd Aquarium. Every once in a while two of them would square off into a squawking fit over which rock they were entitled to stand on. Big deal. Meanwhile, they're helpless captives inside a system that has cut them off from their true natures, and they don't even know it. Same thing in this movie.

LaBute, who writes and directs, is an intriguing new talent. His emphasis is on writing: As a director, he is functional, straightforward and uncluttered. As a writer, he composes dialogue that can be funny, heartless and satirical, all at once. He doesn't insist on the funny moments, because they might distort the tone, but they're fine, as when the Keener character tells Kinski she's a writer—"if you read the sides of a tampon box." She writes ad copy, in other words. Later, in a store, Kinski reads the sides of a tampon box and asks, "Did you write this?" It's like she's picking up an author's latest volume in a bookstore, although in this case the medium is carefully chosen.

The Jason Patric character, too, makes his living off the physical expression of sex: He's possibly a gynecologist (that's hinted, but left vague). The Eckhart character, who pleasures himself as no other person can, is cheating on his wife with . . . himself, and he likes the look of his lover. The Brenneman character is enraged to be treated like an object by her new lover, but of course is treated like one by Eckhart, her husband. And treats him like one. Only the Kinski character seems adrift, as if she wants to be nice and is a little puzzled that Keener can't receive on that frequency.

LaBute deliberately isolates these characters with identification with any particular city, so we can't characterize them and distance ourselves with an easy statement like, "Look at how they behave in Los Angeles." They live in a generic, affluent America. There are no exteriors in the movie. The interiors are modern homes, restaurants, exercise clubs, offices, bedrooms, book stores. These people are not someone else. In the immortal words of Pogo, "We have met the enemy, and he is us."

This is a movie with the impact of the original stage production of Edward Albee's "Who's Afraid of Virginia Woolf." It has a similar form, but is more cruel and unforgiving than "Carnal Knowledge." Mamet has written some stuff like this. It contains hardly any nudity and no physical violence, but the MPAA at first slapped it with an NC-17 rating, perhaps in an oblique tribute to its power (on appeal, it got an R). It's the kind of date movie that makes you want to go home alone.

Roger Ebert's review covers quite a bit of ground. After dispensing with the four-star evaluation before the text begins, he first launches into the theme of the film: the extreme selfishness of all the characters and its effects on themselves and others. This selfishness is manifested in sexual desire and gratification with no love, compassion, or consideration for the other party under the sheets.

The critic then points out the influences on and the parallels between the LaBute film and other notable movies, namely, his own *In the Company of Men* and Quentin Tarantino's *Reservoir Dogs* and *Pulp Fiction*. The egotistic, self-absorbed, and sometimes cruel characters are neither happy nor satisfied despite their comfortable and stylish residences paid for through decent jobs with hefty incomes.

Ebert sees LaBute's considerable writing skills as the strong suit of this film. Clever, biting, and funny, LaBute's dialogue goes far in developing these despicable, yet fascinating group of contemporary people. As the audience condemns these characters for their morally bankrupt lives, it becomes increasingly unsettled as it realizes that those on screen have emerged from the same stuff as those in the theater seats and that the distance between the two is uncomfortably short.

In contrast, we read of Mick LaSalle's interpretation of the same film expressed in the *San Francisco Chronicle*. Here we have the identical film seen through an entirely different prism of reaction and taste.

Not Your Typical 'Friends and Neighbors' Sex Satire Is Full of Empty Provocation

"Your Friends and Neighbors" is the title of writer-director Neil LaBute's new movie but whose friends and neighbors is he talking about? Not mine. Not yours, I'd bet. And not even his, I suspect.

This is an embarrassing film. It's a sex comedy that sets itself up as a satire of middle-class mores, except there's no truth behind any of its observations. LaBute tries to be shocking and only manages to be shockingly puerile—tasteless in a high-school-boyish sort of way.

The picture begins with a close-up of a man (Jason Patric) having sex, gasping out rude compliments about the woman's body and technique. Then the camera pulls back and we see that he's alone, practicing his banter into a tape recorder.

Next we enter the bedroom of a couple, played by Ben Stiller and Catherine Keener, who are actually doing the deed. During the act, he can't stop saying stupid things like, "Do you feel?! Do you feel it?!" She finally pushes him away, and he storms out of the apartment in a huff.

And so on for 100 minutes. "Your Friends and Neighbors" is made up of a series of unsuccessful, pathetic and grotesque sexual encounters, interspersed with conversations in which friends and acquaintances do nothing but talk about sex. Why they should be so fixated on sex is anybody's guess—they're all so bad at it.

More than 20 years ago, David Mamet broke ground in this area with "Sexual Perversity in Chicago," which sent up certain kinds of men and women and lampooned the way people talk about sex. But the talk in "Your Friends and Neighbors" is too false to be a lampoon and too flat to be interesting.

LaBute has his characters constantly asking each other about their most memorable encounters. Jason Patric, as a ruthless Lothario, has a long monologue in which he describes the ecstasy he experienced raping a boy in the high school locker room. The monologue is bereft of any artistic truth. It's just calculated for reaction.

LaBute's first film, "In the Company of Men," was about two junior executives who brutally seduce and dump a deaf secretary. People criticized it for being politically incorrect or praised it for the same reason. Some saw it as an indictment on male cruelty. Camille Paglia, the sharpest critic, said it was too politically correct.

After "Your Friends and Neighbors," LaBute's first effort looks simply like a delicate provocation, with no integrity beyond that. Certainly his second movie rolls out the same tricks: He tries to titillate by showing the most appalling behavior he can devise—for example, in one scene a man explodes at a sex partner for staining his bed sheets. At the same time, by putting all the evil and idiocy on the male characters, he leaves his film open to a feminist interpretation.

"Your Friends and Neighbors" is not a feminist or an anti-feminist film. It's just empty—false, insincere, and a complete waste of time.

Mick LaSalle's scathing review is obviously a far cry from the laudatory comments by Roger Ebert. Where Ebert perceives a great, burgeoning talent in its director/screenwriter, LaSalle was not impressed by the dialogue and characterization. The critic's use of such adjectives as "false," "insincere," and "embarrassing" sum up much of his perception of LaBute's movie. He sees it as supposing to be a "sex comedy" and "satire of middleclass mores"; yet to him, the film lacks any veracity or even integrity, to back up writer/director Neil LaBute's insights.

The Mixed Review

Predictably, most reviews of films fall somewhere between the pan and the rave. A critical piece will praise some features of a given movie and castigate others. Often, comparisons are made between the current film under review and its antecedents, identifying the film as a derivative of earlier—perhaps better—screen entries, or comparing it to other—and superior—works of the filmmaker. The reviewer continues to move back and forth: lauding the acting here, condemning the writing there; applauding well-conceived sequences in one paragraph, chastising the director's inconsistency in the next. The review is "mixed" and thus is a compilation of a movie that is "disappointing," or "falls short," but, nevertheless, has its "good points" and "flashes of brilliance."

Many critics, besides their written reviews, employ a rating system that immediately summarizes their overall evaluation of a motion picture. It is most comparable to an educator's grading system, but instead of letter grades—A, B, C, D, and F—usually stars are used (as with restaurants and hotels). Thus an excellent or outstanding movie typically gets four stars (* * * *), a good film rates three (* * *), a mediocre entry deserves a modest two (* *), a poor cinema feature nets a mere one (*) and a miserably executed reel of celluloid earns no stars whatsoever (—). Some reviewers get so fine as to include pluses or even minuses (B+, A-) or halves to stars (**1/2). Others in their definitions of ratings provide catchier expressions than such standard terms as "superior," "fair," or "poor." These substitutes would include "Don't miss!" "Worth a chance," and "Save your money," among others.

A film about young people, Spike Lee's *Crooklyn* (1994), exemplifies this mixed bag type of review. It has its strong qualities but also glaring weaknesses as well. What follows are two mixed assessments of Spike Lee's semiautobiographical *Crooklyn*. The tone of the first, which is unsigned, "Life from the Stoop and Other Brooklyn Memories" is neutral, even sympathetic, when pointing out the film's shortcomings and broadly admitting its strengths.

Life from the Stoop and Other Brooklyn Memories

This film by Spike Lee is his most autobiographical. Despite its being an arrow shot from the heart, *Crooklyn*, unfortunately, misses the mark in building sympathy for its characters. The adult cast, anchored by such stalwarts as Alfre Woodard and Delroy Lindo cannot be faulted nor can their kids, played by a host of young, naturalistic actors of considerable talent. In fact, that is the problem: they get so "real" that it interferes with the creation of empathy for them within the audience. Perhaps it is this critic's intolerance for excessive noise and chaos that gets in the way of more fully appreciating the film—and *Crooklyn*, within fifteen minutes, provides mayhem to spare.

It must be said that as with many of his previous films (*Do the Right Thing* and *Jungle Fever* come immediately to mind), director Spike Lee together with his siblings Cinque and Joie Lee (who co-wrote the script) meticulously evoke Brooklyn's Ft. Greene neighborhood during one summer in the 1970s. What especially rings true are the various street games invented by the local children to entertain themselves during the long, hot days.

Eventually, the film focuses on the Carmichael family: mother Carolyn, a schoolteacher (Woodard); father Woody, a musician (Lindo); sole daughter Troy (Zelda Harris); and their four sons Clinton (Carlton Williams), Wendell (Sharif Rashed), Joseph (Tse-Mach Washington) and Nate (Christopher Knowings). The kids we soon learn are a rambunctious crew guilty of all the petty cruelties, the whining, the bullying, the selfishness, and the total self-centeredness that are characteristic of so many children. Carolyn is constantly shouting above the din and overreacting, or so it seems, to every juvenile transgression. Easygoing, patient Woody is always the "good cop," the irresponsible, non-disciplinarian. But there is reason for Carolyn's anger: overwork, out of control kids, the pressures of school duties and school politics, and a husband who doesn't pull his weight fiscally—be it bouncing checks or refusing gigs because he doesn't enjoy playing rock 'n roll.

There is an interlude, when the family visits relatives in Virginia and Troy is left there with her uncle, aunt, and cousin for part of the summer. During this time, the young girl is either sullen, arrogant, mischievous, snotty, or utterly charming. This portion of the film is somewhat looser than the rest of the movie. The director is guilty of self-indulgence by filming the Virginia visit using a wide-angle lens, a heavy-handed, disconcerting device to show Troy's alienation with her surroundings.

When she returns home, there is a new and very serious family crisis. She and her siblings act predictably—crying, sulking, getting angry, being confused—rather than nobly. True, kids will be kids, but in so being meticulously faithful to their acting personas, something is lost in terms of character growth. Their reactions to tragedy are minimalistic and, consequently, even somewhat dignified, but their personalities and view of the world are virtually unchanged.

In this review, the critic, because of the film's honesty and strong acting, wishes he could have liked the film more than he had. However, he points out certain flaws where, ironically, the faithful portrayals of the principals make for less sympathetic characters. Admittedly, a strong point in the film is the wonderful evocation of time and place early in the film. However, the "noise and chaos" heard and seen as the storyline unfolds weaken the film. Since this is a review, the writer has hinted at the climax and denouement but has not given it away.

Now we turn to *Edward Copeland's Tangents* series entitled "From the Vault: Crooklyn." This blog, mostly filled with some praise and grudging admiration for auteur Spike Lee, nevertheless, comments about his glaring deficiencies in screenwriting and also chides the film's weak ending.

From the Vault: *Crooklyn*

Without a doubt, Spike Lee remains one of the most talented directors working in film today. Unfortunately, his greatest weakness— screenwriting—continues to plague him, especially in his latest work, *Crooklyn*.

With the exception of his unequaled greatest film *Do the Right Thing*, even his most worthy efforts (*Malcolm X, Jungle Fever*) could have used one or two more rewrites before filming began. With his least successful films (such as *Mo' Better Blues*), their weaknesses were usually the fault of the writing. While *Crooklyn* hardly equals the mess that *Mo' Better Blues* was, it certainly exhibits the same structural problems and lack of cohesion.

Crooklyn, which Lee co-wrote with his siblings Joie Lee and Cinque Lee, marks a departure for Spike in its subject matter, offering a warm, tragicomic look at growing up in Brooklyn in the early 1970s, when the main drugs parents had to worry about their kids falling prey to wasn't crack or heroin but television and sugar.

Alfre Woodard and Delroy Lindo head the Carmichael clan, a family of seven loosely based on the real-life Lees. Woodard plays Carolyn, who teaches school and tries to keep the house in order, including her husband Woody (Lindo), a musician trying to stay true to his art even if that means placing his family in a financial strait-jacket.

Crooklyn takes the point of view of the family's only daughter, 9-year-old Troy (newcomer Zelda Harris). While the film certainly looks through her eyes, it doesn't seem to be a strong enough viewpoint to carry the film's whimsical meandering.

While Woodard, Lindo and Harris all give solid performances, the four brothers tend to disappear into the woodwork, never developing into characters in their own rights. Subplots about a neighbor (David Patrick Kelly) and two glue-sniffing street kids (one played by Spike Lee) appear but never really go anywhere, though the glue sniffers do provide some funny camera angles.

Crooklyn turns out pleasant enough, but by the end, it feels as if something has been left out and it just stops. Despite the good actors and nice touches by Lee, Crooklyn ultimately disappoints. A film cannot survive on 70s vibes alone.

Just by adding an "s" to the word mixed-review, we mean something a bit different than a film that is both praised and skewered by the same critic. Thus the term "mixed reviews" signifies a movie of which the critics are, more or less, equally divided among those who award it a "thumbs up" and those who dismiss it with a "thumbs down." (An obvious illustration of this would be the differing assessments of *Your Friends and Neighbors* by Roger Ebert and Mick LaSalle, respectively, presented and discussed previously.)

Another film we can use to demonstrate the differences that two separate reviewers could have in evaluating a movie is Alexander Payne's *About Schmidt* (2002). We return once again to Roger Ebert, who thought fairly highly of the film, giving it three and a half stars out of four. David Edelstein, however, *Slate* on-line magazine's film critic, wasn't as kindly in his review.

About Schmidt

Warren Schmidt is a man without resources. He has no intellectual curiosity. May never have read a book for pleasure. He lives in a home "decorated" with sets of collector's items accumulated by his wife, each in the display case that came with the items. On his retirement day, he is left with nothing but time on his empty hands. He has spent his entire life working at a job that could have been done by anybody, or, apparently, nobody. He goes to the office to see if he can answer any questions that the new guy might have, but the new guy doesn't. In a lifetime of work, Warren Schmidt has not accumulated even one piece of information that is needed by his replacement.

"The mass of men," Thoreau famously observed, "lead lives of quiet desperation." Schmidt is such a man. Jack Nicholson is not such a man, and is famous for the zest he brings to living. It is an act of self-effacement that Nicholson is able to inhabit Schmidt and give him life and sadness. It is not true to say that Nicholson disappears into the character, because he is always in plain view, the most watchable of actors. His approach is to renounce all of his mannerisms, even the readiness with which he holds himself onscreen, and withdraw into the desperation of Schmidt. Usually we watch Nicholson because of his wicked energy and style; here we are fascinated by their absence.

"About Schmidt," directed by Alexander Payne, written by Payne and Jim Taylor, is not about a man who goes on a journey to find himself, because there is no one to find. When Schmidt gets into his 35-foot Winnebago Adventurer, which he and his wife Helen thought to use in his retirement, it is not an act of curiosity but desperation: He has no place else to turn.

The film's opening scenes show him suffering through a meaningless retirement dinner and returning home to ask himself, after 42 years of marriage, "Who is this old woman who is in my house?" His wife may ask the same question about her old man. They have lived dutiful and obedient lives, he as an actuary for the Woodman of the World Insurance Co. in Omaha, Neb., she as a housewife and mother, and now that the corporate world has discarded them they have no other role to assume. Helen (June Squibb) makes an effort to be cheerful, and surprises him with breakfast in the Adventurer the morning after his retirement dinner, but breakfast is a cheerless meal when it does not begin a day with a purpose. Then Helen drops dead. Warren is astonished and bereft, not at the enormity of his loss, but that he had so little to lose. Here is a man who did not "plan for retirement." "About Schmidt" has backed itself into a corner with its hero, who is so limited it would be torture to watch him for two hours, even played by Nicholson. The film puts Schmidt on the road, in a reversal of Nicholson's youthful journey in "Easy Rider." He and the film are in search of life, and find it in his daughter's plans to marry a man he (correctly) perceives as a buffoon and a fraud.

The humor in the film comes mostly from the daughter (Hope Davis), fed up with him and the family she is marrying into. Schmidt's new in-laws include Randall Hertzel (Dermot Mulroney), a waterbed salesman and a promoter of pyramid schemes, and his mother Roberta (Kathy Bates), who embraces the life force with a bone-crushing squeeze. Schmidt, who has hardly had a surprise in 40 years, now finds himself wrestling with a waterbed, and joined in a hot tub by the topless and terrifyingly available Roberta.

Roberta is intended as a figure of fun, but at least she approaches life hungrily and with good cheer. This is one of Bates' best performances, as a woman of outsize charm and personality, who can turn on a dime to reveal impatience and anger. Her selfishness helps us observe that Schmidt is not a selfish man, mostly because there is nothing he has that he wants and nothing he lacks that he cares about.

Schmidt has one relationship in his life that gives him a place to spill out his fears and discontents. After watching a TV ad for a world children's charity, he "adopts" a 6-year-old Tanzanian named Ndugu. Encouraged to write to the boy, he spills out his thoughts in long confessional letters. It is impossible to be sure if he thinks Ndugu can read these letters, or understand them, or if he has such a painful need to find a listener that Ndugu will do. Certainly there is no one in America who Schmidt would be able to talk to with such frankness.

"About Schmidt" is essentially a portrait of a man without qualities, baffled by the emotions and needs of others. That Jack Nicholson makes this man so watchable is a tribute not only to his craft,
but to his legend: Jack is so unlike Schmidt that his performance
generates a certain awe. Another actor might have made the character too tragic or passive or empty, but Nicholson somehow finds
within Schmidt a slowly developing hunger, a desire to start living
now that the time is almost gone.

"About Schmidt" is billed as a comedy. It is funny to the degree
that Nicholson is funny playing Schmidt, and funny in terms of
some of his adventures, but at bottom it is tragic. In a mobile home
camp, Schmidt is told by a woman who hardly knows him, "I see
inside of you a sad man." Most teenagers will probably not be
drawn to this movie, but they should attend. Let it be a lesson to
them. If they define their lives only in terms of a good job, a good
paycheck and a comfortable suburban existence, they could end up
like Schmidt, dead in the water. They should start paying attention
to that crazy English teacher.

What impressed Roger Ebert most in the film *About Schmidt* was
Jack Nicholson's interpretation of the title character. Nicholson performed against type and subtly painted a character that became
extremely "watchable" and sympathetic. Warren Schmidt of Omaha,
Nebraska, on the surface could be seen as the dullest of dull, with no
apparent wants and needs and totally non-emotive. After his retirement
and the death of his spouse, his life is particularly empty and meaningless. With another actor the character could be maudlin and non-
engaging but director Alexander Payne and Nicholson have sculpted a
person who at times is very funny and, ultimately, not merely sympathetic but, to Ebert, "tragic."

Although David Edelstein was impressed with Nicholson's performance, it nevertheless, was not able to carry the entire movie. His
review focuses more on the deficiencies of the work than its assets.

Omaha Lineman:
Even Jack Nicholson Can't Save *About Schmidt*

Alexander Payne's end-of-life road movie *About Schmidt* (New
Line) is like a Twilight Zone episode in which Jack Nicholson
awakes to find himself a 66-year-old former actuary and assistant
vice president of an Omaha insurance company married to a small,

overbearing woman who looks every bit her own age. This, of course, is not the film's literal premise. But Nicholson is the closest thing we have to a great actor with an expansive, Bogart-like movie-star persona, and he always comes with what a physicist might term a massive amount of "potential energy." When, at the climax of *About Schmidt*, the title character rises to make a toast to the marriage of his only daughter to a man he regards (accurately) as a nincompoop, it is the most loaded moment in a movie this year—not because of anything he says, but because you can hold it between your knees and the bug that you have up your ass, because a Nicholson who doesn't unleash the full force of his libidinous counterculture energy is a Nicholson unrealized.

Since the '80s, it's the "unrealized" Nicholson who has actually been the more exciting: not the mugging, Oscar-winning Jack Nicholson impersonator of *As Good As It Gets* (1997), but the grimly, sometimes furiously contained character actor of *The Border* (1982), last year's *The Pledge*, and now *About Schmidt*. Payne's movie is flat, depressed, and at times—given this director's talent—disappointingly curdled; it needs every quivering molecule of Nicholson's repressed rage to keep it alive and humming.

The movie is a surprisingly old-fashioned specimen of the "tune-out, turn-off, drop-in" genre—in which a funked-out character, suddenly stripped of the opiates of his or her previous life, drifts through what seems like a cold and harsh new world. Here that world is a gray Midwest in which ominously indifferent skyscrapers are bunched together on the flat plains, in which retirements and marriages are celebrated in chain restaurants to the tune of chain homilies.

After the sudden death of his wife (June Squibb), Warren Schmidt spends his days in bed watching TV, the dirty clothes and dishes piling up. In time he writes long letters to a Tanzanian orphan named Ndugu, whom he has sponsored (after seeing an ad on TV) for $22 a month. He tells Ndugu that, as a former actuary, he can calculate with great probability how many years a man will live, and he gives himself a 73 percent chance of being dead in nine. He says, "Life is short, Ndugu." So he takes to the road in a 35-foot Winnebago to try to convince his daughter, Jeannie (Hope Davis), not to marry a cretinous water-bed salesman named Randall (Dermot Mulroney). Schmidt longs, before he dies, to make a difference. Payne and his co-writer, Jim Taylor, have largely discarded the Louis Begley novel (set in an affluent, New York milieu) with which they began. As in *Citizen Ruth* (1996) and *Election* (1999), they're out to chart the distinct dementia of the "red" states in the vast middle of the country. And although Payne has chosen until recently to make his home in

Nebraska, he seems to regard the so-called heartland as a barren place, indeed—a place where souls go unwatered. Schmidt's retirement party is marked by numbingly generic toasts; and even when his drunken best friend, Ray (Len Cariou), lurches to his feet to dismiss the previous encomiums as b.s., Ray ends up spouting a different (and no more insightful) set of chestnuts.

One scene, in which the bored Schmidt goes to visit his "young-punk" successor, has been constructed entirely of clichés: from "Hey, there he is!" to "You look great—you been working out?" This is the code of Midwestern American capitalism, as rigid in its ways as a Japanese tea ceremony—only enacted by people who don't realize that their modes of discourse have been so deadeningly channeled. Payne's Midwest is a land that has apparently not discovered irony.

That's odd, since David Letterman comes from the Midwest, too, and you'd think his slant would have reached Omaha by now. Or is Letterman popular only in the "blue" states, where they sneer at the folks back home? The parade of people whom Schmidt encounters are Letterman-worthy fools—serene in their mobile homes, delighted by their prime rib restaurants, smug in their materialism. There are shots of Randall's dimwitted brother that would not be out of place in a Rob Schneider picture. No wonder Payne is moving to Hollywood, since he's unable to see anything but anomie and zombielike artifice in the Midwest.

The director took some easy shots in *Citizen Ruth*, too, but that movie hurtled along at a rollicking, Preston Sturges-like tempo, and the audacity of its premise (it was a screwball comedy about the anti-abortion movement) went far toward putting it over. But *About Schmidt* needs something more than Payne and his hero's strangely resigned superiority. It needs more, richer, and more conclusive scenes with Schmidt's daughter, Jeannie, whom Davis plays with a post-nasal-drip neurosis I find mysteriously alluring but who isn't enough of a counterweight.

No one in the movie balances Nicholson, not even for one scene. As a loud, bohemian feminist and the mother of Jeannie's boobish fiancé, Kathy Bates brings an enlivening jolt of energy—she summons up your fight-or-flight instincts, as would a coming bulldozer. But her pride in her son is meant to be delusional, and the movie makes the final case against her character with a scene in which she hops into a hot tub and comes on to Schmidt. Yes, it's a double standard: She's in better shape than he is. But audiences have not yet evolved to the point where they can greet the sight of a naked Kathy Bates without wild spasms of horror.

There's a larger disconnect in *About Schmidt*: It's hard to imagine Nicholson ever being at home with his family and accommodating himself to the protocols of a small-city insurance company. Suspension of disbelief only goes so far, even in *The Twilight Zone*. And yet the movie holds you. Its characters are one-dimensional, but there is real emotion in its aura of hopelessness. And Nicholson is capacious in his stillness. He will always be the world's most mythically bedraggled rich guy. It's fun just to pore over his visage, with its pouches within pouches, its left eyebrow ever ready to fly up and his face to assume its rightful leer. The old cliché goes that some actors are so great you could thrill to their reading the phone book. In Nicholson's case, it just might work. Imagine him reading, say, "Bacon, Gladys" and his eyebrow flying up, and the innocuous words that become double entendres and the double entendres that become triple entendres. The potential energy is nuclear.

The subtitle of the David Edelstein review says it all: despite Nicholson's strong performance the film has too many flaws to make it a winner. Although the director Alexander Payne has shown great capability in previous films, Edelstein feels he misses the mark with this effort.

Approaches

Besides boilerplate, some plot, and an evaluation, a review will emphasize some other aspect or two of the film to discuss and develop. This can be about any topic relevant to the film: how it reflects the political climate, the exceptional special effects, the impact of the cinematography, or the music score's enhancement of the mood. Most often, however, the review will center around one of the following:

- The storyline (plot),
- The main character(s),
- Adopted source, such as novel, play, or short story,
- An idea, theme, or political issue,
- The director's (auteur's) unique style or body of work, and
- An actor in terms of his/her style or body of work.

The Plot-Driven Review

The plot-driven review may disperse boilerplate at the beginning, the conclusion, or throughout the piece. The same methodology can be used for the evaluative parts of the essay. However, this type of review mainly concentrates on telling the story, analyzing the characters, and mentioning those aspects of the movie that make it somewhat unique or interesting.

It comes as no surprise that a film noir classic, Jacques Tourneur's *Out of the Past* released in 1947, is being used to illustrate the *plot-driven review*. The film noir genre was a type of mystery which almost by definition relied heavily on plot and vivid character types. Bob Stephens' 1997 review in the *San Francisco Examiner* discusses that motion picture whose intricate twists and turns of the storyline and typed film noir characters make this piece such a good example of the plot-driven review.

Out of the Past: Timeless Noir
For 50 Years, It's Been a Benchmark of the Genre

In the fatalistic universe of film noir, personal choices (however limited by hazardous circumstances) are all that matter. Disoriented by an ever-changing present, fleeing from a terrifying memory or dreading what may come in the onrushing future, a man has no foothold beyond his freedom to make decisions, judgments that are true or unfaithful to his beliefs.

Jacques Tourneur's "Out of the Past" (1947) is about Jeff Markham, an ex-detective who's haunted by an episode that happened years before, an event that caused him to abandon his principles, compromising himself and risking retaliation. Jeff's code of honor is so strong that his sense of failure is undiminished by the fact that he was involved with a criminal when he violated it.

As Jeff, Robert Mitchum double-crosses a crime boss, Whit Sterling (Kirk Douglas), for the sake of love. Employed to track down the hoodlum's runaway girlfriend, Kathy Moffatt (Jane Greer), the honest private eye is suckered into a romance, then betrayed by the gun moll's deceitful, selfish behavior.

Jeff becomes entangled in the femme fatale's cobweb, a snare spun of exploitation and desperation. He's eventually framed for the murder of Whit's accountant and also tagged for the death of a man Kathy ruthlessly shot to death.

Jeff realizes he's doomed, so he lets everything play out in a way that destroys his antagonists as well as himself. His sacrifice relieves Ann (Virginia Huston), whom he really loves, of any obligation to him. Jeff's death makes it possible for her to have a new life with another man, a friend since childhood.

Tourneur is a director who belongs in the pantheon of sound era artists such as Orson Welles, John Ford, and Howard Hawks. Tourneur's dynamic compositions derive from the traditions of still photography and painting. There's a beautiful shot in which he combines the forbidding symmetry of a wrought iron gate, the silhouette of a man in a trench coat who stands apprehensively before it, and, in the background, the serene grandeur of a mountain range. But the director also had a more contemporary grasp of film plasticity. For example, he presents an imaginative sequence in which a pair of panning shots of Jeff waiting in a bar are fused by a subtle dissolve, and we experience the startling passage of time and a surprising cycloramic effect.

Mitchum, a beloved performer who has, nonetheless, been criticized as having a passive approach to acting, is anything but disengaged. His method can be more accurately described as speculative, because what he really does is assay the character of everyone he encounters and carefully examines the psychological layout of the situations in which he finds himself.

The hardboiled repartee that is so trite in other hands fits Mitchum perfectly: He used it to hold people at an evaluative distance, to protect his privacy onscreen and off. Greer is soft, cuddly, and lethal. She isn't frivolous like a lot of noir demi-goddesses. Her sexiness comes from cunning and she never relies on flirtatious self-parody of such actresses as Lauren Bacall and Martha Vickers. Greer's appeal is finally darker, more destructive, in spite of the allure of her Angora surface.

Paul Valentine's portrayal of the hit man Joe Stefanos is unique. Though Jeff and Whit display cool versions of magisterial attitudes in response to crisis, Joe's a violent jitterbug—a man who's anxious to get on with it, someone who thrives on his own restlessness. His homicidal tendencies are contradicted by his remarkably soothing voice.

Dickie Moore appears as a teenage deaf mute and, in his psychic connection with Jeff, he's almost sinister at times. Moore's silent boy is an extraordinary figure who signals intentions and warnings with his hands. His moral presence somehow implies that words are lies and the capability of a spoken language is not to be trusted. Moore's last manual monologue in the film is an unforgettable romantic gesture.

Nicholas Musuraca, the director of photography, is responsible for the wonderful black and white incarnation of Tourneur's vision. "Past" is a movie of irreconcilable contrasts, one that basically compares forms of purity with corruption: Rural life is innocent and urban life is decadent. The working class is less affected by the temptations of money and power, the illegally wealthy are lost in the relentless pursuit of capital and clout. A sunny blonde is virginal and loyal, two shadowy brunettes are conniving and traitorous. The daylight represents life and ethical illumination, while the night remains the precinct of evil and death.

"Past," an inestimable collaboration by Tourneur and Mitchum, is not just one fine noir film among many. It has been a gauge of the genre, even a template, over the past 50 years.

Movie review: "Out of the Past." Cast: Robert Mitchum, Jane Greer, Kirk Douglas. Director: Jacques Tourneur. Writers: Geoffrey Homes (Daniel Mainwaring), James M. Cain, Frank Fenton.

The focus of the previous review by journalist Bob Stephens is clearly on the plot and then the characters who fall into the characteristic persons of film noir: the flawed but self-sacrificing hero, the femme fatale, the innocent ingénue, the evil hoodlum, and others. He also comments on the lead actor, Robert Mitchum and his singular contributions to the film, as well as some of the cinematic techniques employed by the director, Jacques Tourneur.

The Character-Driven Review

This type of review centers on the major character, the protagonist of the film. To illustrate the *character-driven review* best would be the "bio-pic" (biographical movie), which is, of course, the cinematic treatment of an actual person's life, living or deceased. Another type of character-driven film (and thus subsequent review) would be a protagonist inspired by a well-known piece of literature, including the currently very popular comic book super hero—especially in this era of computer generated imaging (CGI) and other special effects. Of course, there have been numerous film characters that have been so overpowering in the imaginations of audiences that they have inspired multiple sequels or some actors are totally identified with the characters: think of the *Rocky* or *Dirty Harry* franchises.

Biographies, plays, and films about artists—musicians, sculptors, painters, writers—usually concern subjects who lead passionate, colorful, and controversial lives while in the process of creating art. This process of dedication to their work often comes in conflict with other people and other aspects of living in society. Most artists seem to be a breed apart. The movie *Frida* (2002) directed by Julie Taymor about the life of Mexican painter Frida Kahlo certainly supports the claim. Former BC student Mary Beth Hofstein wrote the review which is presented next.

Frida

Director Julie Taymor takes the audience on a journey through a life wrought with physical frailty, emotional difficulties, and personal triumphs in her film *Frida*: a movie saturated with imagery as intense as the art of Frida Kahlo itself. Starring Salma Hayek in the title role, opposite Alfred Molina as Diego Rivera, and featuring Geoffrey Rush as Leon Trotsky, *Frida* is an artistic expression of passion and pain that could only have been accomplished with Taymor's vision and courage. Cutting her teeth on the Academy Award-winning *The Lion King*, she proves her ability to weave a biography with imagery. With the help of art director Bernardo Trujillo (*Blow*), she uses the motif of art to give the story soul and bring it to life.

While fictitious depictions of actual events are perilous at best, and biographies doubly so, the screenwriting team of Anna Thomas, Clancy Sigal, Diane Lake, Gregory Nava, and Rodrigo Garcia along with the director succeeded in marrying the known facts of the life of beloved Mexican artist and political activist Frida Kahlo with the legendary stories passed on by witnesses, friends, and lovers over the years without getting mired down in factual minutia. Such details of her life are less important than the impact of her work and the important role she played in the political events of her time. If previously unfamiliar or unimpressed by her art, one will surely come away with a new appreciation for the work as well as its influence on Mexican culture. If unfamiliar with her activism, one will be impressed by her intelligence and strength.

Particularly clever tools were employed to give the audience a sense of who Frida was to herself as well as to those around her. Re-creations of her paintings, the vast majority of which were self-portraits, "came to life" as the subjects moved into the moment beyond what was captured on canvas, animating what had been created. Original art was created to segue from one scene to the next when depicting a major time of change in her life. A deeper understanding of and appreciation for her art was offered by the use of her paintings to punctuate important events as they were depicted in the film.

Judging from her previous performances, this part at first seems beyond Salma Hayek's capabilities as an actress. Surprisingly, she slips into the role of Frida Kahlo naturally and seamlessly. From precocious schoolgirl through ambitious, sensual young woman to self-actualized, successful artist, Hayek gives us a sense of the woman who touched so many lives and meant so much to Mexico and to the art world.

Alfred Molina as Diego Rivera gives his familiar strong performance without upstaging his costar. He portrays the philandering, arrogant artist unapologetically while remaining a character with whom the audience can sympathize.

The cast is well-endowed with recognizable Mexican and Spanish actors such as Valeria Golino as Lupe Marin and Diego Luna as Alejandro Gomez Arias. Antonio Banderas even does his obligatory cameo in all films Latin as David Siqueiros. Edward Norton, who also worked on script revisions with Julie Taymor, plays Nelson Rockefeller.

Simply put, the film is beautiful and passionate. Even those who have read her biography will come away enriched, perhaps seeing Frida Kahlo in a different light for the first time.

Alfred Molina and Salma Hayek in Julie Taymor's Frida *(2002). Miramax.*
Courtesy of Everett Collection.

The critic here shows how the life of Frida Kahlo—a woman passionately devoted to art—has been, in turn, depicted artistically by filmmaker Julie Taymor in her motion picture *Frida*. The director, who with her previous work, direction of the stage adaptation of *The Lion King*, showed her flair for the graphic arts has embarked successfully on a project where her techniques and talents mesh nicely with that of her subject. Ms. Hofstein also comments upon the skillful choice of the cast and the strong performances that the actors give.

As stated before, a very popular cinematic character has derived from the comic and graphic novel industry. Sometimes the re-makes inspire new re-makes which go beyond the mere sequel where so much is still in place—director, producers, writers and many of the actors. For the best illustration of how an established comic book character—or film character for that matter—can mutate, we see this character-driven review written about Christopher Nolan's *Batman Begins* (2005) by Mark Englehart of the *Imdb* (*Internet Movie Database*) staff. Among the things Mark Englehart does is take us through the many "iterations" of Batman that we have experienced over the years through the 2005 cinema rendering of this classic comic book character.

(BATMAN BEGINS)

Review by Mark Englehart
Starring: Christian Bale, Michael Caine, Ken Watanabe
9 out of 10 stars

After all the iterations of Batman that there've been that we've put through, it would seem nearly impossible that there could be anything new to say at all about the Caped Crusader. Amazingly, director Christopher Nolan proves that there is—and then some. Nolan's *Batman Begins* is a literal cinematic re-imagining of the beginning of the Batman legacy, and with its stark yet powerful emotions and design, it rises easily above what we've come to associate with the remakes and adaptations of past movie franchises, which basically just put a new coat of paint (or sometimes, just high-end lacquer) on the old, musty plot and send it out for a spin around the block. *Batman Begins*, while honoring the origins of its hero, is so smart and fresh that it manages to wash away the old taste of all the other Batmans that have cluttered your brain—the TV one, the animated ones, the Michael Keaton one, the Val Kilmer one, the George Clooney one, and so on and so on. It's not so much *Batman Begins* as it is Batman Lives Again.

That said, what makes *Batman Begins* so successful—its darker, more adult tone; its forsaking of glitz for drama; its devotion to the true origins of the hero; its refusal to pander to blockbuster stereotypes—could possibly prove to be its downfall. Thanks primarily to Tim Burton and all the other superhero movies that have come down the pike since the director's 1989 *Batman*—the *Spider-Man* movies and the *X-Men* movies to be most specific—we've come to expect a certain glamour from our comic book movies. We are conditioned to look for the easy archetypes, from the glowering, conflicted hero to the brazen, larger-than-life villain to the sexy, helpless female love interest; it's almost a game of connect the dots, and not get too high-falutin' about it, but moviegoers (myself included) are basically Pavlovian dogs when it comes to summer blockbusters. Ring this bell, ring that bell, we'll go through the paces and oh, the movie's over.

What *Batman Begins* dares to do is throw out almost all the conventions you know and proceed with the basic outline in place; however, it ups the ante in terms of plot (it actually has one), its cast (made up entirely of people who are actors first and maybe movie stars second), its design (appropriately urban without being over the top), and its overall intelligence level. It's not that this *Batman* is hard to follow, but like Nolan's previous films—*Memento* and *Insomnia*—it assumes a certain intelligence from its audience, and isn't about to sink down to the Batman-explains-it-all-for-you cop-out. When you first start watching *Batman Begins*, you'll probably start off being intrigued but may end up asking yourself: Am I watching a drama or an action movie? It's smart, but is it Batman? And your tolerance for such will ultimately dictate how much you will warm to this film.

Batman Begins' mission to distinguish itself from its predecessors is immediate in its opening, which introduces us to both the young Bruce Wayne and his present incarnation. The young Bruce, while playing with childhood pal Rachel Dawes, falls down what appears to be a dry well and is overtaken by a flurry of bats, causing him to cower in panic; the current Bruce (Christian Bale) is holed up in a Chinese prison for reasons unknown, surly and dirty and not about to take crap from anyone. In playing out both these storylines, Nolan and co-screenwriter David S. Gover give us the familiar Batman trappings, but in a sobering, almost more horrifying way. Bruce's parents, the rich-and-gentle sort, are gunned down in a back alley of a decaying Gotham City by the desperate almost rabid Joe Chill; it's a heartbreaking, pointless act of violence, and not the immediate spark of fury that sets Bruce on his stylish mis-

sion of vengeance. The imprisoned Bruce, who catches a break in
the form of Henri Ducard (Liam Neeson), is recruited to join the
League of Shadows, which professes to fight evil; it's not a hot-and-
sexy induction by any means, but with its shades of Crouching
Tiger, Hidden Batman, it does feel a bit more mystical than it
should be. Still, the gritty upshot of these two stories, which con-
verge when a teenage Bruce has the opportunity to off his parents'
killer but is thwarted by fate and not his own conscience, is to show
that this isn't the gothic Batman of Burton but instead a darker,
fiercer version of the hero; one that we're not necessarily used to in
our Pop Culture 101 classes, where Adam West holds court alongside Michael Keaton.

Once Bruce discovers the true methods of the League of Shadows, and in particular its menacing, mysterious leader, Ra's Al
Guhl (Ken Watanabe), it's back to Wayne Manor for the buffed-up
Mr. Wayne, and the mean streets of Gotham City. And these are
some mean streets. This isn't your stylishly run-down Gotham, or
your sunny New York verity of *Spider-Man* or your slick futuristic
X-Men territory—it's one hugely scary city, where corruption runs
rampant thanks to crime boss Carmine Falcone (Tom Wilkinson)
and an ineffectual police force, the only good egg of which seems to
be the sad-sack Lt. James Gordon (Gary Oldman). The one other
person who seems to care about cleaning up the city is district
attorney Rachel Dawes (Katie Holmes), all grown-up and the
movie's lone voice of honor and conscience. Bruce not only has to
contend with a rotting city but a ruthless CEO (Rutger Hauer)
who's taken control of the family business, intending to strike fear
into the hearts of those who instill fear. Bruce creates Batman, and
thus a legend is born.

Nolan cannily parallels the creation of Batman with the creation
of Bruce Wayne himself, and what he drives at throughout the
movie is the fact that neither is separately a man in full; both are
icons indeed, but mere personas to be inhabited rather than people
who actually seem to be living. Does Batman exist when he's not
saving people? For that matter, does Bruce Wayne when he's not
being a playboy on the town to distract from any similarities he
might hold to the Dark Knight? In offering us this version of Batman, the lone superhero with no super-extraordinary powers, this
is the first superhero movie since 1978's *Superman* that seems to
understand that heroes can indeed have feet of clay, and that the
dichotomy of being a mere mortal and someone super isn't breathtaking or energizing, but sometimes downright miserable. And
Bale, a true actor who happens to be blessed with movie star good

looks, brings these two sides of his protagonist together in a way that shows how one can't exist without the other. It's hard to imagine anyone else bringing off this transformation so effortlessly and effectively, hitting just the right emotional notes without ever straying to bathetic territory.

The fundamental plot that eventually drives *Batman Begins*—someone is planning on poisoning Gotham's water supply, and it's the evil Dr. Jonathan Crane (Cillian Murphy), aka the Scarecrow, who's carrying out this plan—it's your basic save-the-world-and-the-girl tale but also carries a deeper dimension to it, in both the way it addresses the plight of the inner-city Gotham and reveals the motivation of those who are behind it. Nolan manages to deftly balance the unfolding scheme with all the fun stuff we expect from the creation of Batman—the establishment of the Batcave (an actual cave), the toys that Batman arms himself with, and of course, the creation of the Batmobile, which here is less sexily sleek than scaringly intimidating. If the movie makes one misstep, it's in the presentation of two characters who could seemingly be combined into one: the butler Alfred (Michael Caine), who helps Bruce create Batman, and the scientist gadget dude Lucius Fox (Morgan Freeman), who is basically an Americanized version of James Bond's Q. Caine and Freeman are both great fun to be around, but switching from one character to another in Batman's metamorphosis, is a bit exhausting and de-energizing.

Not so with the rest of the characters, especially Oldman's Lt. Gordon, who's a perfect human foil to Batman's otherworldliness. Oldman also gives a performance that wouldn't be out of place in a film noir or cop drama; ditto Wilkinson, whose Falcone is a perfect mix of menace and arrogance (his spread-eagle stringing-up on a spotlight, a precursor to the Batsignal, is a nice touch). Neeson easily makes up for his Jedi-induced stupor in the recent *Star Wars* flicks, and Holmes, while not nearly as good as everyone else, is nonetheless solid and effective (her performance is more of a triple compared to the other home runs in the movie). And a lot of credit should go to Murphy, who makes the Scarecrow a palpably realistic villain, one you might be more likely to encounter on the street than, say, the Joker—though there is a nice, um, joke about him towards the end of the film.

Ultimately, though, despite Bale's strong performance, this is pretty much Nolan's movie all the way, and he manages to make a blockbuster that's neither pandering nor stupid nor simplistic. Usually it's not best to describe movies in terms of what they're not, but in today's movie age, where we go in expecting something to be not bad rather than actively good, it's important to acknowledge a movie that not only surpasses our expectations but does so by being something actually great and impressive and almost important. If audiences respond, *Batman Begins* could change the landscape of the summer blockbuster, for the better. Maybe then, like the residents of Gotham City, we'd no longer live in fear of the ugly behemoth that's lurking around the next corner—or in this case, the next opening weekend.

This sprawling, feature-length review by *IMDB*'s Mark Englehart just as easily could have been put in the *director (auteur)-driven* category, but was placed in the character-driven slot because so much print was devoted to the changes in the concept of the comic/film creation known as "Batman." Admittedly, the language at times is a bit self-indulgent with most sentences running to three lines and the liberal use of semicolons, but Mr. Englehart has much to say about this film and how different it is. Notice, true to review format, details of the conclusion and ending are not mentioned, boilerplate is peppered throughout, and evaluative comments are interlaced throughout the piece. *Batman Begins* was released in 2005. Mark Englehart while effusively praising the film was concerned that it wouldn't gain a strong enough acceptance and popular following to furnish a sequel. He need not have worried: in 2008 Christopher Nolan made *The Dark Knight* followed by *The Dark Knight Rises* released in the summer of 2012. In both cases, Christian Bale was again playing Batman.

The Adopted Source-Driven Review

Many motions pictures have been admitted even heralded adaptation from other—usually print—sources such as novels, plays, or short stories. Whether from a best-selling novel, a Broadway musical, an off-Broadway drama, or an arresting short story from a magazine or anthology, Hollywood, over the decades, has considered original written sources as fertile ground for successful movie hits.

An example of a review written about a film inspired by another medium and adapted for the screen comes from the international best-selling novel *The Girl with the Dragon Tattoo* (2011) by the Swedish author Stieg Larsson. The review was written by Broward College student Candice F. Woolcock.

The Girl with the Dragon Tattoo

I imagine that every filmmaker desires and contrives to breathe life into characters from a favorite novel or play that captures his/her imagination. In the case of director David Fincher, he accomplishes this feat and so much more with the screen adaptation of *The Girl with the Dragon Tattoo*. As someone who has read the Millennium Series of novels by Stieg Larsson, the first of which is *The Girl with the Dragon Tattoo*, I can attest to the vivid connection between the film and novel. Not only is the female lead, Rooney Mara, eerily cast as Lisbeth Salander, but the very personality of Lisbeth is translated into reality on the silver screen by this marvel of a semi-unknown actress. The plotline of the film follows the novel almost exactly, yet each twist and turn is vividly exciting and feels as if it were being read for the first time. There are only a few occasions when a film/filmmaker can make one lose oneself in one's own imagination while still being drawn in by another's interpretation of a story. *The Girl with the Dragon Tattoo* is that film and David Fincher is that filmmaker.

The movie, which was released in the autumn of 2011, tells the story of Mikael Blomkvist who, once a celebrated Swedish investigative journalist, in 2002 loses a libel case against an unsavory businessman named Hans-Erik Wennerstrom. Daniel Craig plays Blomkvist, the part owner of "Millennium" magazine. After losing the case, he decides to neutralize some of the negative attention from the magazine by removing himself from the office and editor's chair. During the hiatus, he is approached by Swedish business mogul Henrik Vanger (Christopher Plummer), who sends him on an incredible investigative journey to find the truth about a missing family member of his. Along the way, Blomkvist enlists the help of strange, borderline autistic Lisbeth Salander, who just so happens to be one of the best computer hackers in all of Europe. Together they endeavor to take a trip toward the truth, but they both have to face seemingly insurmountable if not downright deadly obstacles to overcome along the way.

Craig becomes Blomkvist on-screen and makes you believe that he is deciphering every riddle along the excursion to the truth about Harriet Vanger, the long-lost niece of Henrik Vanger. You will feel the twinge of excitement whenever Blomkvist is on the precipice of the next big break. Daniel Craig has the history of playing the ultimate ladies-man, James Bond, and that charisma translates seamlessly into the character of Mikael Blomkvist, even though the two roles could not be any more different. He lends a boyishness to Blomkvist that enables him to be with as many women as he likes throughout the story, but not come off like a complete chauvinist. These qualities in the actor only add to the believability and depth of his character in the film.

Lisbeth is described as a slight girl with jet-black, Goth-style hair and dress and the demeanor of someone who may have Asperger's syndrome. She has trouble socializing, but has no problem hacking into private and government computer systems to get any information she needs to do her job as an investigator. With all of the technical talent that she has, she is still a ward of the state and is assigned a legal guardian; she has formed somewhat of a bond with him over the years. Faced with the sudden loss of her long-time guardian, Salander falls victim to the most heinous of evils that one human being can perpetrate upon another. Such evil is performed by her new guardian, the very person entrusted to preserve her safety and welfare. Yet, however small Lisbeth is described as being, she is a character that would never back down, especially against those who would prey upon the weak. It is in this respect that Mara gives a ferocious performance and bestows upon Salander the dimension and gravity which brings her crisply into the harshness of reality.

This film is full of amazing supporting actors who are stars in their own right: Christopher Plummer, Stellan Skarsgard, Robin Wright, Embeth Davitz, Joely Richardson, and Goran Visnjic, just to name a few; but it is Daniel Craig and Rooney Mara who truly become their characters. I cannot imagine this film without Daniel Craig but especially not with Rooney Mara, for she is *The Girl with the Dragon Tattoo.*

Student film critic Candice Woolcock has shown that director David Fincher has successfully transformed the difficult mystery thriller by Stieg Larsson into a topnotch film. He has done so by means of a script faithful to the book and exceptional casting.

Novels are the most common form of literature to become a movie. Everyone wants to see how a best seller is transformed into a film. Occasionally a popular Broadway musical or drama will get a cinematic treatment. Arthur Miller's *Death of a Salesman*, arguably one of the 10 greatest American plays ever written, has been made into numerous motion picture versions. One of the best is German director Volker Schlondorff's 1985 effort that featured an American cast and was supervised by the playwright himself. It stars Dustin Hoffman, John Malkovich, Kate Reid, and Stephen Lang, who are ably supported by an excellent cast in the other roles.

Death of a Salesman

Volker Schlondorff didn't want to rock the boat too much. Admittedly, Dustin Hoffman's selection to play Willy Loman seemed a bit unusual, not because of Hoffman's acting chops—he's one of America's great character actors—but because of his physicality. He is a short, slight man rather than a larger fellow with a husky frame, which is the way Willy Loman has traditionally been portrayed ever since the play opened on Broadway. But other than that, Hoffman was perfect in the role. And as far as this critic is concerned, no one has played the beleaguered salesman better. For Biff, the choice of John Malkovich was superb. The actor's range was broad and when he had to show emotion, weeping especially, it was hyper-real with not only tears flowing but mucous streaming as well. Kate Reid was strong in her portrayal as his wife. Again the director selected a woman physically different than her predecessors, who were more delicate physically (whereas Ms. Reid would be classified as "full figured"). Stephen Lang as Hap was far more than adequate, showing how he was the "second" son: less favored and denied equal attention and praise although desperate for both. The company, including Charles Durning (Charley), David S. Chandler (Bernard, Charley's son), Louis Zorich (Ben, Willy's brother), Jon Polito (Howard, Willy's boss), Kathy Rossetter (the woman from Boston), and Linda Koslowski (Miss Forsythe) rounded out the exceptional cast.

The production was not filmed on location but on a sound stage built to have the feel of a proscenium stage with painted sets and a cutaway house for the Loman residence. The audience watching this film feels they are observing a play not a movie. The backdrop of the backyard and beyond is easily transformed into a cemetery for the epilog in the same manner that a stage manager or set director would employ for an actual stage production.

The traditional themes of *Death of a Salesman* have been maintained—the pursuit if the American Dream, the desperation of the failing breadwinner, and the dysfunction of a household constructed on a foundation of lies—and still manifest the immediacy and relevance that they had at the time of the play's premiere in 1948.

Death of a Salesman is a timeless classic. This particular film rendition, shot in 1985, maintained the original setting of time and place: post World War II Brooklyn, New York. It also handled the tricky time changes of the two eras, which were roughly twenty years apart (when Willy was in his 40s and 60s and his sons in their mid-teens and mid-30s) by means of costuming, props, and sets. I won't go into the details of the plot—because it is so well known by now—but I will assure the reader that the storyline also was faithfully maintained. Mention should also be made of the sensitive film score with its haunting, recurring theme; it was composed by Alex North and greatly enhanced the mood of the production.

I will conclude with this declaration: without question, this is the finest motion picture adaptation of this Arthur Miller drama that I have ever had the pleasure of watching.

The previous standard-size review, reports on one of the numerous film renderings of Arthur Miller's play *Death of a Salesman*. Faithful to the original in almost every way, what makes it so successful is its finely nuanced direction of an outstanding cast by director Volker Schlondorff.

Some films are adapted from short stories and frequently change the title. In so doing, they often take certain liberties with the plot in general, the ending, the characters, or a combination thereof. Todd Field's motion picture *In the Bedroom* (2001) uses the title as an indication of the emotional barometer of the Fowlers, the couple who is the focus of the movie, especially after the murder of their son. The movie has been adapted from Andre Dubus' short story "Killings" and, for the most part, is faithful to its literary source. Broward College student Andres Benatar discusses the merits of this motion picture in the review that follows.

Murder within the Bedroom

Love is the key component to holding a family together, compromise that, and the unit is weakened, even endangered. Director Todd Field's independent film takes this simple concept and uses it as a manner of balance for the characters of *In The Bedroom*. The film adaptation of the Andre Dubus short story "Killings" explores its rather deep marital issues and translates them to the screen. *In The Bedroom* is a drama about the relationship between a husband and wife—Matt and Ruth Fowler (Tom Wilkinson and Sissy Spacek, respectively)—and the changes they undergo in the wake of a tragic loss. The death of their son Frank (Nick Stahl), has shaken the foundation of their marriage, bringing them to further confront deeper truths about one another. It is these significant differences that truly separate the film from the short story. The more minor details are hardly noticeable, as several names

Tom Wilkinson and Sissy Spacek in Todd Fields' In the Bedroom *(2001).*
Miramax. Courtesy of The Kobal Collection at Art Resource, NY.

and characters have been changed, while the similarities range
from the descriptions of the lead characters, the conflicted situation, and their motivations. The revelations explored within the
film are deep enough to reflect who Matt and Ruth really are not
just as husband and wife, but as people.

In the film, Matt and Ruth Fowler's marriage is shown initially
to be a rather healthy and mutually loving relationship. The casu-
alness they embody is defined by the simple comfort they take in
each other's presence. In the beginning of the film, their son Frank
is in a relationship with a woman named Natalie Strout (Marisa
Tomei), who is older, and triggers a positive and negative opinion
from both parents. On one end, Matt sees the relationship as an
amusing summer infatuation of his son for an attractive older
woman. Ruth's thoughts on the matter, however, are more critical,
since she feels that Frank's primary focus should be on furthering
his education. Nevertheless, their separate views are seemingly
unimportant as their son continues his relationship as well as his
plans for graduate school in the fall, and their own marriage is
shown to be peaceful with rarely any conflict.

The death of their son at the hands of Natalie's abusive but
legally separated husband Richard Strout (William Mapother),
comes as a sudden and tragic loss to the Fowlers. Frank's death and
the subsequent lack of legal action against Strout, ultimately alter

the state of the Fowlers' marriage. Matt and Ruth undergo the usual grieving through their sobbing and tear-filled expressions. However, it is in those very silent moments both Matt and Ruth experience an alienation from each other. The only conversations taking place between them are brief formalities and polite small talk. Never is there a word about Frank or the hole left in their hearts. Behind all that silence is a tormenting feeling of agony that Ruth, a choral instructor, describes as "A rest in music . . . no sound, but so loud."

The breaking point is reached when all their anguish, all their anger, all their doubts as to their parenting, and all their individual forms of grieving collide. Ruth's bitterness towards Matt's calm behavior is piercing, as she blames him for Frank's death. "I don't know what you go through Matt, or if you go through anything. You can't admit the truth to me or to yourself that Frank died for your fantasy piece of ass." Matt defends himself against these wild accusations with harsh, but ultimately defining truths about Ruth. Matt regards her as controlling and bitter, saying how much she had frightened and alienated her son. These insults and resentments soon become apologetic regrets, when clearly the truth points to Richard as the real source of their misery. "Killings" never explores the Fowlers' marriage to such a deep extent. The short story merely presents their current anxiety on the subject of Richard, and what needs to be done to resolve it all.

Beyond the notion of justice, it is the very foundation of the Fowler's marriage that is being ridiculed by Strout's freedom. With very few witnesses and undetermined evidence, little can be done to incarcerate him. On top of that, Ruth has encountered Strout several times, thus making the reality of his presence all the more unbearable. The possibility of their son's killer remaining free so haunts and torments the Fowlers that Matt has finally decided to take some action. He calmly devises and calmly executes a plan to make Richard disappear from their lives. Once put into effect, he then returns home to an eagerly awaiting Ruth. She simply sits up on her bed, calmly smoking a cigarette. Her only response to Matt's arrival is, "Did you do it?" Matt indicates he did and then lies down on their bed. During those final moments of the film, the camera closes upon the tortured expression on his face. Matt now solely carries the weight of his actions, while Ruth merely goes downstairs to make him breakfast, relieved of the load. Life will go on for Ruth, but for Matt the same can't be said.

A comment must be made on the title of the movie and its somewhat obscure double meaning significance. Early on, Matt refers to a section of a lobster trap known as "the bedroom." This chamber can accommodate a male and a female. If, however, two males are caught there with a female, unsurprisingly, the two males will fight. Transpose this to the plot of the film: we have two love triangles; in each case, the same second male instigates the violence. The first is obvious: the lovers are Frank and Natalie with the third being her estranged husband, Richard. The second love triangle is less evident: the imposition of the newly-freed Richard upon the lives of the Fowlers, Matt and Ruth, the surviving parents of Frank, who was killed by Strout. Think in terms of that worn saying: "Two's company, three's a crowd."

If there is any lesson derived from both *In The Bedroom* and "Killings," it is of the slow moral decay of its characters. At first, Matt and Ruth are seen in the film to be loving and socially active people. As soon as Frank dies, their friendship, their marriage, and even their desire to continue life are shattered. Ultimately, they are brought to take desperate measures. Both works have described the anguish further linking them together. The initial complications of their son's relationship, then the grisly murder, and, finally, the events leading up to the resolution remain intact. The dilemma of Richard Strout may be resolved, but Matt, as he finally lies down in bed, never will feel peace again.

Andres Benatar's review briefly explores the influence of Andres Dubus' "Killings" upon the Todd Field motion picture *In the Bedroom* inspired by it. With the exception of some minor parts and characters, the film is substantially true to the story. It differs in some points of emphasis, especially the relationship of the Fowlers after the murder of their son. In addition, the function of the title is explained as helping to consolidate the movie's critical elements: its plot, its central characters, its thematic motifs, and its setting—that deceptively quiet, coastal Maine town one summer.

The Theme-, Idea-, or Political Issue-Driven Review

Often a review will explore a theme, an idea, a political issue (or even an ideology) that is central to a movie. An aspect of the military mindset can be seen in Rob Reiner's *A Few Good Men* released in 1992. It exposes the chilling discrepancy between an outwardly espoused ideology and one that is secretly followed by those wielding significant power. The review is an example of one that is ideology-driven.

However, this film was adapted from a hit play written by its screenwriter, Aaron Sorkin. Therefore, it can be argued that it should be categorized instead as an adopted source-driven review since it is a direct derivative of a stage drama. However, so much of the play focuses on military law versus informal but near sacrosanct traditions, and the general ideology of the United States Marine Corps, that it was decided that this would better serve as an example of an idea-driven review. Such an ideology and how it affects the plot and characters within the movie is reason enough for classifying it in this manner.

Semper Fi . . . But Get a Good Lawyer

The United States Marine Corps: embodiment of the American patriotic ideal; last bastion where loyalty, love of country, and honor remain the rule and not the exception. It is a closed society whose own codes and laws are holy writ, impervious to civilian or even military accountability.

Or is it? A new breed in the military doesn't think so. Personified by Kaffee (Tom Cruise), a lieutenant in the Judge Advocates Group of the Navy, he is cynical, smart, and glib. Stationed in the heart of bureaucratic Washington, D.C., rather than some hard scrapple Leatherneck outpost, this type of naval officer is willing to compromise and cleverly plea bargain rather than sink in flames arguing on the stand for some glorious principle.

Suddenly, Kaffee's normal legal work is interrupted by a case requiring him to fly down to the Marine base at Guantanamo Bay in Cuba. He is assigned the defense of two gung-ho Marines accused of a barracks murder. He must interview the defendants and conduct a preliminary investigation. He learns that this is a case that cuts to the very core of what is meant to be a Marine in today's world. The dead man, Santiago, apparently had been far less than a perfect Marine, not tolerable especially at a forward station like "Gitmo." When he had informed on a fellow Marine, Pfc. Dawson, for a "fence line shooting" (firing at an enemy sentry and thus risking retaliation, a fire fight, or an international incident), the need to harshly discipline Santiago was becoming imperative. Then when he went outside the chain of command to request a transfer, punishment was inevitable: a "Code Red" was set into motion.

(A Code Red is an informal, dangerous, and violent disciplinary action taken by fellow Marines under the sanction of, but officially denied by, a commanding officer for extreme cases of malingering, disloyalty, or negligence endangering fellow Marines. It is illegal under the Uniform Code of Military Justice.)

Two members of Santiago's unit—Dawson and Downey—had enacted the draconian disciplinary measures: they forcibly bound him, stuffed a sock into his mouth and secured it shut with duct tape. Before any extended pummeling or other physical abuse could occur, his lungs hemorrhaged. He died choking on his own blood.

During the Guantanamo visit, Kaffee confronts the base commander Colonel Jessep (Jack Nicholson) who belittles the other's youth, inexperience, and sheltered position. Jessep sermonizes "We're in the business of saving lives. . . . We follow orders or people die." A frontline position requires a Marine to put the unit, the Corps, God, and country first and foremost—never himself before the other four. Apparently, Santiago had trouble adhering to such an iron standard. Although Jessep denied ordering the Code Red, he felt Santiago had to be "trained" rather than transferred, or the other men would be weakened and their lives put at risk.

Santiago's immediate commander Lieutenant Kendrick (Keifer Sutherland) also denied involvement with the Code Red but echoes Jessep's sentiments stating that Santiago is dead because "He had no code. He had no honor."

Kaffee is not impressed with Jessep's professed patriotism nor with a code so rigid that it could lead to the death of a man like Santiago. He is supported in his views by the two other military lawyers working with him on the case, Lieutenant Weinberg (Kevin Pollak) and Lieutenant Commander Galloway (Demi Moore). It is they who prevail upon Kaffee to try the case rather than settle for a reduced charge.

In a dramatic courtroom climax, Kaffee calls Jessep to the stand. It is a showdown with no punches pulled. We see that Jessep "will stop at nothing to keep his honor" while his young adversary "will stop at nothing to find the truth." The outcome of their duel makes for a rousing climax of intense courtroom drama.

Nicholson's Colonel Jessep is one of the great movie performances of the year. He portrays a man who is sinister, zealous, clever, bullying and convinced of his rightness even when it flouts the law he has sworn to uphold and defend. Tom Cruise does a masterful job as the foil to Nicholson's Jessep. Rob Reiner has skillfully directed a fine ensemble of players in this acting tour de force of Aaron Sorkin's script of his own hit play *A Few Good Men*.

Since this is an ideology-driven review, some major concepts of a controversial military code are presented as the first paragraph. The second paragraph shows that this ideology is not universally held and introduces those characters who disavow it. The contending principles eventually become personified by two men who come into direct conflict in the movie's stirring climax.

Finally, for our last example of an idea-driven review, we look at a documentary. Documentaries by their very nature center on a theme or an idea or an issue. Normally, the viewer finds most of his or her documentaries from public television. But occasionally, a full-length documentary makes it to the big screen and is distributed beyond the narrow art house circuit. The controversial film by Michael Moore *Fahrenheit 9/11* (2004) about the United States' questionable entry into the second war in Iraq broke box office records for a documentary, while also broadening the definition of the genre. With its polarizing interviews and voice-overs, its selection of film clips, and its clear-cut political stance, Moore's piece showed that the documentary can be used as an effective influence in the shaping of public policy.

It must be understood, however, that American as well as international documentaries have been created for reasons other than swaying public opinion. Often their main objective is educational or informational: be it about an historical event or figure; some aspect of the natural world; insight into a different culture—past or present; or exposure to a program or movement in a particular area or city. It cannot be denied, however, that even the most clearly informative of documentaries may have ulterior motives, perhaps as means to influence the public or leaders into some action or another.

One documentary that has recently received some very positive reviews and increasing theater distribution is *Mad Hot Ballroom* (2005). The film is witness to a successful experimental program that has existed in the New York City public school system for the last 10 years, namely, the incorporation of ballroom dancing as part of the overall fifth grade curriculum among numerous elementary schools.

Dancing in the Classroom: Off the Streets and out of Trouble

It was a noble concept that led to a noble experiment ten years ago. What if a mandatory course in ballroom dancing at randomly selected schools across the five boroughs was put into play? A course for fifth graders—for the most part, 11-year-olds—who were on the cusp of adolescence? What immediate social skills would accrue? Would there be any long-term benefits?

With these questions in mind, the New York City's school system began a 10-week program in ballroom dancing, culminating in a citywide competition for its participants. Director Marilyn Agrelo collaborated with Amy Sewell on the script and shot the documentary during the fall of 2004.

We look at kids from three different neighborhood schools: one in Tribeca (Lower Manhattan), another in Washington Heights (Manhattan's Upper West Side), and one in Bensonhurst, Brooklyn: different schools with very different demographics. Tribeca has a diverse, multi-ethnic, generally affluent student body, many living in remodeled, gentrified buildings. Bensonhurst's youths hail from middle and working class homes; their area is in transition: it used to be mainly Italian-American but now is almost 50% Asian. Finally, almost all the children from the Washington Heights school are the sons and daughters of recent Dominican immigrants; they come from a section of the city where poverty, unemployment, and crime are rampant.

What all these youngsters have in common is that the onset of puberty is not far off, resulting in all the awkwardness with oneself and those of the opposite gender that it entails. The opening scenes are touching and funny with the physical mismatches, discomfort, and resistance to something new and alien that could be expected. Early on, however, we see the drive and dedication of the dance teachers. Besides helping the kids to feel less awkward when holding those of the opposite sex and letting themselves be transformed from mis-stepping klutzes to graceful dancers, the instructors help their students improve their self-confidence, team spirit, and loyalty; and also, for later on, graceful acceptance of defeat if it comes.

Along the way, we too learn something about these young folks: their dreams, their aspirations, and their fears. For the young Dominicans, the fears are less temporary—such as looking foolish or making mistakes—but more permanent and thus more heartbreaking: such as worries about gangs, drugs, teen pregnancies, and the like. These children seem to have a greater sense of reality than the others.

What Agrelo does is set her cameras at the kids' eye levels and let them discuss with their classmates or directly to the lens what is going on, what it feels like. As the film progresses, not only do we see their physical evolution in grace, rhythm, and step mastery, but also acceptance of the socialization process.

As the weeks go by, the tension builds as each school's team of six couples (five competing, one back-up) prepare for the citywide dance competition. Now their mentors have to teach them how to deal with disappointment, how to cope with defeat when seemingly on the verge of victory; yet, simultaneously, make them realize that there are absolutely no losers since each student, each couple, each team has accomplished so much.

Visually, there are number of memorable scenes that lead up to the nail-biting finale. But these are for the reader to see and enjoy. Although so much of *Mad Hot Ballroom* is affirmative, this viewer noted sadly as the credits rolled, that for some of these boys and girls of eleven, this competition may be the high point of lives that will have too few options and triumphs in the years ahead.

The review points out the immediate aims of the program as well as the ultimate (and overly optimistic) goals. The piece discloses instances in the film that display the enthusiasm and dedication that the program inspired among its primary participants: the students and their teachers.

The Auteur-Driven Review

A number of reviews focus on the director or, as the French say, auteur. This type of director is very independent and uses a heavy hand in other aspects of filmmaking—especially writing and editing, but also cinematography and producing. In films by some strong directors (auteurs), actors are to be shaped like clay, to move as the filmmaker determines. Some directors are more collegial and work closely with the actors and others involved welcoming input and, ultimately, reaching consensus.

Woody Allen has long ago established himself as an American auteur filmmaker of the first order, but unlike so many other directors, he also has a career as a brilliant comic actor. In the last decade or so, he has concentrated on writing and directing rather than acting. Unlike his earlier films, he has left his beloved Manhattan locales for other venues overseas, namely, Paris, London, and Rome.

Now we will look at two positive reviews of his very well-received *Midnight in Paris* (2011) written literally within one day of each other. The two articles both demonstrate that besides boilerplate, evaluative comments, and an overall feel for the plot of the film, critics often broach a particular facet of a movie and develop it. This is very much the case of the successive reviews of the same Woody Allen offering by Peter Travers of *Rolling Stone* and then Karina Longworth of *The Village Voice*.

Midnight in Paris

Owen Wilson, Rachel McAdams, Carla Bruni
Directed by Woody Allen
Rolling Stone star rating: * * * ½
By Peter Travers—May 19, 2011

They love Woody Allen in France. And in *Midnight in Paris*, which just opened the Cannes Film Festival, the Woodman returns the favor. Not since 1979's *Manhattan*, in which he rhapsodized over the New York of his black-and-white dreams, has Allen used a camera to make such urgent, passionate love to a city.

Midnight in Paris opens with a prologue, shot with the poet's eye by the great Darius Khondji, which shows off the City of Light from dawn to darkness in images of shimmering loveliness. Pity the actors who have to compete with such an object of desire. Owen Wilson stars as Gil, a Hollywood screenwriter on a return visit to Paris, this time with his fiancée, Inez (Rachel McAdams). "This is where Monet lived and painted," Gil enthuses. Inez isn't into water lilies or Gil's dreams of writing the great American novel like Hemingway and Fitzgerald. She'd rather party with Paul (Michael Sheen), a fake intellectual who thinks he can one-up a Rodin museum tour guide (a cameo from France's First Lady, Carla Bruni).

Allen has fired at these targets before. What's fresh about *Midnight in Paris* is the way he identifies with Gil's idealization of the past, of the Paris that represented art and life at their fullest. Wilson is pitch-perfect at locating the right blend of humor and gravity that the role demands. Gil finds a kindred spirit and a muse in fashion designer Adriana (a superb Marion Cotillard). What's at risk is a lifeline back to the present. As a filmmaker, Allen has grappled with the temptations of repeating himself instead of forging a fresh path. You can feel that conflict here, and watching him work it out is exhilarating.

Midnight in Paris is infused with seductive secrets no review should spoil. But for all the film's bracing humor and ravishing romance, there are also haunting shadows. That alone makes it a keeper.

Travers begins his relatively short review by comparing *Midnight in Paris* with Allen's earlier *Manhattan* (1979) in that both pay homage to their titled cities. Through a series of voice-overs, still shots, and running clips of the sights and sounds of these cities, the initial minutes of both unfold. He tells us that besides the characters and plot, this is a film about artistic temperament, art, and living life at it fullest.

Karina Longworth emphasizes other aspects of the movie in her considerably longer piece. She comments more at length of the character of the protagonist Gil (Owen Wilson), his fiancée Inez (Rachel McAdams), and the differences in their personalities and world views. She also discusses the time-travel motif and how it affects the film. Like Travers she also praises the work of cinematographer Darius Khondji, especially in his use of lighting.

Midnight in Paris: Woody & Owen's Excellent Adventure

By Karina Longworth—Wednesday, May 18, 2011

A nebbishy screenwriter who longs to publish a novel, Gil (Owen Wilson) is tentatively working on a book set in a nostalgia shop— much to the open frustration of Inez (Rachel McAdams), his all-too-modern, rich-girl fiancée, who has a tendency to talk about him in catty, judge-y tones as if he's not in the room even when he is, and who makes no bones about preferring Gil the casher of Hollywood paychecks to Gil the wannabe artist. The couple has accompanied her parents on a trip to Paris in advance of the wedding, and if Gil, who once gave up the chance to live there for real, had his way, they'd never leave. "I tell ya," he tells his future wife, "if I had just stayed here and written novels instead of getting into the whole grind of writing movie scripts . . ."

The latest in a long line of actors playing a "Woody Allen type" in a Woody Allen film, Wilson bends his own recognizably nasal Texan drawl into an exaggerated pattern of staccatos and glissandos that's obviously modeled on on the writer/director's near musical verbal cadences; the word "lunatic," for instance, begins with a long, hard "LEW," modulated over three connecting notes. His performance— "Woody Allen" in quotes and beach-blond drag—adds an extra layer of distance to a script thick with allegory. A deceptively light time-travel romance, *Midnight in Paris* uses fairy-tale devices as a way to get the filmmaker's familiar, real-life-sourced themes: desire as both magical salve and instigator of insanity, and the fear of death that makes us forget past miseries just long enough to pursue plea-sures that'll almost surely end in pain.

One night, as Inez flirts with an obnoxiously pedantic American academic (Michael Sheen), Gil drunkenly wanders off alone. A car pulls up, the strangers inside offer him a ride, and the next thing we know, he is at a bizarre party full of flappers dancing to Cole Porter. When a vivacious young couple introduce themselves as Scott and Zelda, he comes to understand that he's been transported to Paris, circa the 1920s. Before the night is through, he begins a flirtation with Adriana (Marion Cotillard), a stunning serial muse, and forges a bond with Ernest Hemingway (Corey Stoll), who offers to show Gil's novel-in-progress to his good friend and mentor, Gertrude Stein (Kathy Bates). Gil runs out to grab his manuscript—and promptly gets lost in the present day. But the next night, the clock strikes midnight, another mysterious car drives up, and Gil is once again transported to his personal nostalgic paradise.

Allen only lightly milks the sci-fi potential of his premise, barely probing into the wonky details of how Gil's presence in the past could alter the space-time continuum. (The one time his reticence feels like a missed opportunity: when Gil gives Zelda Fitzgerald a Valium and she subsequently disappears from the film.) The high concept is a means, not an end: Allen sends Gil traveling through time not because he's terribly interested in the mechanics and fantastic possibilities of inter-dimensional travel, but because it's a backdoor way to investigate the problem of time—our inability to slow it down or stop it, to make anything good last or prevent inevitable misery—within ordinary life.

Shot by Darius Khondji (who collaborated with Allen on the much-maligned *Anything Else*), *Midnight* is a striking study in aesthetic contrasts. The present day is white, fluorescent, blindingly bright—the atmosphere equivalent of a hangover. In the past, it's permanently just-pre-last call, and every room pulses softly with smoky, amber light. No wonder Gil, drunk on the rush of being able to control his transport through time (and often just drunk), gets cocky and attempts to close the gap between past and present, for the first time in his life going after what he really thinks will make him happy.

But ephemerality proves to be a curse in every epoch. Allen— whose contemporary output is often unfairly dismissed as trifling, even though his films of the '00s have been shot through with an intense, cumulative despair as often as they've been shot thanks to the miracles of foreign financing and tax credits—gives the episodic ebb and flow of satisfaction an expectedly upbeat spin. Or does he? *Midnight* concludes with a rushed coupling that could be read as falsely optimistic. Or maybe it's just the beginning of another crest of hope and momentary joy, doomed to dissipate just after the end credits—or, more likely, in the next film.

Ms. Longworth's longer review takes a somewhat different tack than Travers' although both praise Woody Allen's 2011 effort. She also analyzes the film as not so much as a return to optimism of Allen's much earlier films but rather one with more of a balance between darkness and light, optimism and pessimism.

This next review, written by Broward College student Andres Benatar, is somewhat lengthy and discusses a very moving and highly acclaimed film by a troubled and controversial director, Roman Polanski. Released in 2002, *The Pianist* is based on the true life experiences of Polish concert pianist Wladyslaw Szpilman.

The Pianist (* * * *)

Genre: Bio Drama
Director: Roman Polanski
Cast: Adrian Brody, Thomas Kretschmann, Frank Finly, and Maureen Lipman

Director Roman Polanski brought to the cinema a brutal and painful to watch exploration of one man's struggle for survival in one of the world's darkest times. *The Pianist* is the story of a passionate and strong-willed pianist, Wladyslaw Szpilman. His experiences during the Holocaust have been adapted from his memoirs and conveyed in a dark and painful tone by the director. The Holocaust was undeniably a time of great suffering and sorrow for many. Jews from all over Europe were confronted by death in the gas chambers fostered by discrimination, blind hatred, or, simply, the Godless apathy of many Germans. During those atrocious times, many Jews struggled desperately to survive. The story of this particular Jew is told by Polanski with enough anguish that by the time the credits roll, audiences will remember indelibly what so many endured at the hands of true evil.

Wladyslaw Szpilman was a Polish pianist whose love for the piano could not be more clearly defined in this remarkable tale of courage, misery, and determined survival. Adrian Brody has delivered a performance that is believable in every account, and no doubt worthy of his Best Actor Oscar. He hasn't gone over the top in his interpretation to capture the beauty and sadness of his character. Just by watching Brody, the audience can believe that he is Szpilman by his mastery of the Polish accent, finger movements playing Chopin on the piano, and demonstration of confidence, vulnerability, and despair of the musician.

The story began with the termination of his career in Polish radio and ended with his eventual return to it. During the intervening five years, Spzilman's life was destroyed bit by bit. Being Polish Jews who were living in the midst of the Holocaust, the Szpilman family faced many atrocities as the Germans continued their invasion of Poland. The moment the Germans marched into Warsaw in 1939, many Jews were subjected to humiliation, persecution, debt, starvation, and, ultimately, death. The madness ranged from the limit of zlotys Jews could carry to their forced relocation within the Ghetto to their eventual deportation to the death camps. One scene of the film in particular showed a unit of German soldiers invading a Jewish home within the Ghetto. As part of their search, they ordered everyone to stand, except for the paraplegic member of the group who was allowed to remain sitting. The subsequent demonstration of their inhumanity showed no limits, as they first tossed him off the balcony, hurtling onto the pavement and then continued the bloodshed as they gunned down the rest of the family. The Spzilmans could do nothing but excruciatingly witness this ordeal.

Life in Warsaw transformed to death, either by the lack of food or the lack of humanity displayed by their Germans overlords. It was by the hand of God, or, more precisely, by that of a Ghetto policeman that Szpilman was saved from boarding a train to the death camps. Alone, Szpilman survived and lived in the Ghetto as a laborer, secretly working for those who were willing to fight, while hoping for an eventual chance to escape his confines. His wish was granted as he made it out the walls and back into the very world that had rejected his kind. Surviving in the Ghetto was grueling, but attempting to live outside it was another story. Near the film's conclusion, his long urge to play the piano had been fulfilled by the presence of Wilm Hosenfeld, a man recognized today as one of the few members of the Nazi party to willingly hide and assist Jews. Food, shelter, and kindness were the very things Hosenfeld provided Szpilman. His last words of farewell to the grateful pianist were powerful: "God wants us to survive."

The Pianist is no doubt one of the best films of 2002, as Mr. Brody brings the revelation of the renowned pianist to life so that audiences can experience further what this man had lived through. Adrian Brody portrays Szpilman on a professionally effective level, embodying a feeling of sensibility in his charm, his curiosity, and even more so in his passion for music. The scenes of Szpilman playing the piano, and the very sadness that defined him were represented by the rhythm of notes, as they embodied a longing expression of escape from that depression. On a physical level,

Brody succeeded with both the weight loss as well as the piano practice regimen required to perfectly portray this damaged, yet inspiring character. Mention should be made of the supporting cast's remarkable performances in helping capture the forms of suffering so accurately.

The film itself serves as a lesson not just in history, but also in morals. Szpilman lost his family to the Third Reich, went into hiding as the war continued outside his apartment window, and deliberately risked his life, all the while harboring doubts he felt about his own place in the middle.

Roger Ebert of the Chicago Sun-Times wrote in his review of the motion picture: "By showing Szpilman as a survivor but not a fighter or a hero—as a man who does all he can to save himself, but would have died without enormous good luck and the kindness of a few non-Jews—Polanski is reflecting, I believe, his own deepest feelings: that he survived, but need not have, and that his mother died and left a wound that had never healed."

After viewing the film, it is obvious that the direction is excellent. When we notice how much Polanski delves into the life of this man, we start to see that this film is more of a personal tribute because Polanski himself had lost loved ones to the Holocaust. *The Pianist* is more than just a dedication to Szpilman, but it is also a dedication to all the Jews who became victims to the evil that was Adolf Hitler and the Third Reich. It shows how well a filmmaker like Roman Polanski can capture the victims' burdens and convey them through filmmaking, thus reminding us of the humanity we as people must never discard.

Andres Benatar's review of *The Pianist* discusses the outstanding directorial skills of Roman Polanski in making this film about a horrific time that he personally experienced in Poland as a child. The critic also praises specifically the attributes of Adrian Brody's performance that garnered him the Academy Award for Best Performance by an Actor. Finally, Mr. Benatar commented on the life of the subject of the film: the Polish pianist Wladyslaw Szpilman, who happened to be a Jew, and suffered greatly because of it.

Actor-Driven Review

Often films revolve around stars and are considered vehicles to showcase their talents or appeal. Such stars have the power to pick the scripts since they are the box office draw. That is why we speak of a Brad Pitt

film or a Meryl Streep project; or, if we go back in cinema history, especially to the comedies of the 1930s, we speak of the films of Mae West or
W.C. Fields or the Marx Brothers—no one remembers who the directors
were for these star-driven motion pictures.

Film critic David Ansen views Jocelyn Moorhouse's *A Thousand
Acres* (1997) certainly in positive light. The film is based on the celebrated Jane Smiley novel of the same name. His review especially
praises the acting performances of Michelle Pfeiffer and Jessica Lange.

A Powerful Duet from the Heartland:
Pfeiffer and Lange Triumph in *A Thousand Acres*

There are many ways in which *A Thousand Acres*, Jocelyn Moorhouse's film of the Jane Smiley novel, doesn't do justice to the
Pulitzer Prize-winning book. But anyone in search of a powerful
emotional experience, and anyone who wants to see two of the juici-
est performances of the year, shouldn't miss it. Michelle Pfeiffer
and Jessica Lange—both of whom, remember, were written off at
the start of their careers as disposable Hollywood blondes—have
done as much to light up American movies in the past two decades
as any other actors I can think of. Paired as the Cook sisters, Rose
(Pfeiffer) and Ginny (Lange), in this loose transposition of "King
Lear" to the Iowa farmlands, they make an incandescent team.

Rose and Ginny are two of three daughters of a powerful and
revered Iowa farmer named Larry Cook (Jason Robards). The third
daughter, Caroline (Jennifer Jason Leigh), has become a lawyer in
the city. The tragic events in Smiley's novel, as in "Lear," are set off
when the patriarch quixotically announces his plans to divide his
land among his three offspring. But Smiley turns Shakespeare on
its head—for the heroines here are the arch villainesses Goneril
and Regan, and the Lear figure is a malevolent patriarch who has
inflicted ghastly psychological damage on his children. From under
the family's Grant Wood surface, poisonous fumes rise.

Rose, the mother of two, recovering from a mastectomy, is a
woman fueled by rage ("The more pissed off I feel, the better I
am"), while the childless Ginny, passive and repressed, tries to
smooth over the buried antagonisms that are wrenching this
deeply dysfunctional family apart. These complex, fully realized
women are Smiley's triumph, and Lange and Pfeiffer, playing an
eloquent emotional duet, bring them vividly to life.

Moorhouse and her fellow Australian screenwriter Laura Jones
succeed where it counts, capturing the close, sometimes bitterly

fraught relationship between the sisters. The men in the tale—
Rose's unstable husband (Kevin Anderson), Ginny's virtuous but
obtuse mate (Keith Carradine) and the neighbor's seductive son
Jess (Colin Firth)—are merely sketched in. The storytelling, full of
dark secrets and impassioned outbursts, can seem melodramatic at
times, and Moorhouse doesn't have much feel for the Iowa landscape or for the community that demonizes the two sisters. But if
the movie is not all it could have been, when Pfeiffer and Lange are
on the screen, you don't want to be anywhere else.

By coincidence, the two stars had neighboring offices at Orson
Pictures back in 1992, when both received early galleys of Smiley's
novel. They immediately turned to each other and smiled: this was
the project they had been waiting for. "In the beginning we didn't
really decide who was going to play what character," says Pfeiffer,
who admits she always wanted to play Rose. "I loved her struggle,
loved her fight. She had this uncontrollable urge to speak the
truth. This movie scared me a lot. This was the one that I knew I
could fail on in a big way." Lange was scared, too, at the prospect of
playing Ginny. "Ginny's passive. I've never had to play a character
like that before. At the beginning of the film I used to walk around
the set and say, 'God, I haven't got a clue what I'm doing here.' But
I always had the novel as my guideline. I kept it with me every second of the day."

Though it was a five-year struggle to get the movie made, the
shoot itself, according to the stars, was mainly harmonious. "Jessica
and I didn't know each other very well before this movie. I didn't
even really talk to her until we were literally walking to the set to
do our first scene together. But the work was effortless." Lange
agrees: "There was not one moment in the suspended reality that I
didn't believe she was Rose and that she was my sister."

The problems came after the shooting ended, when Moorhouse
("How to Make an American Quilt") turned in her cut. Everyone
was disappointed. The story meandered; the emotion got lost. The
producers hired an outside editor to come in and work alongside
Moorhouse's editor. The director stormed off, threatening to take
her name off the movie.

With the input of the stars and the producers a new version
emerged. "My feeling was the storytelling was not clear," says Lange
of that first cut. "I had no problem shooting with Jocelyn," says
Pfeiffer. "Postproduction was the hard thing. It may have been that
she was too close to it. We were all too close to it. It took bringing in
a new editor who was objective and brutal. It's still Jocelyn's movie."

In this age of the auteur, interfering with a director's "vision" is a
great heresy. But in the real world, not all directors are created

equal, and not all directors are always right. Movies are a collaborative art. Whatever Moorhouse's side of the story is (she declined to be interviewed), she has kept her name on the picture, and she deserves credit for creating the conditions that allowed Pfeiffer and Lange's magic to blossom. It may have taken fights to get there, but the movie still feels like a labor of love.

For the most part, David Ansen's review is quite complimentary to the movie. The acting performances alone of the two principal females in the cast are excellent enough to carry the movie. Ansen is also intrigued with novelist Jane Smiley's premise of taking Shakespeare's *King Lear* and totally changing it not only in terms of setting but also in the characterizations and plot. The critic also provides some interesting tidbits about the pre-production and post-production conflicts.

————————————————— **Lengths** —————————————————

Movie reviews come in all sizes and, as such, function quite differently. The thumbnail sketch is a quick summary of the plot, players, and genre and usually does not exceed 150 words or so; whereas the short review can reach about 350 words. A piece of medium length is typically anywhere from approximately 400 to 750 words long. Feature length reviews exceed that last number considerably The longer the review, either the more detailed it becomes or the broader its scope. The Andres Benatar review discussed previously on Roman Polanski's *The Pianist*—which counted more than 1,000 words—*would* be a clear-cut example of a feature-length review.

The Quick Summary and Short Review

Some quick summaries, as stated before, give the bare essence of a review. At the other end of this shorter length piece would be a review of up to 500 words. Here you get a concise review but definitely have more of a feel for the movie. In the much shorter version, the expected conventions of the review are still followed but in a more abbreviated form—even if it is as brief as the "thumbnail summary" of a paragraph or two.

Our first example is a thumbnail summary (only 124 words long) of *Sorcerer*, William Friedkin's 1977 taut thriller/adventure. It has the basic elements of the review including one particular sentence that could stand as an evaluative statement about the movie.

Sorcerer

Director William Friedkin's *Sorcerer*, a color remake of Georges Clouzot's 1953 black and white thriller, *Wages of Fear*, is just as much a nail biter as the earlier French version of the Georges Arnaud novel. Four fugitives, in order to escape from a Latin American town, agree to transport ultra-sensitive, highly explosive nitroglycerine in a rickety, old truck (ironically christened "Sorcerer") through bumpy jungle roads and narrow, mountain passes. Their destination is a raging oil fire that their dangerous cargo would help extinguish. At times, the suspense is painful in its intensity. The international cast, headed by Roy Scheider, also includes Francisco Rabal, Ramon Bieri, Bruno Cremer, Amidou, and Peter Capell. The running time is 122 minutes; the movie is rated PG.

The thumbnail review above for *Sorcerer* consists in large part of important boilerplate about the movie. But also included are the premise of the plot and its complication. None of the climax and ending is even hinted at. The word "nail biter" and the phrase "the suspense is painful in its intensity" suggest both the genre and its effectiveness within it.

Another short review—this time of 488 words—comments upon the Clint Eastwood treatment of an episode in the life of Nelson Mandela, the inspiring former president of South Africa. The film, released in 2009, stars Morgan Freeman as Mandela and Matt Damon as Francois Pienaar, the captain of the national rugby team. The following essay is written by Harrison S. Barrus, a student at Broward College.

Invictus

The pillars of history oftentimes are built upon the shoulders of great men. Nelson Mandela is one such great man and Clint Eastwood's stunning biographical portrait *Invictus* is his story.

Invictus is set at the end of Apartheid just after Nelson Mandela is freed from prison and steps into the shoes as president of a divided South Africa. Eastwood's story revolves around this time as the leader uses the South African rugby team to bridge the gap between the racially divided South African blacks and the white Afrikaners.

Clint Eastwood's motion picture and his depiction of the racism affecting South Africa, though often heavy handed, does accurately portray the very real, very passionate, and very divisive feelings of the country at that time.

Some of the highlights are memorable, as in the treatment of the Rugby World Cup matches. There is a gritty realism in the games that, at times, feels as if you are participating in the contest itself, or, in another instance, one of the fans desperately rooting for the underdog team. The emotion is so palpable that you feel the experience of the hopes and dreams of a broken nation being rebuilt and forged.

Morgan Freeman's characterization of Nelson Mandela is another highlight of the film. His portrayal of the kindness, determination and perseverance that embody the man during this momentous and moving struggle are spot on. Mandela's carefully measured speech, so embodied with sincerity and passion and emotion, ring true with Freeman's performance.

Matt Damon's role as captain of the South African rugby team is another moving example of acting that is equal to—at times, even outshining—Morgan Freeman's masterful command of Mandela's person. As Francois Pienaar, the young rugby captain, charged with winning the World Cup by Mandela, Damon is highly credible, mastering the nuances of the Afrikaner-tinged accent perfectly. We feel his momentary helplessness at being overwhelmed by his burden of responsibility to not only bring forth the former glory of the national team, the Springboks, but exceed it, and in so doing unite the country through athletic victory. With both Freeman and Damon on screen together, you can truly glimpse a part of the relationship that the actual Mandela and Pienaar must have shared. Their shared time together especially takes their performances to another, even higher level.

As a whole, the film is a deeply moving biographical venture—a somewhat new genre for Eastwood to explore. But he has a deft hand, as he makes sure that Morgan Freeman's Mandela embodies the careful deliberateness of a man who is carrying the weight of a nation on his shoulders. He lets Matt Damon's Pienaar, in turn, capture the strength of an ordinary man called upon to serve an entity far greater than himself. Together, their joint performances are something to behold.

Invictus may have its flaws, but it, nevertheless, moves forward in credibly demonstrating how ordinary men who are called to greatness can succeed against all odds.

This modest-sized review talked about the unusual relationship between two men—one black and one white, one the elected leader of a nation and one the captain of a prestigious rugby team—and how that special relationship changed their country's history.

Standard Size

The medium-length review of a few typewritten pages (500 to 750 words or so) enables the critic to develop more deeply those aspects of the film and comment upon them more fully. All parts of the shorter review are in place; however, they are just treated more extensively.

Irish director Neil Jordan's *The Crying Game* was to some quite controversial, while to many others it was one of the quality films of 1992. The 691-word review that follows discusses some of the movie's more important elements.

Friendship, Love, and the Irish Republican Army

This Neil Jordan film (writer and director) has two very distinct parts where the first segment inextricably and continuously influences the second. *The Crying Game* is an unusual film, a powerful film. Coming midway in the second section, its great surprise— after the initial shock wears off—does not hinder the audience's increasing absorption with the two central characters and their intensifying relationship.

The first portion of the film takes place in Northern Ireland. Just outside a country fair, an off-duty black English soldier is kidnapped by a number of I. R. A. gunmen. He has been set up by the woman he has just met and to whom he has been making heavy amorous advances at a secluded spot. The woman, Jude (Miranda Richardson), is a member of the band of irregulars.

The soldier has been taken hostage and placed for safekeeping in an abandoned greenhouse in retaliation for the British internment of a local I. R. A. leader. The words of Maguire (Adrian Dunbar), head of the kidnappers, are chilling: "[He should] be treated as a guest until further developments. . . . Give 'im a cup o' tea."

The captive, bound and barely enduring a suffocating thick woolen hood over his entire head, mumbles appreciatively, "Thank you, soldier," when his captor removes the hood. As the hours mount, a wary then friendly relationship builds between Jody (Forest Whitaker) and his guard Fergus (Stephen Rea). Each recognizes the humanity of the other; Fergus, not surprisingly, permits Jody to remain unhooded and his hands unfettered. Their conversation meanders from the political to the personal with the two often intertwining.

"You're tough, deluded people, and it is not in your nature to let me go," Jody claims.

"I got signed up to get a job," counters Fergus.

"We do our tour of duty and we're finished. . . . If this were all over, [we'd be] having a pint on a rock," Jody ruefully comments. The sequence is reminiscent of a similar confrontation between a captured British soldier and an Irish irregular in Edwin O'Connor's troubling short story, "Guests of the Nation."

The men view each other as obedient soldiers without any personal animosity toward each other. In time, Jody trusts Fergus enough to share intimate details of his life and shows his captor a snapshot of his striking lover. Despite the affinity of the two men, the possibility that Fergus may be forced to execute his bound companion is never far from either's mind. In a moment of panic, Jody pleads that Fergus contact his sweetheart, Dil, if his life is taken.

Soon Fergus is ordered to kill Jody. Torn between duty and sentiment, the Irishman allows the British soldier to escape momentarily then desperately chases him through the woods. Before Fergus can make up his mind to shoot to kill or shoot to miss (and thus risk his own life), Jody crashes through a thicket and onto a paved road only to be instantly struck, dragged, and crushed to death by a British personnel carrier en route, ironically, to liberate him.

The movie's second segment has Fergus on the lam from both the pursuing British and his vengeful I. R. A. collaborators (who had been attacked at the hideout and suffered some losses). Altering his appearance somewhat, he flees to England. He goes to Jody's home town and gets a job as a construction worker. Soon he seeks out Dil (Jaye Davidson), keeping his oath to Jody. Dil, indeed, is every bit as beautiful and alluring in person as in her picture.

In time, Fergus and Dil strike up a friendship which eventually deepens into a love affair. Their interracial romance takes some unusual twists and turns. But they cannot escape their pasts: Jude, the sole surviving kidnapper, surprises Fergus and threatens violence to Dil unless Fergus participates in an assassination of an English judge.

Suffice it to say, the film ends with Fergus in prison for a crime he did not commit but for which he confessed so as to shield Dil from harm. In the last sequence, we see Dil during one of her frequent visits to the incarcerated man, demonstrating the same faithfulness to Fergus that had been shown to Jody.

The review traces how *The Crying Game* comes full circle. Politics directly affects the first portion of the film. This, in turn, leads to an intensification of the human issues and relationships in the lengthy second portion. The climax merges the two with politics strongly impinging on the human story by movie's end. Any evaluative statements are found exclusively in the initial paragraph as are the major credits. Perhaps too much of the plot is detailed in this review; however, the major themes that the film presents are fully developed.

Next is another medium-sized review that gives us the essentials in under 600 words. It expounds upon James Cameron's blockbuster *Avatar* which many thought was a shoo-in for the Academy Award for Best Picture of 2009.

Avatar: James Cameron Transports Us to a Truly New World

This reviewer is old fashioned: I love a clearly-crafted plot; I demand well-conceived, credible characters; I require a setting with enough verisimilitude and attention to detail to transport me to another time and place; and I need a theme worthy of consideration. What I am not interested in is a surfeit of special effects and computer-generated imaging (CGI) at the expense of the other vital cinematic components; nor can I tolerate an obscene abundance of action, weaponry, and explosions that diminish the film's basics as well. That being admitted, and despite such reservations, I confess to being drawn in by all the hype attendant to James Cameron's 3-D sci-fi epic *Avatar* (2009).

When I emerged from the darkened cineplex two and a half hours later, I was a believer, enveloped in a state of stunned bedazzlement. I had just been witness to one of the great cinematic experiences of my life. *Avatar* was unlike any other science fiction epic that I had ever seen: sure there were influences of other futuristic adventures of the past—*Star Wars* and *Jurassic Park* immediately come to mind. But although this motion picture borrowed from others, it then took such gleanings far beyond.

This review is intended to be relatively short, so I will gloss over such aspects as plot, characterization, and theme. Instead I will concentrate on how the special effects and computer generated imaging affected me. Suffice it to say that the plot was engaging and kept me enthralled for the entire 160+ minutes. The characters were unique enough in conception, complexity, and appearance to more than keep my interest even though most of the actors playing them were relatively unknown. The themes of a military losing its moral objective conjoined with crass corporate greed trying to explore, endanger, exploit an unspoiled natural world and its inhabitants were not new—however, their development was more than sufficient to suspend my disbelief.

That being said, let me state what made this such a unique movie-going experience. What Cameron did was visually create a world not only unlike any I had previously seen, but one that had never entered my wildest imagination. Foremost of these was his creation of the floating cloud worlds of Pandora, moon to some star out in the galaxy. Conceive of steep, heavily forested tropical islands not emerging from some ocean but floating in the sky. Or think of potted bonsai communities with not only their miniature trees, plants, moss, rocks, and man-made objects—tiny wood bridges and miniscule porcelain dwellings—being removed from their ornamental receptacles and hanging in mid-air. Then think of blue, ten-foot high humanoids with tails, the Na'vi, peopling this cluster of air-borne islands. And then we have the creatures, wild and domesticated, which are both fantastic and phantasmagoric. Finally, you have the battle scenes, also unlike anything we have seen before.

I will not go into further details about the plot and themes here since this is intended to be a modest review in length. Nor will there be an analysis of how the storyline relates to the interplay and growth of the characters—again for the same reason. In ending though, it should be stated that this film is James Cameron's baby: he conceived of the idea, wrote the screenplay, invested his money in the project, and directed it (including close involvement in many of the technical processes and innovations used in the production). This close involvement has made this an unforgettable experience that will influence the future of filmmaking considerably.

Feature

The feature-length review is long—sometimes the length of an in-depth critique. The main difference, of course, is that it is still a review and follows the restrictions of what it should divulge in terms of boilerplate and plot and what it should not—namely, in most cases, both the climax and finale—since it still operates under the assumption that most of the readership has not yet seen the motion picture. Similar to the critical analysis, however, the feature-length review explores to considerable depth a number of aspects of the film that might be given shorter shrift in a briefer review.

The silent movie has been a relic of cinema history ever since 1930 . . . until its spectacular rebirth in 2011. *The Artist,* a French movie but shot in the United States and directed by Michel Hazanavicius, was virtually the first silent film made since the Great Depression—and what a comeback! It won the Academy Award for Best Picture among other Oscars that it gathered back in February of 2012. The following feature length review needs that amount of verbiage to analyze the many merits of the film and to show that it may not only be a revival but a breakthrough as well. The review was written by Andres Benatar, the Broward College student whose name by now has become familiar to you.

The Artist (* * * ½)

Genre: French Silent Comedy/Drama
Directed by Michel Hazanavicius
Cast: Jean Dujardin, Bernice Bejo, John Goodman, and James Cromwell

"My. The talkies have been running rampant over the years." The silent film began in the year 1877, lasting for only a 50-year period, until sound began to be grafted onto the motion picture. The "talkies" were introduced around the year of 1927, soon to take over the film industry. Within a year or two, the public referred to

Jean Dujardin in in Michel Hazanavicius' The Artist (2011). The Weinstein Company. Courtesy of The Kobal Collection at Art Resource, NY.

films with sound as if there were no other cinema. This was not the case back in the days of silent movies, as the very first picture to ever win an Academy Award for Best Picture was the silent film *Wings* in 1927. It is now the year 2012, and *The Artist* had just snatched the same plaudit.

The year is 1927 and *The Artist* focuses on the rise and fall of George Valentin (Jean Dujardin), an actor with enough charm, charisma, and enthusiasm to remind us what it took to capture the physical romance silent films embodied. The body language, combined with the sheer use of ever-changing background music and the occasional occurrence of title cards was what truly defined a silent film. There were moments of delight, wit, excitement, and sadness to further challenge any performer's capabilities. In a screen world without sound, the audience had to follow George Valentin and make their own interpretations of him. It's obvious that he lives a rather frivolous lifestyle, always within the constant spotlight of his stardom. He is often cast as the lead of great hits such as *A Russian Affair* or *A German Affair*. The music ceases as the camera rolls and the audience claps to every act of heroism displayed. It is only when the world starts to talk that the music really starts to play.

One consistent and accepted principle in any industry, whether it be film, the media, or the publishing industry, is change. Attendant to the principle of change is the need to adapt, and that in and of itself serves as one of the great lessons of *The Artist*. George's place as a famous actor seemingly secure, nevertheless faces the ongoing risk of being replaced. Back then as today, there are a number of actors whom many producers and directors would kill to cast or even keep on a payroll. Although it isn't easy to substitute an actor with incredible talent, if he or she is unwilling to adapt, then that star suddenly becomes expendable.

George reaches that point as he witnesses the rise of the film industry into a more modern age. His producer, Al Zimmer (John Goodman), has deemed this new era of sound "the future." As sound films dominate, silent films lose their appeal in such mutable times. Adaptation has become a critical necessity. George's own denial and ignorance of that principle becomes his downfall. His expendability is shown further with the rise of an actress who does more than hold her own with the talent Dujardin brings to the film. As "America's newest sweetheart," Bernice Bejo displays an equal amount of life, joy, and even more honest innocence in her portrayal of Peppy Miller. Miller's passion for acting is motivated by her own admiration of Valentin, as she is cast from the background roles of a simple stage dancer to the star role of romance films.

Everything in life always goes through its own phase of development. Whether the subject is to revolve around an industry, a person, or even a theological principle, the bottom line is that as time moves forward, we must also move forward or then we fall back. This alone serves as the central theme of *The Artist*. The silent film era began by capturing the physical dimensions expressed by the performers. Title cards and live music could help add some necessary information and instill mood respectively, but the full story was still not being told.

How this sea change in the industry affects George is presented in a simple manner, yet with a level of sympathy so engaging, that audiences in observing his mastery of physical expression become totally absorbed with the resolution of his professional struggle.

This reviewer in watching this, his first feature-length screening of a silent movie, found the experience not only enthralling, but necessary. *The Artist*, in its direction tells a simple, yet familiarly entertaining story. Themes of arrogance, passion, determination, and love further invoke life within the speechless characters, and make the format fully authentic and vital. Director Michael Hazanavicius has delivered a film not only worthy of high praise from the Academy of Motion Picture Arts, but also given new hope to the industry. *The Artist* is a significant effort to explore not just a past era of filmmaking, but in doing so propels the craft to reach even higher plateaus of accomplishment. After the silent movies, the talkies were the next step in filmmaking; then came color followed by computer generated imaging. In a generation or two, who knows where we'll be?

As can clearly be seen, this feature-length review covers a great deal of ground. First we learn a bit about the history of the silent movie. It is significant that *The Artist* takes place in 1927, the year *Wings* won the Academy Award for Best Picture. The reviewer then gives us insights into the main attributes of the principal characters and the demons that both drive them forward and hold them back. The need to change and adapt to move on is the theme of the movie. This holds true for individuals, such as movie star Georges Valentin as well as for industries (silent movies). If he (or it) doesn't, he (it) falls back and perishes. The final paragraph of the review praised the boldness of the concept and its execution by the cast and its director.

Before its numerous examples of different types and lengths of the film review, this chapter first pointed out the two most typical functions of the review: to summarize and evaluate. Consideration of the audience and formulation of the format (including boilerplate) followed. Next, the tone and style of reviews were established, as well as the word choice necessary to form them. In discussing these concepts, the chapter introduced the following types of reviews: the serious review, the humorous review, the pan, the rave, and the mixed review. Approaches or points to be emphasized in a review comprised the next section and included the plot-driven review; the character-driven review, with the "biopic" and superhero films as examples; the theme-, idea-, or ideology-driven review; the auteur- driven review; and, finally, the actor-driven review. The chapter's last section covered the varying lengths of a review. Placed into categories as well, these included the quick (thumbnail) summary and short review, the standard-sized (medium length) review, and the feature-length review. To illustrate these concepts, excerpts and complete examples written by professional critics, the author, and college students were provided throughout.

Chapter 4 concerns itself similarly in format and development with discussion of the critical analysis, otherwise known as the analytical critique (or "critique"). As in Chapter 3, it is organized by sections on Audience and Format and then Approaches. The latter section forms the bulk of the chapter focusing on different approaches one can take in writing a critique. These include critiques that are cinematic-driven, idea-driven, character-driven, actor-driven, and auteur-driven.

4

TYPES OF FILM CRITICISM:
THE ANALYTICAL CRITIQUE

Dooley Wilson, Humphrey Bogart, and Ingrid Bergman in Michael Curtiz's
Casablanca *(1942). Warner Bros. Pictures.* Courtesy of Everett Collection.

The *analytical critique* (also known as the *critical analysis*) assumes that the reader is **familiar** with the subject in question. In cinema, it would be the particular motion picture that is to be discussed. In broad circulation periodicals—such as newspapers and popular magazines—it is far less frequently published than the review.

Audience and Format

The *critique* is normally directed to a somewhat different audience than the review.

This audience is often composed of aficionados of film who have background knowledge about the medium. As a result, the critique is more scholarly in tone than the review although no research is cited (unlike the documented research paper). Often it is also longer than the review and will develop its thesis in depth. Its title will be fully functional—rather than be clever, or whimsical, or merely announce the movie in question, unlike so many titles of reviews—and will announce the subject matter and the specific film(s) that are to be discussed in the critique. The title is a key to the paper.

The critique's format differs considerably from that of the review in what it does and does not require. Boilerplate is restricted to a need-to-know basis. The same is true for the plot summary. The reader is assumed to be already familiar with much of this information. The critique may concentrate on only one portion or sequence in the film and exploit it fully—clearly a different emphasis than the review. In fact, since the thrust of the critique is so overwhelmingly analytical—with its incumbent explanatory passages—even evaluative comments are optional. The thesis statement is made early in the essay, although not necessarily in the first paragraph. The minor inferences (supporting points) with their accompanying examples—likely from the film itself—make up the bulk of the paper. The longer critical analyses are often divided into subsections. These, in turn, can be indicated by using additional spacing, bullets, subtitles, Roman numerals, or some other clear-cut designation. To summarize, the critical analysis will feature the following:

- A functionally descriptive title including the film's name,
- An in-depth development of the thesis and minor inferences with specific examples,
- An acknowledgement of credits limited to those that are relevant,
- An optional plot synopsis and evaluative commentary, and
- Division in subsection for longer critiques with additional designations.

—————————————————— **Approaches** ——————————————————

There is even greater latitude in the critique than in the review: one can discuss anything of interest or importance in a film as long as one's points are justified. Despite this breadth of subject matter, most critiques will either be centered on cinematic technique or cinematic elements; central ideas or topics that the films expose; or characters, actors, or auteurs.

The Cinematic Technique- or Cinematic Element-Driven Critique

The technical aspects of filmmaking—the cinematography, sound, music score, lighting, set design, location setting, special effects—all can greatly affect the outcome and impact of a motion picture. Specifically, how any or some of these do so makes for fascinating speculation and development. The success of what has now almost become a television and cable subgenre, "The Making of . . . [supply name of first-run feature]" is a testament to the interest that this facet of filmmaking engenders.

Following are some sample titles of critical analysis studies that focus on cinematic techniques or elements:

- The Use of Lighting to Instill and Reinforce Mood in Francis Ford Coppola's *The Godfather*
- Quentin Tarantino's Controversial Upending of Traditional Plot Structure in *Pulp Fiction*
- Interplay between Setting and Characterization in Jane Campion's *The Piano*
- Sergei Eisenstein's Cinematographic Genius: the "Odessa Steps" Sequence of *Battleship Potemkin*
- Orson Welles' *Citizen Kane*: An Explosion of Creative Camera Angles and Shots
- Make-up Magic in Arthur Penn's *Little Big Man*: the Aging of Jack Crabb from Callow Teenager to 121-Year-Old Man.
- Using the Interplay of Sound and Silence to Build Suspense in Alfred Hitchcock's *The Birds*
- The Design, Blocking, and Shooting of the Chariot Race Set Piece in William Wyler's *Ben Hur*
- High Tech Animation Techniques in Steven Spielberg's *Jurassic Park*
- "Living Kaleidoscopes" Choreographic Effects in the Musical Production Numbers of Busby Berkeley's 1934 *Dames*

Director Ridley Scott's *Alien* is a masterpiece of the hybrid genre of horror/sci-fi. Besides doing extremely well at the box office, it was highly influential in its merger of the science fiction and horror genres. Many aspects of the movie contributed to the success of the production: its restrained, naturalistic acting; its Hitchcockian building of suspense; and, finally, the use of set design and lighting to insinuate the mood. However, the critique that follows focuses on the more technological visual aspects of the project. Initially, after a brief overview of the premise, we explore the use of set design: both interior and exterior with commentary on how lighting aids and abets the set design. Final mention must be made of the alien creature itself, where the merging of natural looking features blends with starkly industrial elements to bring to life a truly fearsome monster.

Production Design of Ridley Scott's *Alien* as a Means for Inducing Suspense and Horror

In 1979, Ridley Scott's *Alien* had its theatrical release and eventually came to be as influential a space epic at the *Star Wars* entity that preceded it in 1977. Unlike the George Lucas effort, this wasn't a sprawling space "opera" with a huge cast of extras and myriad of characters with set piece battle scenes and such. The technical look of the two films was very different. We must remember that although both employed many special effects, both were produced when CGI was in its infancy. The *Stars Wars* look in most scenes was slick and futuristic, its movement quickly paced; whereas those elements of *Alien* were decidedly different. Although supposedly taking place in deep space and in the distant future, the film's sets had a gritty, steamy, industrial feel to them. Indeed, the craft was a commercial hauling and salvage vessel towing millions of tons of mineral ore back to earth. The pace, at first, was more leisurely, and the characters were believable and common rather than fantastic and super heroic.

This critique will show the great impact that set production, lighting, and the design and functioning of the creature itself had on the project as a whole.

The film opens with an exterior shot of a massive spacecraft methodically lumbering through space as if carrying a heavy load—which it indeed is. It has a dark exterior with many crenellated nooks, crannies, and functional accessories. It is lit reflectively by some unseen moon as the ship laboriously but steadily passes by it. This is no streamlined entity traveling towards worlds to explore or conquer, nor is it a highly maneuverable and deadly war machine zipping through space at warp speeds ready to fight the good fight. In contrary, this plodding conveyance is comparable to its twentieth century antecedents that plied the sea lanes of our planet as freighters and tankers.

It is symbolically named "Nostromo," after the character in the eponymous Joseph Conrad novel, which, not coincidentally, takes place in a mining camp in a fictitious South American country. Like the Conrad work, *Alien* also turns out to be a story of duplicity and deception.

"Nostromo's" interior is as can be expected: modern, functional, and cold with indirectly lit panels and multi-colored knobs, dials, switches, and buttons for its many screens and control panels. It is run by a human crew overseen by its overbearing computer "Mother" (shades of "Hal" from Stanley Kubrick's *2001: A Space Odyssey*). During the opening scenes, the crew has been settling down for their cargo-towing trip back home. Suddenly, they are notified that there seems to be a ship in distress, so following space protocol, they send a small craft with three crew members to investigate.

When they reach the disabled ship, they enter a dark, dank interior that looks less like the interior hull of a spacecraft than the steel and cable version of some giant organic beast's body cavity. There they investigate a large chamber that seems to have living creatures, incubating in what appears to be giant eggs. What is unclear is whether the distressed ship's automatic pulsating signal is one of distress (an "S.O.S.") or one of warning ("Keep Out!").

Suddenly, one of the giant pods erupts and a creature hurtles out and crashes into the helmet of Kane (John Hurt), one of the crew members, tightly covering the man's face with bony, clawed tentacles in an otherwise gelatinous, pulpy body. Formal company policy declares that all alien creatures must be quarantined off the ship, but this dictum is overruled by the captain, despite the protests of Ripley (Sigourney Weaver), the second in command. Kane, miraculously is still alive so the host and alien are returned to Nostromo to an isolated section of the living quarters. By the next day, he appears fine, all signs of the alien have disappeared, and he sits down with his crewmates for a hearty breakfast. Suddenly, he starts convulsing as a somewhat altered alien bursts out of Kane's stomach, letting its host hemorrhage to death as its screaming reptilian form with a mouth full of razor-sharp teeth scurries away into the bowels of the ship.

The hunt begins through the dark and dirty monochromatic interiors with their metal walkways and railings like some heavy industry manufacturing area. The light is dim with a yellow cast and the hunters carry search lanterns and such. As the story develops, so does the creature which grows larger, constantly mutating and killing off crew members while subsequently being nourished by their remains. Its calling card is viscous, oozing, gooey matter with acidic powers that eat through metal and any other solid substance in the ship. The hunters of the crew decidedly become the hunted as they search in increasing terror through the maze of the ship's dim, backlit corridors and steamy, wet passages, and an array of flickering electronic devices that offer little comfort.

The monster itself is a terrifying yet fascinating creation. Critic Ted Gershuny of *Magill's Survey of Cinema* describes it thusly:

> The alien form at first is raw, quivering, and fleshy, like the underside of some crustacean. It oozes yellow bile that eats through the floor of the big space vehicle. And its spawn, in the ship, is "born" from the guts of the first infected crewman. . . . Guts and the tearing at guts provide the driving images in *Alien*. As the monster grows, its metallic teeth are glimpsed briefly in double and quadruple rows: mouths full of teeth, arms reaching out with teeth, all accompanied by the din of shrieks, wind, and synthesized cacophony. The monstrosity of the alien lies precisely in its otherness from the world of technology. (38)

The critique immediately prior concentrated on some of the more visual technical aspects of the film *Alien*, including the exterior and interior sets, the lighting, and the construction and movement of the "monster" itself. Their total effect was to merge the genres of science fiction with horror in a way that was very different than what had been done in the past and would be highly influential for future films made in both genres.

Filmmakers are constantly learning from each other as the art and science of moviemaking expands. Certain masters of the cinema, however, create technical, narrative, and aesthetic breakthroughs that bring the entire industry up to a higher level. One such pioneer was actor/director/choreographer Gene Kelly who together with co-director Stanley Donen presented their 1952 masterpiece *Singin' in the Rain* to delighted audiences across America and the world. Three instances in the film were particularly memorable in their use of simple sound stage props or atmospheric effects to create choreographic set pieces that were among the movie's high points.

Props and Atmospheric Effects That Inspire Innovative Choreography in Gene Kelly and Stanley Donen's *Singin' in the Rain*

The name Gene Kelly was synonymous with dance on the big screen in the 1940s and 1950s. His dancing in many of his hit films was characterized by athletic grace and an opportunistic incorporation of props and other studio effects—wind machines and lighting, for example. Nowhere is this more apparent than in the 1952 musical comedy *Singin' in the Rain* in which he starred, sang, danced, and co-directed with Stanley Donen. *Singin' in the Rain* is arguably America's most beloved musical, and unlike most of the later musical productions of the century, it was written directly for the screen rather than adapted from a Broadway hit.

The film takes place in Hollywood during the late 1920s as the entire movie industry is grappling with the traumatic transition from silent films to the new "talkies." This is affecting everyone connected with the industry, including leading man and former vaudevillian Don Lockwood (Kelly) as well as his wisecracking, hoofing sidekick Cosmo Brown (Donald O'Connor). With the advent of sound, they see a golden opportunity to collaborate on the writing and staging of song and dance numbers for the screen. This, in turn, logically leads to a number of wonderful songs and choreographic routines that are delightfully woven through the film. In many of these set pieces, everyday objects and studio props together with common staging effects—such as a wind machine, simple lighting, and a flat set—are used as integral parts of extremely innovative and entertaining dance numbers.

The dance set pieces featuring Donald O'Connor are particularly funny, raucous, and freewheeling—such as "Make 'em Laugh" and "Moses Supposes." He uses well-upholstered sofas, tabletops, and a mop, all left randomly on the sound stage during a break. His numbers incorporate tap, ballet, and ballroom steps for his antics. One number has him even dancing onto a vertical wall and then back flipping to get a laugh.

A different mood is invoked during the "dream sequence" of the extended "Broadway Melody Ballet"/"Gotta Dance!" scene. Cyd Charisse, a sexy, leggy gangster's moll is suddenly transformed from a vamp to a sweet, idealized woman for this fantasy dance number. On an empty sound stage, wearing a 25-foot white silk scarf that billows up in the air—from a wind machine—she dances a graceful, romantic pas de deux with Kelly. Against a screen backdrop of projected sunset hues, this ballet number is remarkable for its simple ingenuity and sheer beauty. (Admittedly, it does break the mood of the entire Broadway Melody production piece.)

Finally, we come to the eponymously named dance sequence, perhaps the most famous in the history of the American film musical. On a rainy evening, Don Lockwood has just left Kathy Selden's (Debbie Reynolds) apartment, realizing that they are in love with each other. His exuberation is such that even the nasty weather cannot dampen it. While singing the title tune, he again uses found objects to aid his choreography. He rhythmically cavorts with his umbrella—both opened and closed; he jauntily hangs from and then twirls around a lamppost; he boldly stomps into and splashes through puddles as an underwater tap dance: in sum, he makes his joy infectious.

There are other memorable song and dance numbers throughout the film involving the principals as well as the corps of dancers. In many of the numbers, simple props found in an apartment or studio floor are used as foils for creative choreography. The pace of comedy, dance, and song rarely flags. Memorable moments are scattered throughout—first reel to last—in this most satisfying of American movie musicals.

The prior critical analysis shows how some accidental "found" objects at a movie sound stage site are incorporated into a set piece dance routine that soon becomes one of the highlights of the film. In all the instances given, there are never more than just one or two dancers in the scene as opposed to a full dance company performing an intricate production number. The effect of each of the three examples is different: the first is comically slapstick, the second wistfully romantic, and the third is exuberantly joyous.

Former Broward College student Casey Cook points out and then develops his insights upon the interplay of sound and silence that Alfred Hitchcock incorporates into his 1963 suspense/thriller *The Birds*. Hitchcock uses this juxtaposition of the two opposites as a means of building suspense and keeping the audience off balance.

The Use of Sound and Silence in Alfred Hitchcock's *The Birds*

Alfred Hitchcock's unconventional use of sound and silence in his *The Birds* builds suspense by playing against audience expectation. By the time of the 1963 release of *The Birds*, film audiences had been conditioned to the language of suspense, in no small part by

Hitchcock himself, through such groundbreaking films as *The 39 Steps*, *North by Northwest*, and *Psycho*. A key component of this language was the use of sound, building tension with silent and quiet passages, and releasing it with sudden, loud noises, either through a sound effect corresponding with the onscreen action, or via a large swell or accent in the musical score. In *The Birds*, Hitchcock turns these expectations upside down, and, in doing so, creates disconcerting and effective suspense.

From the opening title sequence, Hitchcock is surprising in his use of sound, eschewing any musical score. The director maintains this stylistic choice throughout the movie, and the absence of music provokes a vague uneasiness in the viewer from the start. The only sound present in the introductory credits is the fluttering sound of bird wings—an otherwise innocuous sound becomes slightly ominous through its insistence.

Early in the movie is a scene when Melanie, played by Tippi Hedren, charters a small boat and travels across the bay to play a trick on Mitch, played by Rod Taylor. The majority of this scene plays with no dialogue, adding an underlying tension to an otherwise lighthearted sequence. Dialogue only resumes after the initial attack of a seagull on Melanie, which provides the payoff to the suspense. The lack of any dialogue and minimal sound in this builds tension, but, conversely, lulls the audience into a sense of complacency and sets up the shock of the attack.

Hitchcock uses another odd stylistic choice that adds tension when he overlaps dialogue from a character speaking on the phone with other characters having a discussion in the background. Typically, in a movie this background dialogue would be played as "busy noise," adding a realistic murmur without distracting from the foreground dialogue. In *The Birds*, the background conversation is distinctive enough to confuse the audience, leaving it unsure as to which conversation is advancing the story. As it turns out, in both cases the conversations are insignificant in terms of the plot, but represent another unsettling use of sound that adds to the unease of the audience.

In a pivotal scene, Mitch's mother Lydia (portrayed by Jessica Tandy) discovers the first brutal evidence of the birds' murderous intentions in the form of the corpse of a neighboring farmer with his eyes pecked out. The image of the farmer's mutilated face is delivered in three sharp cuts that close in on each beat of time, but the release of Lydia's horrified scream is muted, stuck in her throat, and it's left to the viewers to supply her full-throated scream in their minds. The scene is yet another unexpected use of silence over sound to misdirect the audience, stealing its release from the suspenseful scene with an added layer of discomfort.

In the absence of a musical score, Hitchcock uses bits of singing in key scenes that precipitate attacks by the birds. In the first instance, Melanie is playing the piano in the calm post-dinner ritual of Mitch and his family, creating a relaxed mood that is soon jarringly upset by a swarm of birds pouring down the fireplace and into the room. In the second, a schoolroom of children is singing in class, while outside, in the playground, the birds start to flock menacingly on the swings and jungle gyms. In both scenes, Hitchcock uses singing in the context of the story to suddenly add tension and is able to maintain and work around his deliberate choice to use no score.

Hitchcock's use of silence over sound to build suspense is driven home in a key segment of the final reel. In order for the family to escape, Mitch must drive his fully occupied car slowly through thousands of perched birds that have surrounded the house. The muffled starting of the car engine is barely hinted; his consequent slow roll through the massed stationary birds is almost completely silent, with no discernible noise from the car. The random chittering of the birds over the purring of the slowly revving engine keeps the audience focused on the threat of the birds' presence, and the high vulnerability of the carload of humans as they try to escape.

Throughout *The Birds*, Hitchcock's use of silence and sound confounds the expectations of a newly sophisticated audience by building suspense in unexpected ways, thus adding new textures to filmmaking. In particular, the absence of a musical score—which he has used so successfully in his other films—is striking, and has influenced such notable and disparate filmmakers as George Romero in his *Night of the Living Dead* and Stanley Kubrick in his *The Shining*. Although not included among Alfred Hitchcock's greatest masterworks, *The Birds* is a powerful example of how he further developed the suspense genre and his overall influence on modern film.

Casey Cook's essay is a clear example of a critique that centers around technical cinematic elements; namely, the interplay of sound (dialogue, sound effects, occasional music) and silence as a means to create and build suspense. He shows us, using different scenes in *The Birds*, how its famed director Alfred Hitchcock did away with a musical score and used music sparingly, reduced the amplitude of sound on some occasions, and used simultaneous foreground/background dialogue to build tension in the film.

The Idea-, Topic-, or Ideology-Driven Critique

Besides studying the various cinematic devices or elements of a film, the critical analysis often explores the ideas evoked from a movie— what the picture says about us, our way of life, our nation, our world. Some films boldly explore social issues and are political, even propagandistic. Others prefer to look closer to home within the family or within the individual. Hundreds—maybe thousands—of films have been made with larger objectives than merely providing diverting entertainment and reaping the resultant monetary compensation. Many motion pictures are about ideas and concepts—social, historical, political, scientific and the like. The movie public wants to learn, to ponder, to be ethically affected not just amused, and is willing to pay for it. Sure, the movie industry churns out releases that offer well-crafted escapism which gross billions; but those same studios also produce sensitively written, well-acted cinema offerings that provide the public more intellectually, morally, and aesthetically.

The following critical analysis topics deal with ideas, concepts, and problems about our society and/or ourselves as they are presented in specific motion pictures:

- Walt Disney Studios' *Bambi*: An Animated Fairytale as a Harsh Introduction to Life
- The Assault upon Political Integrity in George Clooney's *Ides of March*
- Offensive or Liberating? Mel Brooks' Use of Racial, Scatological, and Sexist Humor in *Blazing Saddles*
- Religious Allusions and Symbolism in Ingmar Bergman's *The Seventh Seal*
- Elements of Racism in the Military Generally and on an Army Base Specifically in *A Soldier's Story*
- The Motif of the Star-Crossed Lovers as Portrayed Repeatedly in *The English Patient*
- California for the Ills of America in Joel Schumacher's *Falling Down*
- Multi-Symbolic Use of the Rose in Sam Mendes' *American Beauty*
- The Interplay of Evil, Cowardice, and Courage in Fred Zinnemann's *High Noon*.
- Of Minstrel Music, the Mississippi, and Miscegenation: George Sidney's Adaptation of Edna Ferber's *Showboat* (1951)

Symbolism is both a basic literary element and cinematic element as well. In simple terms, a symbol is something with one standardized meaning that also has a different particular meaning. For example, spring in one sense is a season of the year, while in another it can *symbolize* "rebirth" or "youth." At times, the symbol can be multi-faceted as the following paper will demonstrate.

Disco Dominance: Symbolism in *Saturday Night Fever*

To many of us, disco music is nothing more than a type of rock 'n roll music that was popular during the late 1970s. To some others, who might have experienced the disco scene more directly, it was also part of a subculture. Yet for Tony Manero (John Travolta) disco music and the dancing that accompanied it symbolized his essence: for himself, the extent of his talent; to his peers, the measure of his worth; and as to his prospects, the future of his prospects.

The film takes us to a time when the "disco scene" was a popular cultural phenomenon that swept across many cities of the United States during the late 1970s and early 1980s. The world of disco included a special type of pop music and new dances to move to it. These dances were quite stylized, yet left room for creative improvisation, especially by the better dancers. Additionally, a new form of men's fashion was not only an outgrowth of the craze, but a de rigueur necessity. It included such items as three-piece polyester

John Travolta and Karen Lynn Gorney in John Badham's Saturday Night Fever *(1977). Paramount Pictures.* Courtesy of The Kobal Collection at Art Resource, NY.

suits with bell-bottom pants in white or pastel colors, polyester shirts—minus ties—of black, loud colors, or outrageous patterns, and, of course, platform shoes.

This era is expertly captured in John Badham's 1977 *Saturday Night Fever*. The film can be perceived as a hybrid, merging the coming of age drama with the musical; for without the music and dancing, there would be no story.

The music impacts us immediately as the opening credits scroll. To the "Bee Gees" hit song "Stayin' Alive," we see the bottom torso of a young man swinging a closed can of paint rhythmically as he struts to the music. There is such grace and power to his strides that it seems as if his walk is really a syncopated dance. Finally, the camera pulls back to a full body shot. He is a young man in his early 20s with perfectly combed hair, fitted trousers, a polyester shirt, and a short length faux leather jacket. An attractive young woman enters the screen from front right striding towards the young man and swinging her hips sensuously. As she passes him, he does a quick double take without missing a beat to catch her movement going away. This little sequence—all visual—already gives us some insights into Tony Manero.

Young Mr. Manero definitely has some studly qualities which we learn of in succeeding scenes. We see Tony spending almost excessive time grooming his hair and primping himself in the rest of his toilette. He spends most of his income on his clothes, and his wardrobe is quite extensive. Although he gets little respect at home—indeed, he is treated like a child by his parents—everywhere else he holds his head high. He works at a local paint store as a salesman/gofer, like a number of his friends, holding a job rather than climbing a career ladder.

To Tony and his set, one's value and standing is defined by the quality of one's moves on the disco floor. This defines their machismo and sexuality even more than muscles or a smooth tongue. Their local Mecca in Bay Ridge, Brooklyn on Saturday night is the 2001 Odyssey. The place is all pulsing strobes, flashing lights, lights and glitter all in sync with the highly amped music. The twirling, preening, gyrating, dancers are a mass of flowing movements colorfully attired in the most stylish of clothing. The attention to looking good and dancing well is comparable to those waltzers of the 19th century or those devotees of the gavotte in the 18th. And in this place Tony is king, even admired by his older brother, Frank, Jr., a young Catholic priest who sheds his collar whenever possible and prefers to be addressed just as "Frank," not "Father." Although they all live for Saturday night, Tony is more ambitious. During much of the movie, he is in the process of defining and clarifying his values. Sure he likes being numero uno on the dance floor, and not only at the Odyssey but other disco clubs as well. But his being disco royalty in Bay Ridge is not enough. He sees that he has real talent as dancer and wants to take his ability to its natural limit. By movie's end, he wants the destiny of a career in dance, not in Brooklyn but in Manhattan and on Broadway. This is his dream.

Saturday Night Fever is a motion picture that melds aspects of the ethnic, rite of passage, and slice of life dramas with the music and dancing of the musical. But no one breaks out into song to express his or her feelings of the moment. It is sexy, it is gritty, but it does show the rite of passage and painful, personal growth of its protagonist, Tony Manero. In the film, disco music and the subculture that surrounds it acquire symbolic importance that become evident by movie's close. One could say that disco music is the defining agent for Tony Manero which ultimately helps him escape the stranglehold of a demeaning family and a confining neighborhood environment.

During the World War II years, 1941–45, Hollywood produced a number of films directly for the government as documentaries, instructional films, or pure diatribes of propaganda. But a number of movies created to entertain the general public had patriotic and even propagandistic elements to them as well. Perhaps the best known of these was the beloved classic *Casablanca*, which besides being a romantic drama with aspects of the thriller to it, was clearly made to put the country behind the war effort. The United States entered the conflict officially on December 8, 1941, only a few weeks after the film was completed.

Broward College student Harrison S. Barrus looks at the film as a work that merges the three aspects of romance, thriller, and propaganda.

Elements of Propaganda, Romance, and the Thriller in the Classic Film *Casablanca*

Early In the year 1942, America had become fully involved in fighting in the second World War which had swept through Europe and Asia. During this period, Hollywood had begun producing propaganda films, one of which was the classic *Casablanca*. Although this motion picture features other aspects—such the romantic drama and thriller—a key intention was for propaganda purposes.

Propaganda, indeed, was a primary motive. During World War II, the feeling in America—especially preceding the attack on Pearl

Harbor—was still one of isolationism and lack of support for the war movement. Thus, as a propaganda film, it was these issues that *Casablanca* was commissioned to address.

In *Casablanca*, the feeling of isolationism is clearly seen in the person of Rick Blaine and the way his character clearly expresses that he is out for himself and no one—and nothing—else. Public lack of enthusiasm for the Allied war effort is due in part to the fear and hopelessness of confronting the overwhelming threat of the Third Reich. This feeling is perfectly illustrated when we first meet Major Strasser who states, "We Germans must get used to all the climates, from Russia to the Sahara," as if Germany's conquest is all but complete. The feeling of fear and hopelessness is shown through the course of the film as we watch the refugees in Casablanca try desperately to escape the German oppression.

This despair and cynicism is reversed in two instances in the film. Midway, at the Café Americain, a group of German officers decide to boisterously sing their national anthem. In defiant response, the French and Allied sympathizers drown the Nazis out with "The Marseilles." And then later, in the closing moments of the film, we watch Rick and Captain Renault walk off into the distance, having saved the day against overwhelming odds, and newly committed to the Allied cause. From this gesture, we are given the idea that if the reclusive underdog Rick Blaine can put others ahead of himself and triumph, then America as a whole can do the same.

The second major characteristic of *Casablanca* is that it is a romantic drama, played out in a straightforward fashion. A man meets a woman, and through a series of events, they fall in love. Something happens that causes them to fall away from each other— this against the backdrop of the ensuing invasion and occupation of Paris by the Germans. Eventually, the couple is reunited in Casablanca in the romantic climax of the film. Their earlier meeting in Paris is recounted through a series of flashbacks concluding with their unexpected break-up. When we meet Rick at the outset of the movie, just a few years have passed, but Rick has been shaped by these former events and has turned into an isolated, seemingly cold-hearted man. When Ilsa Lund unexpectedly appears with her husband Victor Laszlo, the memories of their past flood back to an agonized Rick Blaine. It is Rick and Ilsa's original love affair and her sudden abandonment of him into the cold recluse at the film's outset. Towards the conclusion of the movie, the reasons for her disappearance back in Paris are brought to light and explained. How the love triangle is resolved is unconventionally: Rick has made the choice to sacrifice his happiness for the greater good—forcing Ilsa and her husband to catch a plane to freedom in Lisbon, Portugal, and then on to the United States. Laszlo is a Czech patriot whom the Nazis plan to kill if he remains in Casablanca or returns to Europe. Thus, it is the choice of putting Ilsa's future happiness above Rick's personal feelings that not only gives closure to the romance but ties this element of the film with the propaganda function with the idea of putting the greater public good ahead of individual desires.

The final element of the thriller fits *Casablanca* into the conventional Hollywood mold. We have the exotic locale, the overwhelming odds, and the underdog protagonist emerging triumphant at the end. The setting of Casablanca in Morocco, North Africa is not only perfect but historically accurate. It is a place filled with diverse cultures—especially during wartime—and unique characters. The overwhelming odds of opposing the Third Reich's ever-increasing iron-fisted grip on Casablanca are chilling to watch. Here is Rick Blaine, the one-time freedom fighter and gun runner, presented as the quintessential underdog hero. He maneuvers to save the lives of Ilsa, Victor, and himself under the noses of the ever-present and tightening German threat. If this isn't enough, we place characters like the amoral Signor Ferrari and the ethically ambivalent Captain Renault into the mix, adding another layer of intrigue to the plot.

As with the romantic component, the thriller ingredient supports the propaganda factor by showing that even the most oppressive enemy can be brought down. As the credits roll by, it is evident that the combined strength of the romance, the thriller, and the propaganda vehicle makes *Casablanca* the timeless classic that it has become.

Harrison Barrus in his critique has shown how a great American film from 1942, *Casablanca*, actually helped our early war effort by galvanizing the support of the American public behind it. It did so by combining the genres of the romantic drama and the thriller with blatantly propagandistic cinema.

The Character-Driven Critique

Many critical papers about film analyze the characters who people the movies. Often such analyses are either psychological portraits of a character or investigations of what motivates certain characters to take the actions they do. Frequently, the complex and, at times, changing relationships between characters are delved into through this form of criticism.

Some sample titles of critical analyses that focus on aspects of characterization in a motion picture are:

- Captain Queeg's Descent into Insanity in Edward Dmytryk's *The Caine Mutiny*
- Aspects of an Overwhelming, Inspiring Personality in Morton DaCosta's *Auntie Mame*
- The Metamorphosis of Willard into Kurtz to Complete His Mission in Francis Ford Coppola's *Apocalypse Now*
- Psychological Profiles of the Jurors in Sidney Lumet's *Twelve Angry Men*
- The Minor Characters of John Ford's *The Grapes of Wrath* as Indicators of the Impact of the Great Depression
- An Obsession with Unattainable Beauty: The Portrayal of Gustav Achenbach in Luchino Visconti's *Death in Venice*
- The Private Investigator as Philosopher in Dick Richards' *Farewell, My Lovely*
- Two Father Figures with Two Different Sets of Values in Robert De Niro's *A Bronx Tale*
- The Insidiousness of Alcoholism on the Lives of Good People in Blake Edwards' *The Days of Wine and Roses*
- Instances of Over-Reactive, Excessive Violence in Martin Scorsese's *Goodfellas*
- The Principled FBI Chief Agent Versus the Unscrupulous Gangster Kingpin in Brian De Palma's *The Untouchables*

Blake Edwards was an established maker of clever film comedies from the late 1950s until the middle 1980s. One of his most fortuitous accomplishments was teaming up with comic actor Peter Sellers, who brilliantly embodied the character of bumbling Inspector Jacques Clouseau in *The Pink Panther* series of films. By tracing the course of a number of films in which Peter Sellers appeared and the roles he embodied in them, one can appreciate his genius for zany characterization and physical comedy. These qualities are showcased abundantly in *A Shot in the Dark* from *The Pink Panther* body of motion pictures that he made with Edwards. It should be apparent that his unique abilities extended to many of his other films made with other directors both in England and the United States as well.

The following character-driven critique looks at the genius Sellers had for the unique blend of physical comedy and comic characterization. These qualities he especially demonstrated in the memorable cinematic creation of Inspector Jacques Clouseau.

Slapstick, Sangfroid, and a French Accent: Peter Sellers as Inspector Jacques Clouseau in *The Pink Panther* Series

We have had other cinema slapstick comedians and other celluloid comic geniuses. Each has had his or her own trademarked mannerisms and props. Charlie Chaplin has his derby and rubbery cane and a mixture of impishness and vulnerability as the Little Tramp. Mae West had her walk, that suggestive saunter; her talk, filled with double entendres; and her designs, always out to get men and then put them down. W.C. Fields had that short, fat body and bulbous nose; talking out of the side of his mouth in that singular non-Southern drawl, he was a misanthropic windbag and deflator of all sacred cows—children, pets, motherhood—with clever turns of phrase. To them we add Peter Sellers as Inspector Jacques Clouseau.

No one has taken on a character better than Sellers did with Clouseau. Introduced in 1963 in *The Pink Panther*, the Clouseau character was improved upon in *A Shot in the Dark* (1964) with the introduction of Commissioner Charles Dreyfus (Herbert Lom) his boss and nemesis and Clouseau's comic foil Kato (Burt Kwouk), his Vietnamese houseboy to whom he is teaching karate. Sellers' long-running character appeared in six films of *The Pink Panther* series—the last being released after Sellers' demise and comprising out-takes patched together to become *The Trail of the Pink Panther* (1982). Blake and Sellers also teamed up for *The Party* (1968) where Sellers devised a character every bit as funny as Clouseau in Hrundi V. Bakshi, a rather inept actor from India who has come to the United States to make it big in Hollywood.

What Sellers demonstrates in *The Pink Panther* films and *The Party* is a magnificent capacity for slapstick physical humor and characterization. Within each of these movies, he has developed signature routines, identifiable with him alone. Clouseau, in ways, is a throwback to the physical comedy redolent in the Mack Sennett two-reelers of the Twenties up through the Jerry Lewis farces of the Fifties. Nevertheless, combined with Sellers' genius for vocal mimicry and his ability to totally immerse himself within a character, he was able to invent not only funny film personas but also creations with distinct personalities as well.

In *A Shot in the Dark*, Sellers delineates Inspector Jacques Clouseau, a police investigator who is gullible, stupid, incompetent, and physically maladroit; even so, he is quite vain about his sexual charm and detective prowess. Possessing a remarkable sangfroid when someone else would be visibly upset, he constantly tries to keep the illusion of order—or at least its outward semblance—despite the obvious reality of the ridiculousness of the moment. Impeccable in dress and appearance—with expensive well-styled clothing, neat haircut and meticulously trimmed moustache—he acts as if nothing were extraordinary as he tramps into a luxurious apartment sopping wet (after falling into a fountain while exiting his car) to investigate a murder. He is oblivious to the consequent sloshing noise of his steps and their sodden tracks all over the costly carpeting. In another sequence of the movie, he espouses his forensic theories to Maria Gambrelli (Elke Sommer), the young maid whom everyone suspects of the killing but Clouseau: she is too pretty and engaging in his view. When she suddenly clutches his sleeve, she unintentionally rips it off entirely from the suit jacket. After momentarily noticing the now useless material hanging on his arm and then dispensing it, Clouseau continues his monologue not visibly upset and totally ignoring the absurdity of his sartorial situation.

A Shot in the Dark has numerous farcical moments. Some have even become standard features in the remainder of his *The Pink Panther* films, among them: his ongoing karate matches with Kato and his persecution at the hands of Commissioner Dreyfus. The Inspector knows little about karate—as his stylized karate chops would indicate, yet he insists on teaching Kato the martial art and instructs him to attack without warning any time of the day or night. Kato takes this to heart and assails his teacher in the dead of night. But Clouseau is ready, having gone to bed wearing his heavy canvas karate kimono. They grapple, with the Inspector knocking out his valet unintentionally. These sudden assaults occur throughout the movie, each at an even more inappropriate time. Yet, on each occasion, Clouseau's shortcomings in self-defense are outmatched by his servant's even greater ineptitude in attacking.

If Clouseau always keeps his cool, Dreyfus is the opposite. Reduced to a gibbering maniacal killer by film's end, he is desperate to the point of insanity to rid himself and his department of the bumbling sleuth forever. Another aspect of Sellers' ingenious characterization is his "Belgian" accent and inventive mispronunciations. When Maria hits her head, what results is "bwemmp" (bump); those creatures that fly at night and eat clothing are "mewths" (moths). Whether his accent is accurately French or falls short is not the point: it is funny and consistently maintained. (The same can be said for the lilting singsong of his Hindu thespian in *The Party*.)

There are other comedic instances throughout *A Shot in the Dark*. As mentioned before, the receptions to both *The Pink Panther* and its immediate sequel *A Shot in the Dark* were strong enough to inspire the producers to cultivate the character into a movie series.

Perhaps the greatest compliment to Sellers was that after his death in 1980, *Curse of the Pink Panther* (1983) featured a successor but flopped badly enough to end the series permanently.

Obviously, it was neither the clever gags, the plots, not the concept that had made the Clouseau films such a huge moneymaker, but rather the unique qualities of Peter Sellers which captured increasingly large audiences as he remodeled and refined his memorable cinematic product in sequel after sequel.

This collaboration between the gifted English comedic actor Peter Sellers and the A-list American director Blake Edwards had been so successful, that they had teamed up to make six films in *The Pink Panther* comedic series. The films have all been anchored by the character of Inspector Jacques Clouseau. The Inspector is a hilarious blending of investigative incompetence and personal cool, of physical comedy and mispronunciation hilarity. The previous critique highlights aspects of Sellers' portrayal of this memorable Paris police department employee.

The Actor-Driven Critique

Actor-driven critiques are another type of film criticism. They concentrate on the achievements of a player in a particular role or techniques perfected by him or her. When an actor's work is studied as a complete entity in order to discern growth or emerging patterns, a comparative analysis format is usually employed. For more on comparative analysis, see Chapter 5.

Following is a sample listing of critical analysis titles that concentrate on specific actors' qualities or their unique interpretations in specific movies:

- Marlon Brando and Method Acting in *On the Waterfront*
- John Wayne as the Archetypal Hero of the American Western
- The Voice of Teen Angst: James Dean in *Rebel Without a Cause*
- The Character Actor as Personified by George C. Scott
- The Character Actress as Personified by Kathy Bates
- Handsome to a Fault with a Touch of Self-Deprecating Humor: Cary Grant, the Ultimate Leading Man
- The Simpleton as Wise Man: Tom Hanks as *Forrest Gump*
- Nicole Kidman Plays Against Type in *The Hours*
- Jamie Foxx as *Ray*: A Multifaceted, Multilayered Interpretation of Blues/Jazz Man, Ray Charles
- The Remarkable Incorporation of Facial and Bodily Contortions in the Comedy of Jim Carrey

The critique which follows discusses aspects of Charlie Chaplin's unique creation, "The Tramp," introduced in a short film of the same title. Because of the success of the film and especially of the particular character, in a number of his subsequent two-reel comedies, Chaplin reintroduced him and embellished him until he is there in all his pathetic glory in the feature length silent movie *The Gold Rush*.

Here the critic speculates that *The Tramp* might have been influenced by an earlier familiar character of classic Spanish folklore, the "Picaro"; or at least, shares many of the same qualities. This comes close to being a comparative essay; however, since the bulk of the paragraphs analyze what Chaplin did to make this character so unforgettable, it can be ultimately considered a critical analysis rather than a truly comparative essay.

Charlie Chaplin's Comedic Innovations as he Re-invents the "Picaro" in his *The Tramp*

In 1915, Charlie Chaplin, then under contract with Essay Studios in New Jersey came up with the idea of a character that caught fire with the general public. In a two-reel film (approximately 20 minutes), Chaplin devised the Little Tramp. After seeing *The Tramp* a few times, this critic perceived the parallels between the Chaplin creation and a "the Picaro" of 16th century Spanish character found in stories and novels of that time and beyond.

Picaresque literature of the 16th and 17th centuries revolved around the Picaro or rascal who could be quite mischievous but sometimes had some good points. He was always poor and existed by his wits. Such a scamp rarely had a roof over his head, and was always on the move either by choice or by necessity. Often he fell afoul of the law or at least those with power and authority, and most often bested them. But even when he didn't, he escaped from tight situations with his skin intact. Although not weak physically, he depended on his brains rather than brawn. Often his adventures were told humorously in the first person with the hypocrisy of his tormentors or opponents readily depicted. Always of a lower social class, he was often illiterate. The stories were episodic with a thin plot as the rogue moved from one exploit to another. His profession was that of being a Picaro, nothing more or less. He was consistent in his character and did not change because of his experiences. He was a rascal, but often quite loveable in being so.

Now we look at the Chaplin version. His small film, *The Tramp*, clearly defines the qualities that are decidedly picaresque but something more as well. First and foremost he is a romantic at heart or, more accurately, he is a sucker for a pretty face, especially that of an innocent in distress. All his qualities, picaresque and otherwise, are fully displayed in his film. As it opens, we see him walking down a country road. His supple walking cane is slung over a shoulder with a "hobo" bag tied to the end of it. His clothes are shabby and he looks poor but there is a certain élan to what he is wearing despite its condition. Charlie's character is small and slight. On his head is a black derby. Under his long suit coat is a vest with a white shirt and cravat beneath. Matching baggy trousers cover his clodhopper shoes to complete his ensemble.

It is midday, so he sits under a large tree on this summer day to partake of lunch. He opens his hobo bag drawing forth a sandwich which he places carefully on the ground nearby. At the same time we see an unsavory, unshaven vagabond, who, when Charlie is momentarily preoccupied searching his pockets for eating utensils and implements, steals his meager food and runs away. Crestfallen, Charlie pulls some grass, draws forth condiments from his maw of pockets, salts the grass and eats it as illustration of his fastidiousness and salvaging of a bad situation.

The following scene put him into direct confrontation with a gang of marauding vagrants and paradoxically brings out his softer qualities. A young woman, the virginal farmer's daughter, is walking across a field for some reason counting a wad of cash in her hand. The same thief who stole Charlie's lunch now grabs her money and leaves after threatening her. She screams and calls for help. Charlie, nearby, chases the evil-doer and attacks him with a hidden brick in that hobo bag and retrieves the money. The crook goes back to his confederates and they go after Charlie and the girl. Using his wiles, a bit of bluffing, and surprising aggressiveness, our courageous hero beats them off. He is very much a Picaro in many of his attributes but with a gallant heart for the lady in distress.

When she brings him back to the farm she introduces him to her father who immediately offers him a job as a hired hand. Here we see another parallel between the Little Tramp and the Spanish Picaro: they don't do too well with normal occupations. He gets in scuffles with the hired hand and in trouble with the farmer, but all this is forgiven as he defends the household from an attack by the three thugs. During the process he becomes slightly wounded and plays his temporary disability for all that it's worth. But now

Leo White, Charlie Chaplin, and Edna Purviance in Charlie Chaplin's The Tramp *(1915). Essanay Studios.* Courtesy of Everett Collection.

he has a new foe: the daughter's fiancé or steady boyfriend comes to visit. Although Charlie is introduced to him as a hero, the Tramp realizes the battle for the girl is already lost. Broken hearted, he signs a note of goodbye and prepares to leave. He departs as a gentleman, but his depression doesn't last very long. Once on the road, he squares his shoulders, picks up his pace, clicks his heels, and marches off to the next adventure just like a Picaro would 350 years before.

Audiences found Chaplin's character of The Tramp so endearing and entertaining that Chaplin brought back many aspects of that character back in film after film, including his acclaimed full-length silent class *The Gold Rush.*

The Auteur-Driven Critique

The auteur-driven critical analysis concentrates on certain trademarks, quirks, or talents that have become synonymous with a noted filmmaker. This is an area that may also be served by the comparative analysis. However, in the analytical critique, we are restricted to techniques or qualities as evidenced in one specific work. Sample critical analysis titles that center on the filmmaker would be:

- Sam Peckinpah's Excessive Use of Violence in *The Wild Bunch*
- A Story Told from Four Points of View: Akira Kurosawa's *Rashomon*
- The Concept of Auteurism as Exemplified by Francois Truffaut in His *The 400 Blows*
- The Widescreen Epic as Defined by David Lean in *Lawrence of Arabia*
- Adult Relationships in the Seventies in America as Seen through the Lens of Director, Screenwriter, and Actor Paul Mazursky
- Roman Polanski's *Chinatown*: Film Noir Revisited . . . and in Color
- Post-War Italian Neo-Realism as Evidenced by Vittorio De Sica's *The Bicycle Thief*
- John Cassavetes: An Auteur Who Didn't Use a Script and Who Didn't Direct His Actors in Creating *Shadows*
- He Made Audiences Laugh during the Great Depression: Frank Capra Introducing Screwball Comedy with *It Happened One Night*
- Cecil B. De Mille and His Formula for the Biblical Spectacle as Evidenced in *Samson and Delilah*

Many consider Italian director Lina Wertmuller as the greatest female director of her era. She wrote all her scripts, which usually had a consistency in their philosophical, political, and ideological content. Given great control of the films she made, Lina Wertmuller would be a strong example of a *femme auteur*. As a result, the following is an auteur-driven piece on her 1974 film *Swept Away by an Unusual Destiny in the Blue Sea of August*. It was written by Colin L. Westerbeck, Jr. in *Commonweal*. It was reprinted in this edition not only because it makes some fascinating observations about the movie and Wertmuller's methods in conceiving and executing the work but because it had been miscategorized by the author of this book. The paragraph immediately following explains the error in detail.

(It should be noted that in the Second Edition of *Critical Approaches to Writing about Film*, this essay by Colin L. Westerbeck, Jr. was considered as an auteur-driven *review*. However, upon further study, this should have been more accurately categorized as an auteur-driven *critique*. There are numerous reasons for this change in categorization. Unlike the usual review, the Westerbeck essay mentions the climax and the ending of the movie—usually, taboo for a review. As you read it, you probably noticed a lack of evaluative commentary either of the film or the actors involved in it. Instead, throughout the essay, the critic discusses Wertmuller's cinematic style and how it impacts the portrayal of various aspects of her characters. He also comments extensively on the film's premise of their being marooned on an uninhabited Mediterranean isle.)

Robinson Crusoe

In any film that takes place on a sailing boat—Victor Fleming's *Captains Courageous* (1937) and Roman Polanski's *Knife in the Water* (1963) come to mind first—the director is going to find the opportunities for beautiful photography irresistible. Lina Wertmuller's new film, *Swept Away by an Unusual Destiny in the Blue Sea of August*, is no exception.

The film begins on a sailboat, and Ms. Wertmuller takes about every one of those opportunities she has to dazzle us with the scenery. During the day the boat nuzzles into the blue grottos of the Mediterranean coast. At dusk it glides before an orange and blue sunset. After nightfall, the mistress of the boat, Raffaela (Mariangelo Melato), emerges from below decks into the brilliant, silvery backlighting of moonbeams bouncing off stainless fittings.

Even when Raffaela and one of her sailors, Gennarino (Giancarlo Giannini), get separated from the boat while out in a dinghy, life on the water remains a luxurious, stunning sight. As an aerial shot draws back from them lost at sea in their little boat, the camera picks up the swarming iridescent highlights of the sun on the water. And when they at last fetch up on a deserted island, they are enfolded by green foliage, bleached limestone, and pearl gray twilights. They are enshrouded in the sort of photography whose colors are so rich they seem actually to fill the air between us and the landscape we are looking at.

Yet none of this photography ever allows us to feel that Wertmuller only wants to send us pretty postcards. There's too much trouble in this paradise for us to get that impression. During the establishing shots at the very beginning of the film, before we get even close enough to make out who is speaking, we can hear Raffaela delivering a marathon diatribe against everything and everyone who isn't idle, feckless, and fashionable like her. She is a rich bitch of the worst sort—the sort that flaunts it—and when she discovers that deckhand Gennarino is a Communist, she takes special delight in torturing him. When they are stranded and then marooned, it's like locking up a cobra and a mongoose in the same wicker basket. At first she continues to browbeat and bully him, but once they get to the island he's had enough. Now it's his turn, since she must depend on him for survival, to get his licks in. He makes her work for every morsel of food he provides, and slaps her around for good measure whenever he has the least excuse.

Thus Wertmuller's film becomes in large measure a contradiction, or at least a conflict, between what we see and what we hear. This is why the film is funny. All comedy is the result of some sort of incongruity or disproportion. The clown's shoes are too big and his hat is too small, the punch line of the joke is either an overstatement or an understatement, swatting a fly is wanton but blasting it with a cannon is hilarious. The incongruity that Wertmuller creates here is one between the visual and the aural scales of her film. Again and again, as in those establishing shots at the beginning or that aerial shot of the dinghy, we see her characters from a great distance. Extreme long shots show us Raffaela's party lolling on the deck of the sailboat, or the tiny figures of her and Gennarino traipsing across their island.

The scene in those shots is always lovely and tranquil, and the figures close together. Despite the distance from which we are watching, however, we hear the characters speak in these shots as if we were in their midst; and their dialogue is always pure discord. Raffaela is squawking about something, or Gennarino is, or each is shouting at the other simultaneously.

The disparity between the sights and sounds of the film makes us choose continually between believing what we hear and what we see. Those who choose the former think Wertmuller is full of passionate political commitments to socialism or feminism or revolutionism or whatever. This is unfortunate, especially since her popularity has been based on the misconception that she has such trendy commitments. (Perhaps she sees where her bread is buttered; she has even encouraged this misconception.) The fact is that Ms. Wertmuller is not a politician: she's a filmmaker, and she knows that what we see is what ultimately must matter in a movie. Politics is the great subject of debate in her films, but what her characters have to say about politics is always just a lot of hot air and bombast. More than once Raffaela makes fiery speeches defying Gennarino, and in the next cut Wertmuller gets a laugh by showing her doing precisely what she was inveighing against so eloquently.

Lina Wertmuller's comedy is really not a form of satire, then, but something much more personal and warm-blooded. To her the world is not as strident and disagreeable as it sounds in this film, but as beautiful and as sensuous as it looks. When she suddenly jumps her camera off at a distance from her characters, it is in part to keep their ideological bickering in perspective—to show it as only a small hubbub in a very pleasing landscape. This is not to say, though, that Wertmuller is a sentimentalist, or that the rich pastel world she envisions here is without sadness. Like her two earlier films, *Love and Anarchy* and *The Seduction of Mimi*, this film ends unhappily because of the foolhardiness of a man.

Eventually, grudgingly, Gennarino's and Raffaela's loathing turns into love, but Gennarino is still too mistrustful to be satisfied with that. He affects their rescue so that she will have to prove her love for him by continuing it back in the civilized world. In the penultimate scene, he calls her at the hotel where she has been reunited with her husband. When she comes to the phone, he tells her he's calling from the gas station across the street and is looking right at her. But now that vision of them to which we have become accustomed is turned inside out. We no longer see them together and at a distance, arguing at the top of their voices. This time they speak softly and secretively as he explains how he's arranged to take her away again. He tells her nothing else matters, and she seems to assent. The trouble is that while they are saying these things, we are seeing them only in separate close-ups because they are no longer close enough together to be contained in the same long shot. And now as before, it is what we see, rather than what we hear that we are compelled to believe.

Westerbeck initially discourses about the director's use of cinematography to put certain thematic elements in opposition: namely, the disparity between "what we see and what we hear." This is a major comedic component of the film as well. Her politics—socialism and feminism—are disclosed but the critic believes them to be subordinate to what she is trying to achieve as a filmmaker. Love overcomes politics and even socioeconomic class when given the right environment, but when both characters are returned to "civilization" at movie's end, the baggage of their former lives is seen to erode and then overwhelm their formerly shared passion.

In the late 1980s the National Film Board of Canada helped subsidize the making of an unusual film. The movie—a hybrid of sorts—combining elements of cinema verite, fictional narrative, and standard documentary, was released in 1990.

Originally titled *The Company of Strangers* (it has since been renamed *Strangers in Good Company*), this "indie sleeper" went on to win a host of national and international cinema awards for its director, producer, and scenarist (who sadly died before its release). What follows is another example of an auteur-driven analytical critique.

Strangers in Good Company: No Plot, No Script and an Amateur Cast . . . But It Works!

The overriding premise is quite simple. Put seven elderly women—all strangers to each other—in an old school bus driven by a hired middle-aged driver and have the vehicle break down in the middle of nowhere (or, more precisely, the Quebec wilderness). Then see what happens. And oh yes, in doing so, make sure to have no contrived plot, no detailed script, and no professional actors in front of the camera. Is this a recipe for disaster? . . . not at all the case for Cynthia Scott's *Strangers in Good Company.*

The film begins by the women emerging from ground fog, a somewhat heavy-handed although realistic symbol, since they are isolated and dislocated. And yet there is no panic. Despite their ages and assorted infirmities, they are basically in good spirits and united in seeking shelter first. They eventually find it, an abandoned farm house. The women soon find that there is no means of communication since this was before the pocket-sized (or purse-sized) cell phone era. They are soon able to prioritize—at least for the immediate future—they have shelter, night is approaching, so sleeping arrangements and accommodations are paramount. And this is where the magic of this motion picture begins to manifest itself.

Their director has given the women the barest of outline of instructions: be yourselves in meeting this crisis and getting through it. If this were a real-life situation, their dilemma could grow to be quite dire, even life-threatening. Yet in order to either rescue themselves or find others to aid them, they must collectively problem-solve and help each other. In so doing, they must share parts of their lives with the others. This is "improv" acting at a very high level.

We first see them as a group which is easy to stereotype—a bunch of old ladies in trouble; we wonder if they even realize how much. As the film progresses and a the group coalesces into a single unit, the women open up to each other and, in so doing, become rounded, endearing individuals not only to each other but to the unseen audience as well.

From the rooms of the farmhouse itself and its outbuildings, they find old bedding and straw and settle down for the night, good humoredly making the best of it. Two of the women decide to sleep for the night on the covered porch using a threadbare blanket. They all make it through the night with no mishaps. When they wake up the next morning we see through their eyes that their environment is both beautiful but dangerous and they must plan and work to get food, water, and devise strategies to either leave or get help. Informally, the group divides up to work on these separate issues. In so doing, their individual pasts and personalities come to the fore. The women discover a near-by lake and attendant but vacant boathouse or perhaps bungalow on the water adjacent to the shore. This serves as a source for more provisions and additional shelter. Unfortunately, there are no rowboats or canoes.

For food, two of the women gather berries. Another group goes to the lake, digs for worms and tries to devise a fishing pole and makeshift hook but without success. Finally, one of the women, Alice Diabo, a Mohawk Indian, develops a portable trap of sorts out of some discarded nylon stockings. The result: fish for dinner. One of the others captures frogs; the amphibians' grilled legs will also add protein to the evening meal. Interspersed with these life sustaining projects are more introspective moments and recreational activities.

Some of the conversations are very personal, even confessional. Cissy Meddings, a widow and an emigrant to Canada with a delightful Cockney accent, has had a stroke but has recovered and now fondly reminisces about her lovely gardens back in the south of England. When she asks Mary Meigs, an artist, about former husbands and such, Mary confesses that she is a lesbian. To which Cissy replies non-judgmentally, "Oh, that's good." For recreation they all play cards or sing and dance. Winifred Holden, among other things, used to be a belly dancer and, despite her years, still has remarkable grace and rhythm. The youngster in the group, Michelle Sweeney, their bus driver, is a black woman originally from Cleveland, Ohio, who bubbles over with spirit and sass. Then there is the reticent duo of Beth Webber, a woman who wears a wig covering up her thinning white hair is not too fond of the outdoors, and Constance Garneau, once a trailblazing broadcaster, who is the oldest of the group. She blames herself for the predicament they are all in and seems tired of life. But perhaps the most admirable of the group is Catherine Roche, a nun who tries to fix the bus engine—and almost succeeds—then, despite her arthritic feet, decides to take it upon herself to backtrack the country road for twenty miles in order to seek help.

The next day when we see the pontooned bush plane circle the lake before landing on the water, we know that Catherine has succeeded and the film has a happy conclusion.

Director Cynthia Scott, her scenarist Gloria Demers, and cinematographer David da Volpi have put together a motion picture that is heartwarming and funny, poignant and insightful. A little gem that film critic Rita Kempley of *The Washington Post* so aptly calls "a kind of road movie standing still."

The preceding piece is an auteur–driven critique that shows how very unusual concepts for a film, combining disparate types of filmmaking, merge into a most enjoyable hybrid format. It is indeed a little independent Canadian film that although made more than twenty years ago, is timeless and shouldn't be missed.

In Chapter 5 we are now ready to discuss another type of critique, the comparative analysis. The comparative analysis looks at the parallels or differences between various aspects of films, directors, or actors. It may also compare and/or contrast assorted works of a given artist.

5

TYPES OF FILM CRITICISM:
THE COMPARATIVE ANALYSIS

Janet Leigh and John Gavin in Alfred Hitchcock's Psycho *(1960). Paramount.*
Courtesy of The Kobal Collection at Art Resource, NY.

The *comparative analysis*—also called the *comparative critique*—like the critical analysis, assumes that the reader is knowledgeable about the movies or people in question. The range of topics is limitless. Essentially, the writer finds similarities between two or three or even four items or aspects, makes the statements about them, and then backs up these assertions in the bulk of the paper.

—————————————— Audience and Format ——————————————

Typically, the audience for a comparative film analysis would be students of film or those interested in the cinema with a broad background and deep knowledge about the motion picture. Like the critique, the comparative analysis is more scholarly in tone than the review although, again, no research is cited. Because at least two films or directors or actors are compared on any number of aspects, the comparative analysis is usually longer than the review. Most often, it submits a thesis and develops it in depth. Like the critical analysis, its title is fully functional, descriptive, and sometimes lengthy. It announces the subject matter and the specifics that will be compared and developed.

Like the critique, the format of the comparative analysis differs from the review in what information is necessary and what is not. Boilerplate is restricted to the bare essentials, and the essay may assume that the reader has considerable background information about the film(s) in question. The same is true for the plot summary. Again, the reader's familiarity with the plot is assumed so plot summarization may be brief. The comparative analysis will concentrate mainly on those portions of the film relevant to the thesis. Since so much of the comparative piece is analytical and explicatory, there may be less of a focus on evaluative commentary.

In the comparative analysis, the thesis is made early in the essay, although not necessarily in the first paragraph. The minor inferences (supporting points) with their accompanying examples make up the bulk of the paper but follow a structure somewhat different than the critique (critical analysis). The paper will either emphasize the similarities of the aspects being compared or contrast their differences. Occasionally, the paper will first discuss the parallels and then switch to those points that differ. (A more detailed discussion of the structure—namely block or point-by-point—will be discussed in the next subsection of this chapter.) Like any long critical analyses, the comparative analysis can be divided into subtitled sections. To summarize, the comparative analysis features the following:

- A functionally descriptive title including the film's name,
- An in-depth development of the thesis and subordinate points with specific examples,

- Two or more major points compared with the emphasis being either on their similarities, differences, or one then the other,
- Acknowledgement of credits (boilerplate) limited to those that are relevant to the essay,
- Optional plot synopsis and, in some cases, a less evaluative tendency,
- Longer critiques, possibly broken into subtitled sections, and
- A structure that is either block or point-by-point.

Structure

Structurally, the comparative analysis differs from the critical analysis (critique) because the critique uses a more standard format where the thesis is followed by development of the minor inferences (supporting points). With the comparative analysis, however, the writer has the option of either employing *block style* or *point-by-point* style. Either of the two styles (structures) appears after the introduction which includes the thesis statement. The following formulas provided illustrate the differences between the two structural styles.

Full Block Style

The block style initially introduces the entire thesis statement—which is often derived from the title—and contains the *thesis* together with the *minor inferences* which elaborate upon it. Then, if block style is employed, the writer first develops the points (Points 1, 2, 3 below) about the first half of the thesis (Film A below). Next, in a corresponding fashion, the writer develops those same points for the second half of the thesis (Film B below).

FULL BLOCK
Thesis Statement = Thesis + Minor Inferences
Thesis (Films A and B) + Minor Inferences (Points 1, 2, 3)
Film A: Point 1, Point 2, Point 3
Film B: Point 1, Point 2, Point 3

Incorporating this formula, we can come up with a topic that uses comparative analysis as a means of developing it. The following title is an example:

Terrence Malick's *Badlands* and Oliver Stone's *Natural Born Killers*:
Parallel Motifs of Alienated Youth, False Heroes, and Violent Endings

The aforementioned title will be converted into block style by first discussing *Badlands* (1973) in terms of the shared motifs of alienated youth, false heroes, and violent endings. Then, in similar fashion but in a separate section, we will converse about *Natural Born Killers* or *"N. B. K."* (1994) along the same lines.

Film A:	**Point 1**	**Point 2**	**Point 3**
Badlands:	alienated youth,	false heroes,	violent endings

Film B:	**Point 1**	**Point 2**	**Point 3**
N. B. K.:	alienated youth,	false heroes,	violent endings

Admittedly, there are additional similarities between these two movies in terms of plotlines, set pieces, characterization, geographic locale, and the like. A complete comparative analysis of the two films will contain numerous variables showing these additional similarities. However, for simplicity's sake, only three variables were selected to illustrate the concept of comparative analysis in block structural format and how it can be applied to a cinematic topic.

Point-by-point Style

In point-by-point structure, the same thesis statement is used but its elements are turned around. We start with Point 1 (the first minor inference) and discuss in it terms of Film A; then we treat Film B in a similar manner. The same procedure is used for elaborating on Point 2 and then Point 3. The formula looks like this:

POINT-BY-POINT
Thesis Statement = Thesis + Minor Inferences
Thesis {Films A and B} + Minor Inferences {Points 1, 2, 3}
Point 1: Film A   Film B
Point 2: Film A   Film B
Point 3: Film A   Film B

Using this formula, we can see how we would first be discussing "youthful alienation" (Point 1) and how it applies to *Badlands* (Film A) and then consider the same motif's use in *Natural Born Killers* (Film B). We will then focus on "false heroes" (Point 2) and how that motif is shown in the Malick film followed by Stone's treatment of it. Finally, "violent endings" (Point 3) will be considered in *Badlands* and then in *Natural Born Killers*. Notice that when we use the point-by-point structure, we turn around the thesis statement:

Parallel Motifs of Alienated Youth, False Heroes, and Violent Endings Seen in Terrence Malick's Badlands *and Oliver Stone's* Natural Born Killers

Point 1: Alienated Youth:	Film A *Badlands*	Film B *Natural Born Killers*
Point 2: False Heroes:	Film A *Badlands*	Film B *Natural Born Killers*
Point 3: Violent Endings:	Film A *Badlands*	Film B *Natural Born Killers*

Approaches

As with the critique, a number of topics can be examined in a comparative manner. Directors' styles can be compared. Benchmark films from the *oeuvre* of an established star can be contrasted, highlighting his or her growth from bit player to sought-after commodity, commanding millions per film. Or an actor's transition from light comedy to serious dramatic roles can be analyzed and his or her effectiveness compared in each. Cinematic techniques and special effects moving into obsolescence because of computer-driven imaging and such is another area ripe for comparative analysis. Why a certain cinema genre has arrived, flourished, waned, and disappeared can be developed through comparative study of causal factors and the environment necessary for nourishment. The following approaches listed are only partial; there are other means and topic areas just as appropriate.

The Movie-to-Movie Comparative Analysis

Often movies are compared for common elements or are contrasted for their effects on audiences. The topics that can be selected for comparative papers are vast. Following are selected sample titles that give some indications of directions one can pursue when writing a comparative analysis paper on film:

- Cinema's Depiction of the Iniquitous Power of Television as Portrayed by Elia Kazan and Budd Schulberg's *A Face in the Crowd* (1957) and Sidney Lumet's *Network* (1976),

- Fifty Years of Film Noir as Represented by Howard Hawks' *The Big Sleep* (1946), Roman Polanski's *Chinatown* (1974), and David Fincher's *Se7en* (1995),
- The Changing Portrayal of the American Indian in the Western Movie: From John Ford's *Stagecoach* (1939) to Kevin Costner's *Dances with Wolves* (1990),
- When Good Men Fight Evil in the Lawless American West: George Stevens' *Shane* (1953) and Delmer Daves' *3:10 to Yuma* (1957),
- Italian Postwar Neorealism Explored in Two Representative Motion Pictures: Vittorio De Sica's *The Bicycle Thief* (1948) and Giuseppe Santie's *Bitter Rice* (1949),
- War under the Waves: Wolfgang Petersen's *Das Boot* (1981) and Robert Wise's *Run Silent, Run Deep* (1958),
- The Tragedy of Heroin Addiction in Fred Zinnemann's *A Hatful of Rain* (1957) and Otto Preminger's *The Man with the Golden Arm* (1955),
- Lewis Milestone's *All Quiet on the Western Front* (1930) and Stanley Kubrick's *Paths of Glory* (1957) as Anti-War Films about "The Great War,"
- Sidney Lumet's Gritty New York City Versus Woody Allen's Idealized Borough: *The Pawnbroker* (1964) and *Manhattan* (1979) respectively, and
- When White Men Are Raised and/or Adopted by an American Indian Tribe: Arthur Penn's *Little Big Man* (1970) and Elliot Silverstein's *A Man Called Horse* (1970).

One movie can be shown as the logical outgrowth of another. Former Broward College student J. David Bright has compared two thrillers that have killer sharks as the catalysts if not protagonists of the movies. The films that he examines are Steven Spielberg's *Jaws* (1975) and Renny Harlin's *Deep Blue Sea* (1999). His point-by-point paper focuses on the use of special effects—especially those used in the creation of these large marine predators—and their bearing on the two motion pictures.

The Impact of Modern Special Effects: *Jaws* and *Deep Blue Sea*

Special effects are an aspect of films that should be used to enhance the impact of plot and characterization. However, as special effects have improved, they have had the reverse effect. An excellent way to see this is to compare two films with similar premises that were made 25 years apart, the classic Steven Spielberg thriller *Jaws* and the more recent *Deep Blue Sea* by director

Renny Harlin. There are a few definite similarities between the two movies, but there are many more differences to be found.

Of course, the most notable similarity between these films is that they are both about killer sharks in search of human prey. However, the way that Spielberg and Harlin decided to show these creatures is very different. The shark in *Jaws* is a rogue killer great white who has somehow ended up in the waters off of Maine, a place it does not normally live. Being that this film was made in 1975, the special effects are not exactly up to par with what today's younger audiences have come to expect. At times, the fake shark that is used can seem somewhat mechanical, and it is probably for that reason that Spielberg decided not to linger on it for a prolonged period with one camera shot. He did intersperse some shots of a real shark underwater to increase the effectiveness of these scenes. The sharks of *Deep Blue Sea* are genetically-enhanced mako sharks that begin to wreak havoc on an underwater research laboratory. Here Harlin used fake sharks as well, but it is obvious that the technology had come much farther in this regard by 1999, when this film was made. These creatures don't display as many of the lifeless spasms as their predecessor in *Jaws*, and move with much more fluidity. Rather than incorporate shots of real sharks, Harlin opted to go with computer-generated makos for his underwater sequences. This decision, although more technologically advanced, detracts noticeably from the effectiveness of the scenes, as it is still quite obvious that they are not real.

A major difference between these two films is the amount of screen time that the sharks actually get. Although Spielberg's model shark may have been more primitive, it is only seen in glimpses until the climax of the movie. Instead, he used underwater camera angles from the point of view of the shark and reaction shots of its victims from above the surface. This serves to increase the suspense of the overall movie by leaving the audience in the dark about what exactly is going on. Harlin was much too confident in his special effects, giving his sharks much more face time. They are shown up close and personal with the first five minutes of the film. The only purpose this serves is to remove all suspense.

The most glaring difference between *Jaws* and *Deep Blue Sea* is characterization. Spielberg uses interesting characters that the audience makes a connection with and cares about. Most of them are not especially attractive physically, but are more like people you see walking down the street. This gives the film a greater sense of realism. Also, much of the dialogue is deep, giving a closer glimpse into the minds of these people. Harlin's characters, however, are shallow and underdeveloped. Most of them are either model-types physically or major Hollywood names, such as

Samuel L. Jackson and LL Cool J. The dialogue between these personages is trite and reveals almost nothing about them.

Although there have been a number of advancements in the field of special effects in the past 30 years since *Jaws* was released, this film still stands the test of time. By comparing it to a recent picture with a similar plot and improved special effects techniques, this is even more evident. Where Spielberg relies on strong characterization and uses special effects to enhance his plot, Harlin relies almost solely on his special effects team to drive *Deep Blue Sea*. Consequently, he ends up with a collage of forgettable characters and a mediocre plot that will most assuredly not be remembered a quarter century from now.

Using a point-by-point format, J. David Bright's comparative analysis discusses the similarities and differences between Steven Spielberg's *Jaws* and Renny Harlin's *Deep Blue Sea*. His paper focuses on the difference in the emphasis on special effects of both films. The older film by Spielberg relies more strongly on plot and characterization to tell the story, whereas Harlin's film depends too heavily on his special effects-created super mako sharks to carry the film. Spielberg's more minimal use of the special effects has created a great white shark to illustrate that "less is more" in his superior motion picture.

The second example of the movie-to-movie comparative critique is done in full block style. The following comparative piece looks at two mobster bosses, who on the surface seem to have much in common. Yet, when analyzed more closely, they differ in significant ways. One is the patriarchal and courtly Don Vito Corleone of Francis Ford Coppola's 1972 classic *The Godfather* while the other is the overly independent volatile and vicious Tony Montana of Brian De Palma's 1983 thriller *Scarface*.

Differing Portrayals of Crime Kingpins: Francis Ford Coppola's *The Godfather* (1972) and Brian De Palma's *Scarface* (1983)

Given that both are ruthless, demand loyalty, and are smart, there are significant differences between the Sicilian-born Mafia don, Vito Corleone (Marlon Brando) and the Cuban-born drug lord Tony Montana (Al Pacino). The obvious differences are generational—1950s for Corleone as opposed to 1980s for Montana as well as geographical; the Greater New York City area for the first and Greater Miami for the second. But there are the other differences that have to do with style, personality, and ethics that separate them.

Of course there are similarities. They both grew up poor in Sicily and in Cuba and immigrated to the United States. Corleone immigrated to New York City and Montana to Miami. Both turned to crime to survive with early success.

But there are aspects of these two men that make them very different from each other. They contrast in their personalities and temperaments, in their style of operating their growing crime empires, in their attitude toward wealth and power, in their ethics, in their stance on dealing drugs, and in the position of family in their lives.

Don Vito Corleone

Vito Corleone, don of the Corleone crime family, is a quiet, seemingly self-effacing man; he is contemplative and deliberate before making a decision. He is extremely loyal to those loyal to him. When involved in acts of retribution, he does so in a premeditated fashion rather than being ruled by passion and the heat of the moment. He believes in self-control as his actions attest. His personality and credo are mirrored in his son Michael (again, Al Pacino) and adopted by him as well. Whereas another son, Sonny (James Caan), is the complete opposite: impulsive and completely ruled by passion whether it is in violent punishment or lovemaking. Vito Corleone accords himself modestly and avoids braggadocio, preferring to negotiate and compromise to calm the waters of contention.

Yet Don Corleone could be ruthless in protecting his power and/or his family and, for one so deliberate, could act with great speed and thoroughness. His actions could be deadly and quite comprehensive where both rivals and their minions would feel the brunt of his retaliation.

The Don is a family man first and foremost. However, his family is divided into two branches which sometimes intertwined. One branch includes his immediate nuclear and extended blood family. The other is his extensive crime family with its lieutenants, "button men," "soldiers," and retainers. He shows each an equal degree of dedication. Despite being outside the law, he has a code of ethics and honors his commitments to the letter, but like a medieval lord of the manor, Corleone demands fealty and loyalty of those he serves and protects. "Serve and protect," the motto of many municipal police departments could have been his own motto. In fact, he has regarded the police and politicians to be corrupt and/or inefficient and feels he could do a better job for his people if they need and ask for his help. But first they have to honor him as their "godfather."

Despite what he does for a living, he outwardly makes efforts to appear as a successful businessman as opposed to powerful mobster. The need for not only "respect" but "respectability" is apparent in so much that he does. Perhaps this is best illustrated by his hopes and dreams for Michael whom he doesn't want to enter the family's "business." Michael leaves for college and returns with a degree; he goes off to war and returns a hero; perhaps law school is next and then years later it would be senator Michael Corleone: class, influence, culture, and respectability at last associated with the family name.

As the film opens, the Don is in his office during his daughter's wedding at the family compound in Long Beach, Long Island, to transact a little "business." Traditionally, this is the time when his people ask for special favors. A number of them who visit do so. But each request, in order to be granted, requires the use of Corleone's enormous influence and power, which might include extremely violent methods to get the request fulfilled. The two following incidents cited are quite significant.

The first has the local undertaker, Amerigo Bonasera (Salvatore Corsitto) pleading for justice. His daughter has been assaulted and disfigured and after going to the police has been ignored. Now he comes to Don Vito for justice. First Corleone belittles the man for trusting the police and, especially, for not coming to him in the first place. Then he explains the reason for it: Bonasera formerly had not wanted to make Corleone his godfather and become obligated to him. But now he is more than willing to do so. Don Vito ponders for a while and then begrudgingly agrees as long as Bonasera can return the favor at some future time with his services. Bonasera agrees. Soon thereafter, the transgressors who abused the undertaker's daughter get severe retribution at the hands of Corleone's men. But later on, when Sonny Corleone is ambushed and brutally machine-gunned to death, Bonasera repays his debt by using the skill in his craft to make Sonny's face and body suitable for viewing in an open casket.

A second incident occurring in the Corleone study during the wedding shows another side of Corleone. His own sense of ethics is displayed when it comes to what he would and would not do to acquire even greater wealth and power. He draws the line on hard drugs—the manufacturing and distribution of heroin—by refusing to join and support the efforts of another crime boss, Virgil "The Turk" Solazzo (Al Lettieri). The decision is not made lightly and Don Vito clearly realizes it probably will have dire consequences. To Corleone, gambling, graft, prostitution, and even murder are all part of his conducting business, but hard drugs are totally outside his personal code of ethics.

Tony Montana

The younger mobster Montana is an ex-convict among the many others booted out of Cuba during the Mariel boatlift. Upon arriving on South Florida's shores, he is immediately placed in a detention center and virtually penniless—but not for long for both. He brings with him an acute sense of self-preservation, self-aggrandizement, and impatience with menial labor. Such attributes are shared by fellow countryman and friend Manny (Steven Bauer). After a brief stint selling hot dogs from a street cart, the two make themselves available to South Florida drug lord Frank Lopez (Robert Loggia) for various illegal "jobs." Tony soon becomes indispensable to Frank.

Montana's character and personality are polar opposites of that of those previously disclosed about Vito Corleone. Whereas the Don is circumspect and respectful of others, Montana is flamboyant and verbally aggressive. In fact, if we try to draw parallels with any of the Corleones, Montana resembles Sonny more than any of the others. He has a hair-trigger temper and overreacts violently to a situation. He talks big and employs bluff and bluster in getting what he wants. Some of his lines in the movie are not only memorable but offer clear insights into whom he is. When asked what he wants from life, he replies, "Me, I want what's coming to me . . . [which is] . . . the world . . . and everything in it." Or, upon getting his first "hit" contract from Frank Lopez and learning of the benefits that would accrue if carried out successfully, he boasts: "I kill a communist for fun, but for a green card, I'm gonna carve him up real nice." These lines give some indication that Montana wants everything writ large in quality and quantity: beautiful women, sports cars, drugs, the fast life, and other expensive possessions. And that he will do anything to get them. But does he appreciate them; understand the subtleties of their desirability? No, he just wants them . . . and on his terms.

Tony's ascent to power is quick and ruthless. His willfulness is accompanied by a talent to impersonate a man who knows what he wants and is dangerous enough to get it. Loyalty falls by the wayside to reach his destination. He betrays his mentor Frank to take over the drug cartel and capture Lopez's lady, Elvira (Michelle Pfeiffer).

Corleone's business involved gambling and prostitution but never narcotics. Montana's occupation involves drugs, especially cocaine: not only selling it but using the substance excessively as well.

There is little love between Tony and Elvira. For him, she is a beautiful bauble to have and display. For her, he is an excellent and unlimited source of prime cocaine for her uncontrollable drug habit. Forget children and the outer trappings of respectability and illusion of normalcy. He has no use for a wife and a family; the goal has always been to steal and possess, not love and cherish. Tony does have a near incestuous protective passion for his sister Gina (Mary Elizabeth Mastrantonio). He goes so far as to even kill his best friend Manny to prevent any deepening of a relationship between them.

And as for respectability as an ultimate goal: that never enters the picture—unless it is perversely defined as synonymous with envy and fear.

The comparative critique that you have just read compares Don Vito Corleone of *The Godfather* with Tony Montana of *Scarface*. Although the paper initially glosses over their similarities, it concentrates mainly on their differences. Using a full block mode, it contrasts the two gangsters in terms of their personality, character, ethics, family values, loyalty, and craving for respectability. It should be noted that although both films approach three hours each, the pacing of the two decidedly differs.

The Original-to-Remake-or-Sequel Comparative Analysis

"Imitation is the highest form of flattery." "You can't argue with success." These two adages serve as introductions to our next area for comparative analytical study: the many remakes and sequels created over the years of original films that met with some degree of success, either critically or financially, sometimes both. Hollywood during the last thirty years or so, has been especially prone to repeatedly mine the mother lode. A movie hit is analyzed and converted into a formula which is repeated over and over again—often with diminishing returns. In most cases, the sequel is not as good as the original expressly because the formulation of what was originally a unique concept could only be brought to fruition once, not a second time.

Remakes recognize a good story. The rationale behind making them is that it is the right time for a new generation of filmgoers to see a movie classic renewed. Or it could be viewed as a good star vehicle to showcase whoever happens to be hot that year. Whatever the motive may be, remakes, because they are contemporary, can appeal to new audiences. Conversely, they are often resisted by older filmgoers, enamored with the earlier version and its stars. Occasionally, a remake will be produced of a foreign language film which might have had relatively little exposure in the United States. Examples would be Martin Brest's

Scent of a Woman (1992) from the 1976 Italian film of the same name by Dino Risi, Jim McBride's *Breathless* (1983) from Jean-Luc Godard's 1961 French New Wave film (also of the same title), and William Friedkin's 1977 *Sorcerer*, the remake of H.G. Clouzot's 1955 *The Wages of Fear*.

Following is a list of titles using comparative analysis applied to film sequels and remakes.

- A Comparison of Shakespeare's *Richard III*: the 1955 version directed by Laurence Olivier and the 1995 offering directed by Richard Loncraine,
- *Rocky* (1976) and *Rocky V* (1990) by John G. Avildsen and Its Sequels Directed by Sylvester Stallone *(II, III, IV, Rocky Balboa)* Made in 1979, 1982, 1985, and 2006 Respectively: The Continuation of a Myth,
- The Original *King Solomon's Mines* (1950) by Compton Bennett and Andrew Marton and the Remake's (1985) Misconceived Change in Tone by J. Lee Thompson,
- *The Manchurian Candidate* Original (1962) by John Frankenheimer and the Remake (2004): by Jonathan Demme: Different Eras and Different Directors, but Same High Quality,
- John Badham's *Saturday Night Fever* (1977) Excites, While Sylvester Stallone's Sequel *Staying Alive* (1983) Disappoints,
- The Initial *Star War Trilogy* Made in 1977, 1980, and 1983 by George Lucas: Formulas for Box Office Success,
- Richard Linklater's *Before Sunrise* (1995) and *Before Sunset* (2004): Same Stars, One Decade Later,
- Adopted from the Same James Jones Novel, but You'd Never Know It: *The Thin Red Line* the 1964 Original by Andrew Marton and 1998's Flight of Fancy by the Self-Indulgent Terrence Malick,
- Broad Differences between the Biographical *Moulin Rouge* (1952) by John Huston and Its Adaptation as a Musical by Baz Luhrmann (2001), and
- Akira Kurosawa's *Seven Samurai* (1954) Becomes John Sturges' *The Magnificent Seven* (1960).

The motives behind remakes vary, although a healthy profit margin is a universally shared inducement. Remakes face the same biases of sequels and a comparable anticipatory interest. Although a number of years, even decades, may pass between the original and the remake, the time span between the original and the sequel is usually much shorter. *A Shot in the Dark* (1964), for example, was released just a few months after its precursor *The Pink Panther* (1963) finished its first run. Few expect the sequel to be as good as the film it is emulating and yet everyone wants to see it just to prove that point. At times, though, the sequel is every bit as worthy as the original: witness the accolades for *The Godfather II* (1974) or the original *Star Wars* (1977) follow-up *The Empire Strikes Back* (1980).

Usually, the sequel comes hot on the heels of the original, especially if the former showed a profit. Whenever possible, as much of the original crew—both in front of and behind the camera—is kept for the sequel. Contract commitments and salary demands of some of the cast because of newly found marketability force replacements. This and the often perceived need to rush the new product to theaters before the fickle public's interest wanes, results in sequel productions that are often markedly inferior. As stated before, formula often substitutes for creativity as repetition replaces craft.

Alfred Hitchcock, "The Master of Suspense," has been one of the most influential and widely imitated directors in Hollywood history. In 1998, director Gus Van Sant paid homage to Hitchcock by shooting anew the classic *Psycho* (1960), but this time in color and since it had been almost 40 years since the release of the original, obviously with an entirely different cast. He made the film with the identical number of frames that Hitchcock incorporated and, where possible, used the same buildings if they were still standing. We turn to former Broward College student Holly Griffith for her insightful point-by-point comparative critique comparing Hitchcock's classic with Van Sant's imitative tribute to him.

Hitchcock's *Psycho* and Van Sant's *Psycho*: Contrasts in Characterization, Detail, and Scene

Alfred Hitchcock's *Psycho* was a riveting and shocking horror movie in 1960. The heart-pounding, unforgettable shower scene will forever be etched in the memories of many moviegoers. *Psycho* was creepy and full of suspense even in black and white. Although Gus Van Sant has resurrected *Psycho* in its original plot and soundtrack, his 1998 remake of the classic thriller incorporates enough changes to make this modern version different. The actors' characterizations, the updated details, and the changes made to some scenes together contribute to the differences between Hitchcock's original and Van Sant's re-creation.

The differences in the characterizations of the leading roles are striking. Anthony Perkins portrays Norman Bates as seemingly innocent and childlike. Perkins is friendly and personable when we first meet him, but his personality suddenly changes from these likable qualities to a strange and totally different Norman. This sudden change makes Perkins as the original Bates scarier and more unpredictable than the Norman played by Vince Vaughn. The element of surprise that Perkins lends to his role really adds to the suspense. On the other hand, Vaughn acts strange and somewhat sinister from the very beginning, which detracts from Hitchcock's element of surprise. Perkins plays a more nervous Norman since he stutters and, therefore, appears less confident than Vaughan's characterization which has Bates more in control. The portrayal of Marion Crane is also different in each motion picture version. Janet Leigh of the original lends more credibility to the role. She is more love struck in the opening as opposed to the more casual attitude of Anne Heche's interpretation. Leigh appears genuine and interested in the conversation with Norman when he first discusses his birds and his "Mother." However, Heche seems detached from the conversation and does not act as guilty as Leigh does in her role as Marion.

Changes in detail also contribute to the differences in the original and the remake. While Van Sant attempts to duplicate Hitchcock's structure and running time, he still takes liberties in updating this classic movie to fit the 1990s. Color replaces black and white which enhances the new *Psycho*, especially in the bloody shower scene. The use of color also helps create a darker, more sinister set piece; whereas the black and white original incorporates more light. Technological advances in cinematography are a plus in the Van Sant endeavor as well as the digitally remastered soundtrack. Some other detailed changes are small. The stolen money becomes $400,000 instead of $40,000 and cars, clothing, and Marion's license plate all receive the '90s look. In addition, Norman's house is newer and the motel has a new neon sign. Van Sant also seems compelled to add more shock in his version. There is more blood in 1998 than in 1960 to appeal to a contemporary audience; the cleanup in the bathroom after Marion's murder lasts longer. Van Sant also focuses more on Norman's stuffed birds than in the original and this adds to the overall eerie feeling. The birds look more threatening as if they are signs of the horror to follow. Van Sant depicts Norman's "Mother" more realistically with a white wig. This feature is not as believable as Hitchcock's portrayal of the character. In 1960, her character was darker and in shadow and, therefore, scarier. There is also nudity in the remake. The new Marion is seen with less clothing in several scenes, and her entire naked body is slumped over the bathtub in the infamous shower scene.

Finally, minor changes within many scenes of Van Sant's *Psycho* add up to a significant departure from Hitchcock's original. For example, the opening scene in the 1998 remake has Marion Crane and her boyfriend spending most of their time in bed while unmistakable sounds of sexual encounters from other hotel rooms can be heard in the background. And a very different parting shot in the same scene shows Vigo Mortensen's full nude figure as opposed to the clothed John Gavin of the first *Psycho*. Van Sant also took a giant step when he decided the peephole scene needed a boost by having Norman involved in an unmistakable sexual encounter with himself while spying on Ann Heche who is wearing less clothing than her counterpart Janet Leigh. Another scene change for added shock value takes place in the Bates' mansion when "Mother" stabs the detective. The stabbing itself is more graphically depicted and also the killer's figure is actually shown, whereas her presence is not as obvious in Hitchcock's movie. Just as the opening scene is altered in Van Sant's version, he also makes changes to the ending by spending more time extricating the car from the swamp and, therefore, bringing the scene to a comfortable conclusion. Hitchcock's finale is simple but abrupt as the car barely surfaces the swamp before the screen darkens.

Was it necessary to recreate Alfred Hitchcock's *Psycho* 38 years later? Did Van Sant's take on this classic horror film improve upon its predecessor? The new *Psycho* did take advantage of the technical advances in filmmaking regarding cinematography and sound in order to produce a quality movie. However, the difficulties in capturing the real characters of Norman Bates and Marion Crane are apparent in the remake. At the same time, Van Sant's departure from Hitchcock is obvious as he attempts to cater to today's audiences by adding graphic (as opposed to suggested) nudity, sexual overtones, and bloodier scenes. Yet these ingredients are not necessarily positive additions to an already great suspense film. Van Sant's *Psycho* cannot compare to the original because 38 years ago, it was the film's surprising, unusual twists that captivated moviegoers. Only Alfred Hitchcock is the master of suspense and his expertise cannot be duplicated.

The previous comparative analysis of the original to the remake of *Psycho* clearly delineates the differences between the two versions of the same film. Gus Van Sant's remake obviously updated the Alfred Hitchcock original in order to greater appeal to a modern audience but did not improve on it. Although Holly Griffith does admit that the newer version does have some positive features, she feels it is still not in the same league as the classic original.

In moving on to an example of the sequel, the two films selected do not follow the usual pattern where the later film arrives hot and panting soon after the lucrative original. However most atypically, the acclaimed *The Last Picture Show* (1971) by Peter Bogdanovich had to wait almost two decades before being followed by its more modestly received sequel *Texasville* (1990). This is highly unusual, since a sequel usually appears a year or so after a successful original. Both films are based on the novels by Larry McMurty, who wrote the screenplay for the earlier movie. The point-by-point analysis that follows compares the two motion pictures.

Same Place, Different Time: *The Last Picture Show* and Its Belated Sequel *Texasville*

Most of the team was back in place with Peter Bogdanovich again at the helm. No longer the boy genius of *The Last Picture Show* and having experienced a number of bumps along the directorial road, it was time to return to his roots (of success, at least) and tap them for the hit that would re-establish his career.

Simply stated, it didn't work out that way. The lack of the sequel's success—both critically and at the box office—resulted from a number of factors. One of these that no one could control was age: would the characters be as interesting and their lives as compelling to the viewer 30 years later? Many of the original cast was back in their roles: Jeff Bridges (as Duane Jackson), Timothy Bottoms (Sonny Crawford), Cybill Shepherd (Jacy Farrow), Cloris Leachman (Ruth Popper), Randy Quaid (Lester Marlow), and Eileen Brannan (Genevieve). The original, *The Last Picture Show*, was set in the 1950s. And if there is one major failing of *Texasville* now set in the 1980s, it is that the lives of these same characters after three decades just do not elicit the same degree of empathy as they did before. They have all changed—and not only physically. The texture and look of the film has changed. The town itself has grown somewhat and changed. The point of view has changed. The tone has changed. The theme has changed. And with all that change, much has been lost.

The Last Picture Show was centered upon Sonny, whereas *Texasville* revolves around Duane. In altering the point of view, a ripple effect is created upon other aspects of the film. The tone, once serious and wistful as Sonny himself, now effects the whimsical, ironic humor of Duane. The isolation, loneliness, and slowness of life's passage infused the earlier film. Its "slice of life" style affected the viewers. Although nostalgic for the audience, it was not so for the characters who weren't reflecting on their lives back in the 1950s but living them.

The Last Picture Show was about the aches of young unrequited love, the tests of friendship, the mystery and pain of sexuality, and the devastation of loss through death. There are far fewer rites of passage in the later film. Not too many fresh wounds, just many scars. Everyone is hardened, cynical, blasé, selfish, and tired. Sonny, the mayor of Anarene, is also the proprietor of a convenience store, and the owner of some other enterprises, yet considers himself a failure. He is also losing his mind: not being able to keep up with the events of the day and disappearing suddenly from his shop to sit within the burned-out shell of the old movie theater, he watches moving pictures in the sky. Duane has become rich running an oil business, but presently is millions in debt. Now he fills his idle hours—and there are many of them—by sexually servicing all of the town's unhappy wives and recent divorcees but one: his own missus Karla (Annie Potts). A theme of sexual anomie and moral bankruptcy abounds in the film. Everyone is talking about sex or engaging in it, but no one is finding true pleasure in it—much less love. A spate of unintended pregnancies is the consequence of this lasciviousness, but no one seems to take them that seriously.

The opening sequence sets the tone and theme. In a hot tub behind an enormous house plunked down in the midst of the sterile North Texas prairie, sits Duane, firing an enormous pistol at an expensive, brand new doghouse. He blasts it to smithereens for no logical reason. His boredom, aimlessness, and the uselessness of his possessions are apparent. His family is rotting from moral decay. His first daughter has two little kids, is divorced, and is working on the fiancé of the week with perhaps another pregnancy in the offing. His older son Dickie (William McNamara) is engaged to be married but has gotten one neighbor's wife pregnant and prefers the estranged wife of another. He has also been jailed for speeding through a school zone at 85 miles an hour. Duane and Karla's preteen twins are spoiled brats, fighting with each other and showing no respect for any of the adults around them. Karla is, in turn, angry, sharp-tongued, and runs off to shop when provoked.

Ruth Popper is now Duane's loyal secretary, wasting her good advice on her boss who "because the oil business has gone belly up [has] nothing . . . to do but sleep with any woman [he] can find." Over the years, well after her husband's death, Ruth has never rekindled the romance that she once shared with Sonny, and one wonders why.

Two events are to bring conflict and genuine change to the movie. But both fall short. The first is the return of Jacy to Anarene. The second is the centennial celebration for "Texasville,"

the forerunner of Anarene, to which the film builds to a meaningless climax. Jacy returns to Anarene—if only temporarily—to
recover from the death of her little boy. Having lived in Italy for
years as a third-rate actress, she hopes to convalesce from her loss
at the site of her earliest triumphs as richest and prettiest girl in
town (and also its most selfish and heartless). She soon engages in
mental/emotional dueling with Duane as she co-opts his wife, children, and dog. At one point in the film, she and Karla actually
appear for a pageant rehearsal in identical outfits that they bought
together during a shopping spree. The embers between Duane and
Jacy—always smoldering—never burst into flame, however. Perhaps Duane no longer does "know how to fall in love [or back in
love] with anybody." And perhaps Jacy, despite her strong feelings
for Duane, still has not outgrown her tendency to play with the
emotions of numerous others at the same time. She accompanies
Duane to Odessa where he is desperately seeking to make a financial deal and stay solvent. They get a motel room but have a totally
non-sexual encounter (or so it appears). She is watching a game
show on television while giving him some nickel philosophizing and
a psychological insight into herself which the film never develops
further. She states:

> Game shows are what life's really like. You win things that look
> really great at the time but turn out to be junk and you lose things
> you may want to keep forever just because you're unlucky.

Does she mean Duane or the dead child or both? She continues
to lead Duane—and the audience—on: we expect something passionate to develop between them but it never does. Instead, we just
get a number of wistful glances for what was and might have been.
She says such words as: "I feel like we're the Adam and Eve of this
town" and "You're scared to death you'll feel something you can't
control." Yet such mixed signals lead nowhere. By the film's last
reel, Duane and Karla are slouching towards reconciliation and
Jacy is preparing to return to Europe. At movie's end, we see a
number of knowing looks between Jacy and Duane, Duane and
Karla, and Karla and Jacy. What they know Bogdanovich certainly
doesn't share with the audience.

Texasville sorely misses those characters who have died off:
Ruth's husband, Jacy's mother, Sonny's kid brother, and Sam the
Lion, the philosopher king of the tiny 1950s town now grown to
considerable size by the 1980s. Those characters, their conflicts,
and the relationships they engendered brought a serious, somewhat tragic element to the earlier film. This is totally missing

from the sequel. The characters' flaws as shown and discoursed over in *Texasville* are too excessive to avoid self-parody. Unfortunately, the causal subtext behind them that would make the film more believable and fulfilling is neither viewed nor discussed sufficiently.

This lengthy comparative analysis of an original and a sequel initially is cast in the point-by-point mode. However, midway it segues mainly into a critique of *Texasville*, the sequel to *The Last Picture Show*. The critic points out that a number of factors contribute to the flaws of the later film. These factors have to do with change—and the changes in the sequel do not work. Among these alterations are: the aging of the actors (most of the original cast are reprising their roles); the setting (same place but three decades later); the point of view (the original centered around Sonny, the sequel revolves around Duane); the tone (previously serious and wistful, now whimsical and ironic); and the themes and motifs (in the former: unrequited love, friendship, sexuality's pain and mystery, and devastating loss through death; in the latter: cynicism, selfishness, tiredness, sexual anomie, and moral bankruptcy). Taken altogether, these variables form a sequel that is inferior to the original.

The Literary Work-to-Movie Comparative Analysis

Many movies over the years have used novels, short stories, or plays as their literary sources. As we have already discussed, some adaptations have been literal, others faithful, while some—at best—have loosely based literary antecedents. Immediately following is a list of titles for comparative papers based on the adaptation of literary works into movies:

- Two of the Many Interpretations of Shakespeare's *Hamlet* Almost 50 Years Apart: Laurence Olivier (1948) and Kenneth Branagh (1996) both Directing and Playing the Prince of Denmark,
- Christopher Guest and His "Mockumentaries" *Waiting for Guffman* (1997), *Best in Show* (2000), and *A Mighty Wind* (2003): Some Shared Characteristics,
- The Book *Bonfire of the Vanities* by Tom Wolfe Works but the 1990 Movie by Brian De Palma Does Not,
- Ernest Hemingway's Short Novel *The Snows of Kilimanjaro* Transposed onto the Screen by Henry King in 1952: A Comparative Critique,

- Ernest Hemingway's *The Old Man and the Sea* Converted in 1958 by John Sturges as Cinema: A Comparative Critique,
- True to the Spirit of the Depression: John Ford's 1940 Conversion into a Film of John Steinbeck's novel *The Grapes of Wrath*,
- Homeless and Wandering during the Depression: Gary Sinese's 1992 Adaptation of John Steinbeck's novel *Of Mice and Men*,
- The Blockbuster Best-Seller *Exodus* by Leon Uris and Otto Preminger's 1960 Movie of It,
- The Characterizations within Henry James' Novella *Daisy Miller* Were Developed but an Understanding of the American Expatriate Community Was Missing in Peter Bogdanovich's 1974 film, and
- The Influence of Joseph Conrad's *The Heart of Darkness* upon Francis Ford Coppola's *Apocalypse Now* (1979).

What follows is a comparative analysis using an informal point-by-point structure on director Michael Mann's motion picture of *The Last of the Mohicans* (1992). It was based on the romantic era novel by James Fenimore Cooper and is, perhaps, *too* loosely grounded in it.

Michael Mann Does James Fenimore Cooper's *The Last of The Mohicans*: Gratuitous Action at Any Price

Hollywood, not surprisingly, has done it again. In the remaking of the 1936 movie of James Fenimore Cooper's romantic novel classic *The Last of the Mohicans*, today's moviemakers have jam-packed the film with action and special effects while taking generous liberties with plot and characterization. Perhaps "romantic" is the operative word here, for its associations were quite different back in 1826 when the book was published. Romanticism involved selfless quests and idealized notions of love between men and women. Sexual passion and its graphic depiction were not found on the pages of the typical romantic tome of that day. Having just finished reading the Cooper opus, this critic made the mistake of viewing the film soon thereafter at the local movie house. Thus, the Hollywoodization of the storyline was particularly disconcerting. Despite Cooper's overblown 19th century prose and turgid explications, the original plot was captivating and should have been more closely adhered to in this widescreen epic by Michael Mann (director, producer, and co-writer). Yes, the same Michael Mann who made his mark with *Miami Vice*, that flashy television series notorious for its stylized violence, stylish automobiles, and cutting-edge fashion ensembles.

The tale unfolds in 1757 in the pre-Revolutionary War colony of New York: the French and Indian War is already of three year's duration. The French and their Indian allies are on an offensive, sweeping down from Canada and attacking outposts and farms across the area north of Albany up through the Adirondacks to the shores of Lake George. The actual historical incidents involved are the attack of the British-held Fort William Henry, its ignominious surrender, and the subsequent massacre of its troops and civilians by the Huron henchmen of the French. It is the responsibility of Cooper's fictitious creation Hawkeye (played unconvincingly by Daniel Day-Lewis) and Chingachgook and his son Uncas, his two Mohican blood brothers, to rescue the hostage daughters of the defeated English commandant and avenge the slaughter. As one can expect, there are numerous chases, skirmishes, ambushes, and panoramic battle episodes, but it is in the particulars of the plot and its persona that Mann radically strays from the text in yielding to box office blandishments.

Hawkeye has been depicted as a nonsexual hero by Cooper—a chivalrous knight in buckskin, if you will. Mann, however, has him "making it" with Cora, the elder captive daughter (adequately acted by Madeleine Stowe), in one of the scenes where she is free, 21, and very willing. True, there is no onscreen bunkroom nude scene here at the fort, but by the principals' suggestive dialogue and promising glances, such off-screen cavorting are assured.

Cora, in the book, is murdered by a treacherous Huron warrior in the novel's finale. Her sister Alice, though, survives to eventually find happiness in England. In the movie, however, Alice chooses suicide rather than submit to any Huron indignities during her capture, whereas Cora and Hawkeye, in the film's final sequence, stand together on a rocky crag facing the setting sun and pondering their future.

Major Heyward, the young, gallant English officer that Cooper portrays as a man just a shade less heroic than Hawkeye, is always a willing, helpful collaborator of the woodsman in the quest to free the sisters. Yet Mann shows him as stupid, devious, arrogant, and vindictive—whose only positive act is his heroic death. In the movie, his love for Cora is spurned; in the book, his affections are always directed to and ultimately returned by Alice.

Despite its betrayal of the text and its indifferent acting—with the exception of the masterfully cast Wes Studi as the malevolent

Huron antagonist Magua—the film does have a number of admirable qualities. The cinematography and special effects are exemplary. The battle scenes—both the siege of the fort and the surprise attack from the woods—are well-choreographed and authentic, down to the differing types of European artillery and assorted Indian weapons employed. The action is fast-paced and doesn't give one time to ruminate on the script's inadequacies. The book (at times, exhaustingly so) puts the events in both historical and anthropological perspective. The film hardly makes the effort to do so. This has probably added to its overall positive reception by audiences as an historical spectacle . . . unless, of course, you have just read the book.

The previous essay has discussed a film based on a novel that is also a remake of an earlier cinematic version of the book. The thrust of the critique is the castigation of the director and screenwriter for the excessive liberties they have taken with the original literary work. Wanton disregard for plot and characterization are the film's greatest flaws. Such trampling upon the original author's intentions would especially harm the viewer who was knowledgeable about the written source, James Fenimore Cooper's *The Last of the Mohicans*. Most of the paragraphs that follow the introduction give specific instances of such abuses. In many ways this critique resembles a review, but telling us key instances of plot—including the climax and ending—it goes well beyond the strictures of the review.

Some films are adapted from short stories and often change the name of the title. In so doing, they frequently take certain liberties with the plot in general, the ending, the characters, or a combination thereof. Sometimes the screenplay is written in the spirit of the original piece of literature; other times it uses the original as a launching pad to explore ideas that had been found within the literary source. Tina Rathborne's *The Joy That Kills* (1985) was inspired by the famous short (really short) story by early and secret feminist author Kate Chopin. So much of Chopin's oeuvre explores women's issues and perspectives relating to marriage, sex, individuality, careers, and basic human rights. A transplant from St. Louis, Missouri, after her marriage, Chopin's fictional world had southern Louisiana as its setting. Her short stories and larger works revolved around the Creoles and Cajuns, who populated both the rural and urban (New Orleans) area of the state. The following comparative critique is laid out in a modified point-by-point structure using subheadings:

The Joy That Kills: Taking a Very Short Story and Running with It

Today we would call Kate Chopin's "The Story of an Hour" a very brief "minimalist" piece which hints at certain truths rather than fully identifies them. There are two sentences that inspire the short movie (56 minutes) *The Joy That Kills.* The first is the initial sentence of the actual story: "Knowing that Mrs. Mallard was afflicted with heart trouble, great care was taken to break to her as gently as possible the news of her husband's death." The second passage occurs well into the second half of the tale: "And yet she had loved him—sometimes. Often she had not." These two passages—at the immediate beginning and then later on—promoted a film that rather being totally faithful to the original, used "The Story of an Hour" as a launching pad to place it in a much greater context: a context of detailed and specific setting (time and place), plot structure, character analysis, additional character creation, theme, and symbolism. Thus, by the movie's end, a bare-bones literary sketch has become a fully fleshed short story on film that is faithful to the spirit and to the greater meaning of the original.

Setting

The setting of the entire short story is inside the Mallard household; what city or even state is not mentioned. The film goes right to work in clearly establishing geographic place (the French quarter of New Orleans) and the historic time (1877). Both are very significant. Since the locale is in Louisiana, the date implies not only that the Napoleonic Code (the state's somewhat peculiar legal system) still is in force, but after more than 10 years of Reconstruction and occupation by Union troops, Home Rule has been restored—and thus freedom for the state's (white) residents.

Plot Structure

This short story doesn't waste any time in getting to the point, and announces, "Knowing that Mrs. Mallard was afflicted with a heart trouble, great care was taken to break to her as gently as possible the news of her husband's death." The film, however, adopts a more leisurely pace to work up to this point. As the opening credits are presented, we see 19th century daguerreotypes of exotic places of the world including Egypt, Ireland, France, and Canada (Niagara Falls). Louise Mallard (Frances

Conroy) is looking at these pictures of places that her husband Brently (Jeffrey DeMunn) has visited. She is sitting on her covered, wrought iron porch synonymous with the French Quarter of New Orleans watching for her husband's appearance after his day's work at the office. He finally arrives with yet another picture to look at through their stereopticon—it is of one of the beautiful public gardens in Paris. While looking at the scene, she repeats her familiar refrain of wishing she could visit it with her husband. He demurs and gently changes the subject. As the film progresses, Brently learns of the availability of some property suddenly on the market that he has been coveting. To close the deal, he will have to take a short train trip to another town for a few days. She pleads to accompany him and stay at the hotel while he conducts business. He doesn't think that would be wise given her delicate condition. His wife protests and discloses that her doctor has just given her a clean bill of health. The news upsets her husband who shows signs of being over-protective, even controlling, of his wife. This becomes more apparent when he shares his reservations with Maggie (Rosalind Cash), Louise's faithful servant/companion since childhood.

That evening, the couple is hosting a little dinner party to celebrate their third wedding anniversary. The guests include Louise's physician, Dr. LeBrun (Patrick Horgan), accompanied by his wife, Brently's best friend Richards (Patrick Tovatt), and Josephine (Elizabeth Franz) here transformed from a spinster sister in the story to a spinster aunt in the film. Later that night after the party, the couple pouts: He is jealous that she has shown their precious pictures to Dr. LeBrun and she that he won't let her accompany him on the trip. In a fit of rage, he snaps in two the offending picture of the Mariville Gardens in Paris. Just as quickly he feels remorse and in the most clearly and unexpectedly erotic scene in the vignette, falls to his knees and clasps her legs, begging forgiveness. "Marry me! Marry me!" he intones. "I have, I have," she responds. This unexpected scene in the film harkens back to a different passage from the story and helps support Louise's musings as she sits alone in a state of shock, mourning the sudden loss of her husband:

There would be no powerful will bending hers in that blind persistence with which men and women believe they have a right to impose a private will upon a fellow creature. A kind intention or a cruel intention make the act seem no less a crime as she looked upon it in that brief moment of illumination.

And then the two short, succeeding sentences that could have inspired the entire cinema project: "And yet she had loved him—sometimes. Often she had not."

The remainder of the film follows the story quite closely except there are a few extra people who witness Louise's demise in the film. And, of course, both versions attribute the cause of her fatal heart attack to the wrong reason: "the joy that kills."

Character Analysis/Additional Character Creation

What the story hints and suggests, the film manifests strongly, by creating additional characters and scenes not in the story to make these points plausible. Director Tina Rathborne and co-screenwriter Nancy Dyer devise a series of flashback sequences—immediate and long term—that help explain the conundrums raised by Chopin's sparse tale and lack of supportive evidence in it.

One important new character is Maggie, the black former child companion during slave times, and now—along with her husband and child—is a live-in servant. She has remained all these years Louise's main confidante. But she is also an ally of Brently and distrusts Dr. LeBrun's optimistic prognosis for Louise. And then there is Louise's father (Lee Richardson), an over-affectionate, maudlin alcoholic who cannot get over the death of his wife (perhaps in childbirth). He is also over-protective about his little girl's frail health (again, perhaps from a childhood disease such as rheumatic fever). Finally, making the doctor a three-dimensional character as friend of the family as well as long-term medical caregiver, adds additional tension to the film. Showing Brently as both controlling and loving in a convincing manner is one other objective met by the scenarists.

Symbols & Themes

Symbols abound especially in the film. It is no accident that the dress Louise sews is a pale yellow, a canary yellow at that. For hasn't she been a caged canary all these years kept inside this beautiful house—at times against her will—with its wrought iron doors, windows, and porches so like an imprisoned songbird. And both the story and film depict the storm of passionate grief she initially experiences with the written piece describing the condition of the sky and clouds as if a rainstorm had just passed. The film discusses the new-found freedom of the Confederate States after Home Rule has been restored—but not for Louise except for those brief, ironic few minutes when she imagines herself free because of

Brently's death. Finally, there are aspects of Louise in the film that show her as childlike. She both depends on others a great deal and feels abandonment. For example, whenever her father leaves for a trip, or especially when he goes off to war in uniform on horseback. Another instance is when she is so overwrought at not preventing Brently from catching his train. Then there is the way that she holds and sips her glass of milk, or the way she giggles, or, finally, the way she imagines life outside her home.

The preceding essay discusses how a miniscule short story, "The Story of an Hour" by Kate Chopin, has been converted into a very creative cinematic experience by Tina Rathborne. It would seem that a few key sentences from the story inspired the venture. Rathborne and her co-writer have provided a back story of both recent and distant events, additional characters to support it, and gave the film a definitive and detailed setting which united it with the themes of the story.

The Comparison-of-Individuals Analysis

Another fertile area for comparative analysis concerns those individuals— directors, actors, characters—involved in movies. Comparative studies can be made on such subject areas as:

- Two different actors (or the same actor) playing the same or a similar role in different films,
- Two different characters from two different movies having very much in common,
- Two different (or similar) styles of directors, or
- The same theme but in different films by the same (or a different) director.

The following is a representative listing of titles for comparative papers based on individuals in the cinema:

- Femme Fatales of the Nineties and Their Definitive Films: Sharon Stone in *Basic Instinct* (1992) and Linda Fiorentino in *The Last Seduction* (1994),
- The Motif of Retribution in Clint Eastwood's *Play Misty for Me* (1971) *Unforgiven* (1992), and *Gran Torino* (2008),
- The French New Wave as Interpreted by Francois Truffaut's *The 400 Blows* (1959) and *Stolen Kisses* (1968) and Jean-Luc Godard *Breathless* (1960) and *Weekend* (1967): Similarities and Differences,

- Dark Themes and Dark Settings: Commonalities between Martin Scorsese's *Mean Streets* (1973) and *Taxi Driver* (1976) and Sidney Lumet's *Dog Day Afternoon* (1975) and *Before the Devil Knows You're Dead* (2007),
- John Ford's Treatment of Small Town Life in Wales and Ireland in *How Green Was My Valley* (1941) and *The Quiet Man* (1952) respectively,
- Parallels between Otto Preminger's *Carmen Jones* (1954) and his *Porgy and Bess* (1959),
- Michael Cimino's *The Deer Hunter* (1978) and *Heaven's Gate* (1980): Why One Worked and the Other Flopped,
- Federico Fellini's Representative Early Films: *Variety Lights* (1950), *L'Amore in Citta* (1953), and *La Strada* (1954),
- Federico Fellini's Representative Films of the Sixties: *La Dolce Vita* (1960), *Boccaccio '70* (1962), and *8 1/2* (1963), and
- Some Consistencies in the Feel-Good Oscar-Winning Comedies of Frank Capra: *It Happened One Night* (1934), *Mr. Deeds Goes to Town* (1936), and *You Can't Take It with You* (1938).

The next movie analysis compares an established, well-known actor and the two different roles he has undertaken in two successive projects by the same director. John Turturro appeared in Spike Lee's highly controversial *Do the Right Thing* in 1989 and then played a very different type of character in Lee's *Jungle Fever* two years later.

John Turturro Does Flip Sides of Italian-American Men in Spike Lee's *Do The Right Thing* (1989) and *Jungle Fever* (1991)

John Turturro has long been recognized as a fine character actor whether holding down a leading role as in *Barton Fink* or in a number of supporting parts. Some of his most interesting work has been done for Spike Lee, especially, in two films: *Do the Right Thing* and *Jungle Fever*, made within two years of each other. In both, he plays Italian-American men from Brooklyn. In the first, he plays Pino, the racist son of a local pizzeria owner; in the second, he is Paulie, the liberal, tolerant son—especially in racial matters—of a candy store proprietor.

To better understand Turturro's and the director/screenwriter's interpretation of Pino, one would need a bit of background. Sal (Danny Aiello) is the only white proprietor in what, over the years, has become a predominantly African-American neighborhood in the Bedford-Stuyvesant section of Brooklyn. He has owned and managed a pizzeria for 25 years and is assisted in its operation by his two grown sons, Pino and Vito. The two are very different in personalities and attitudes especially towards their job specifically, the family business in general, the neighborhood in which it is located, and race. Pino feels he's doing the wrong thing, in the wrong place and at the wrong time in his life—but he doesn't have any alternative.

Pino is a bigot and despises blacks. He hates working at a pizzeria in a black neighborhood, serving them, and dealing with Mookie (Spike Lee), their black pizza delivery guy. Pino believes that the only reason they are in Bed-Stuy instead of Bensonhurst (a predominantly Italian section of Brooklyn) is that Sal's Famous Pizzeria wouldn't make it with all that competition from other Italian-American pizzerias and restaurants.

Turturro is able to convey the racism of his character Pino in both subtle and overt means by glances, gestures, tone of voice or harsh statements. He doesn't comprehend his brother's Vito's tolerance of the clientele nor his easy banter and friendship with Mookie. To Pino, Mookie is lazy, shiftless, and untrustworthy and should have been fired months ago—or never hired in the first place. Sal, his father, is perhaps a racist, although he doesn't consider himself as one. At one moment he almost considers his black patrons, whom he has been feeding "slices" since they were young children like family. Yet his Wall of Fame is of Italian Americans only, and he refuses to integrate it with an African American celebrity or two even though the vast majority of his customers are black.

John Turturro's task in playing Paulie Carbone in *Jungle Fever* is more complex since he morphs from being a sucker, who is always taken advantage of or for granted, into a stronger, more sympathetic, and likable character by the end of the film.

Paulie is the son of widower Lou Carbone (Anthony Quinn), an absentee owner of the candy store/luncheonette that his boy runs. The old man may be light in helping his grown son operate the store but is heavy on criticism of him, at times abusively so. Paulie takes the mistreatment and lack of respect stoically despite being essentially the proprietor of the store. Paulie's "friends" are really nothing more than unemployed hangers on who think nothing of walking away with a candy bar or a magazine without paying for it. Again, Paulie is all too accepting of this behavior.

We learn that Paulie has been involved in a longstanding relationship with Angie Tucci (Annabella Sciorra) and has an understanding with her that they are to get married someday. She too is part of a motherless family and has to cook and clean after an abusive father and two oppressive, overprotective brothers.

Once Angie's affair with Flipper Purify (Wesley Snipes) has been established, she breaks the news about it to Paulie. He seems to take it well and doesn't condemn her since he has had some misgivings about the direction they had been heading for a while. But when alone, he breaks down and weeps, realizing his world has been turned upside down. His father suddenly intervenes and beats Paulie, ashamed at his son's weak and "womanish" behavior. This is followed by a litany of harsh criticisms of Angie and her morals, especially since the affair is with a black man, and married at that. Paulie doesn't share the same bigotry as his father and doesn't consider the race of the man who stole his fiancée a significant factor. Word about the split soon gets to the regulars at the shop and the reasons for the break up. They are infuriated and hurl racial epithets as if they themselves were the victims of the betrayal.

Soon thereafter, Paulie takes an interest in Orin Goode (Tyra Ferrell), a young, well-educated black woman who often comes to the store for coffee and a Danish pastry. They soon have more to say to each other than the usual casual pleasantries expected between a shop manager and a regular customer. This does not go unnoticed by the "fellas." When he asks her out and she accepts and the group finds out, they beat Paulie up en route to his date on general bigoted principles. He reaches her residence somewhat the worse for wear but no less eager to pursue her.

The "jungle fever," that curiosity and lust that had been the root cause for the interracial relationship between Flipper and Angie is not echoed in the case of Paulie and Orin. They may not ultimately last together or even get very far but at least they have things in common, mutual attraction, respect for each other, and a sweet, giving nature. Thus by the film's end, we see Paulie in a new light as a man who is principled and open and has the courage to act on his convictions.

The article has contrasted the supporting performances of John Turturro in two of Spike Lee's movies *Do the Right Thing* and *Jungle Fever*. In both films, Turturro has shown great skills in nuanced interpretations that wrings the most out these modest parts. He plays polar opposites in each. In the first, *Do the Right Thing*, he portrays a hateful bigot and yet with enough defensive rationale to make him three dimensional rather than a stereotypical monster. In *Jungle Fever*, always calm, tolerant, and rational, his early weakness and timidity with his peers and father are shed eventually. By story's end, he grows to evince the strength of his beliefs and other attendant qualities that accompany them.

There are obvious parallels between the plays *The Glass Menagerie* and *Death of a Salesman*. They were written and produced in the 1940s and gravitated around two families in desperate financial straits. Each head of the family had a great deal of trouble realistically acknowledging their perilous situation, what to do about it, and the weaknesses of their adult children who they hope to depend on. The films—both very faithful renderings of the dramas—were made within two years of each other in the mid-1980s. As the following comparative analysis will show, two members of each family are remarkably similar to corresponding members of the other. Volker Schlondorff's motion picture of Death of a Salesman was made in 1985. Paul Newman's *The Glass Menagerie* was released in 1987.

John Malkovich, Stephen Lang, and Dustin Hoffman in Volker Schlondorff's Death of a Salesman *(1986). Karl-Lorimar Home Video. Courtesy of The Kobal Collection at Art Resource, NY.*

Parallels between Willy Loman and Amanda Wingfield and between Biff Loman and Tom Wingfield in the Film Versions of *Death of a Salesman* and *The Glass Menagerie*

Before we can begin discussing the particulars of the similarities among the characters within the two families, the Lomans and the Wingfields, we must first mention some generalities that the two works share. The first is visual. Both films look as if they were plays that were filmed in a theater or sound stage rather than movies based on existing dramas and shot on location. This is particularly so with Arthur Miller's *Death of a Salesman* where painted drops and removable sets were used. Next is the resemblance of the clothing which seems to be from the same historical era. *Death of a Salesman* seems to take place from 1929 (or perhaps 1930) until 1946 given how the sons in their middle teens age to their thirties. *The Glass Menagerie*, termed by Tennessee Williams as a "memory play," goes from 1936 to 1944, thus the markedly similar clothing styles worn by the characters in both productions. Both families seem to be living in a state of genteel poverty. Objects in the house are old and worn but, nevertheless, cared for and even cherished with hopes that the good times that have gone will return again. But there are internal factors as well that resonate between the two works.

Both plays are brilliant because of the memorable characters their playwrights created. Willy Loman and Amanda Wingfield have come from different worlds but now, in their late middle years, are remarkably similar.

Willy & Amanda

Despite their efforts, both parents' ability to earn a living has deteriorated and they can't support their family. Amanda (Joanne Woodward), with no training in the world of business, is a telemarketer hawking magazine subscriptions. She's not shy and quite talkative—too talkative—and loses customers before she can close on a sale. To her, it becomes a social occasion rather than a serious business undertaking. Willy (Dustin Hoffman) has comparable problems. He makes too many jokes and has too many rambling, reminiscent conversations. He wastes too much time before closing the sale.

As a result, either in hopes or in actions, both Willy and Amanda look to one of their two children to help them out. In Willy's case, he has pinned his dreams on Biff, who has recently arrived home from out West. Biff had great potential as an athlete back in high school. Willy feels that his son must still have those attractive qualities and would quickly make his mark in the world of business if he only applies himself. As for his younger son, Hap has a job in sales but isn't going anywhere—he is more preoccupied in womanizing than carving out a career for himself. As for Amanda Wingfield, her elder child Laura (Karen Allen) is beset with too many problems to be of any financial help—she has a limp that resulted from infantile paralysis, severe shyness to the point of neurosis, and succumbs to a gradual withdrawal from the real world outside. It is on Tom's (John Malkovich) shoulders to extricate the family from its predicament. All his dreams and creative interests—reading and writing poetry—must be forgotten and dropped as he drudges away at a dead-end position in a shoe warehouse. To escape his frustration and sense of imprisonment, he goes to the movies to fantasize in the world of celluloid adventure and then perhaps has a few drinks to further escape his misery.

Unfortunately, both Willy and Amanda's present has been shaped by events of the distant past that they cannot forget and that still influence them. Back when Willy was still able to make a living as a salesman and both his sons were in high school, his long lost elder brother Ben (Louis Zorich) suddenly appeared at their house. He had sought out his younger brother not so much to renew acquaintances as to offer Willy a golden opportunity to strike it rich. He wanted his brother to join him for an extended business venture up in Alaska. He urged Willy to drop everything—his job, his home, his family—to make a fortune. Willy, with mixed feelings, refused the opportunity, not only because he didn't not want to abandon his family but because he felt there was promise in his sales career. This decision he has constantly questioned then regretted as he has grown older.

Amanda's past decision was even more radical. She was a "Southern belle" from a wealthy family back on a plantation in Blue Mountain, Mississippi. She had many planters' sons, "gentleman callers," clamoring for her hand in marriage. Instead, she met a charming employee of the telephone company who swept her off her feet. They eloped. She got disinherited. They quickly had two children. Eventually he had had enough of domestic life, suddenly leaving his family for the wide, open spaces.

Too often, the respective heads of their households retreat into their past. When life is too disappointing, Amanda likes to fondly recollect those wonderful days of freedom, popularity, and unlimited prospects back in Blue Mountain. Willy's journey into the past is far more serious. He goes back and forth so often that he frequently mistakes the past for the present and vice versa. There has also been a darker incident that plagues him even though he never admits to it.

When his son was a senior in high school, Biff (John Malkovich) was a great football player with athletic scholarship offers from three colleges. During those last few years, Willy had been filling his son's head with the secrets of success. Being "well liked" was the most important precept, as was "it's not what you know but who you know" that would propel him forward. Biff idolized Willy and trusted him. Then catastrophe struck! Biff caught his father in a Boston hotel room with another woman. The boy had come to that city seeking his dad because of a graduation problem he was having. They never spoke of what had happened afterwards, but it ruined their relationship and, subsequently, their lives.

Finally, both parents have unrealistic dreams about their children's future prospects. Willy, even after the Boston debacle, had hopes of Biff rocketing up through the ranks in sales, despite his son's lack of a high school diploma. But Biff had aspirations to work with his hands and preferably outside. Willy has real talent building and fixing things but has always seen little prestige in such skills. A three-piece suit, tie, and hat in an office atmosphere was what he desired for his son. Amanda has no illusions about Tom rising through the ranks at the shoe warehouse. She just hopes he could maintain his position there long enough until his sister gets a husband. Although this seems highly unlikely—given Laura's disabilities—Amanda feels that among Tom's acquaintances at his place of employment there must be some young men worthy of her daughter. Tom is to bring home to dinner such a "gentleman caller" for his sister.

Biff and Tom

Biff has come home to perhaps find himself and in so doing help his parents. He rekindles his closeness with his brother Hap (Stephen Lang) and his mother (Kate Reid) only to find out that Willy isn't doing well at his job—he has been taken off salary and works for straight commission just like an entry level salesman.

Willy is filled with delusions on how successful Biff will be even though the last 15 years for Biff have been one unsatisfying job after another. Biff hates the city and the idea of working there in an office or on the road in sales. He yearns to go out West for a simpler life and work with his hands to farm, to raise cattle, or to work construction.

Tom despises his job in the St. Louis warehouse as well. He dreams of getting a seaman's card, joining the Merchant Marine and seeing the world. But his family, especially his sentimental ties to his sister, is an anchor which keeps him put. When he finally acts on his desires, he moves quickly. Using the money for the family's monthly electric bill instead for his union dues, he soon gets his seaman's card. Soon thereafter, he leaves his mother and sister to ship out on the open seas.

Another tribulation both Biff and Tom have to endure is the constant nagging, sarcasm, and bitter rebukes from their father and mother respectively. Their households are not filled with warmth and peace but tension and rancor. This also contributes to driving the young men away from their families.

Finally, they have friends outside the family who take an interest in them and are willing to give solid advice and even serve as role models of sorts. When Biff was the adolescent football hero, his next door neighbor Bernard (David S. Chandler), a studious type, was always willing to help him cram for exams. He even slipped him answers during tests. As a true friend, he was eager for Biff to enter the University of Virginia on an athletic scholarship. He never knew why Biff gave up at the very end by not attending summer school to make up a failing grade in math and graduate.

To meet his sister, Tom brings home a colleague from the warehouse, Jim O'Connor (James Naughton). Jim is a man who doesn't mind giving advice; usually it turns out to be helpful. He is ambitious and feels the sacrifice of time and effort for schooling or training, especially in some emerging technology, would pay off in the future. He sees television as such a field and is presently enrolled in a night course to get in on the ground floor of an occupation which has such promising horizons. He is also taking a public speaking course to further his advancement. He urges Tom to do the same and, in the meantime, apply himself more diligently at work so as not to get fired. He appreciates Tom's creative talents but feels talk should labor on them at home and not in the workplace.

This is not to suggest that there was any collusion between the playwrights, or that one "borrowed" from the other. Although they were contemporaries, they might not have known each other personally and they did their writing in different regions of the country.

The film adaptations of two of America's most honored dramas, Tennessee Williams' *The Glass Menagerie* and Arthur Miller's *Death of a Salesman*, were released two years within each other. The motion pictures show a number of parallels between the two works. The previous

Karen Allen and Joanne Woodward in Paul Newman's The Glass Menagerie
(1987). MCA Home Video. Courtesy of Everett Collection.

paper first briefly mentions similarities between the films and then
dwells on the likenesses between two of the parents, Willy Loman and
Amanda Wingfield, and between two of their adult children, Biff Loman
and Tom Wingfield.

At the beginning of the chapter, the audience and the format again
have been initially considered. Then, in a departure from the previous
two chapters on the review and the critique respectively, specific structural options of comparison were presented: namely, block style and
point-by-point style. Approaches to the *comparative analysis* (also
referred to as the *comparative critique*) appeared next. They included
movie-to-movie comparative analysis, original-to-remake-or-sequel comparative analysis, literary work-to-movie comparative analysis, and the
comparison-of-individuals analysis. As before, a full complement of sample title listings, excerpts, and complete examples has been furnished.

Chapter 6 studies in depth the documented research paper. The
chapter ends with two entire annotated sample research papers—the
first, analytical and the second, comparative—as well as their respective
works cited pages.

6

TYPES OF FILM CRITICISM:
THE DOCUMENTED RESEARCH PAPER

Robert Duvall and Marlon Brando in Francis Ford Coppola's The Godfather
(1972). Paramount. Courtesy of The Kobal Collection at Art Resource, NY.

The documented research paper is the most formalized means of critical written expression. Not only are ideas, opinions, and theories of the writer necessary, but they now must be supported by the views of "experts" on film criticism and perhaps even those individuals involved directly in the making of the movie(s) discussed. To gather such material, the writer must seek these *secondary sources* from books, periodicals, personal interviews, videos, DVDs, filmstrips, cassette tapes, CD ROMs, and on the Internet to access websites. The approach should be methodical and well planned before being undertaken. Once an outline is devised, the researched material amassed is culled for information that will be used and documented accordingly. When the draft is written, in-text (parenthetical) citations must be incorporated and a "works cited" page created. The remainder of this subsection will address portions of the process in greater detail.

Deciding on a Topic

Much time can be saved if you have some idea of your topic before beginning research. Ideally, it should either be on an aspect of film about which you either have some previous knowledge as a base to build upon or a subject area that interests you greatly—be it a film, director, actor, or period of cinema. If you cannot select your own subject and a list of titles or topics is imposed on you, again, opt for what you know best or what interests you most from among them.

Length of Paper

The length of your research paper will either be externally decided—the professor wants a 10–15 page research paper or one of 1,500–2,000 words. Or, its length will be internally determined by how much time you have to devote to doing research—including viewing some films, videos, or DVDs—and then converting what you have watched and analyzed into a written document.

Subject Area: Neither Too Broad Nor Too Narrow

Probably more important than length, is determining the adequacy of your topic to the given assignment and the time allotted to work on it. If the project calls for a 1,500-word paper (approximately five to six pages) a topic such as "The American Western" would be too broad and general. One could literally write a 600-page tome on such a subject. Conversely, one would be hard put to write a 2,000-word research paper (seven to eight pages) on "The Symbolic Impact of the Train Whistle in *High Noon*," as on such a subject, one or two pages would suffice.

You should support points and assertions with multiple sources, but not so many as to lead to boring repetition. The sample topics that follow are for an assignment of from 1,500–2,000 words. Actually, with each of these options, if you were to write a paper of at least double that length, you could do so fairly easily. You would have to go into greater detail and increase the number of variables covered or being compared. Notice, however, that the titles are specific enough to be focused yet broad enough to avoid being overly repetitive. Again, these titles can be appropriately covered in a research paper of from 1,500 to 2,000 words or one much longer:

- Institutional Racism in the U.S. Army That Fostered Specific Acts of Racism as Portrayed in Norman Jewison's *A Soldier's Story*
- Meryl Streep: A Gifted Actress' Talent for Characterization and Foreign Accents as Seen in *Out of Africa, Sophie's Choice, A Cry in the Dark,* and *The Bridges of Madison County*
- The Thematic Motifs of Futility, Abandonment of Duty, and Outright Desertion in Fred Zinnemann's *High Noon*
- Conflicts Arising from the Collision of a Pre-Arranged, Absentee Marriage in an Exotic, Hostile Geographic Environment in Jane Campion's *The Piano*
- John Landis' *Animal House* as a Comical and Exaggerated Look at American College Life and Fraternity Mores during the Early 1960s
- Mozart and Scarlatti: The Eccentricities of Genius and the Envy That It Incurs in Milos Foreman's *Amadeus*
- Two Women, a Wedding, and Plastics: Driving Forces in Mike Nichols' *The Graduate*
- All the Elements of the Film Noir Movie as Seen in Jacques Tourneau's *Out of the Past*
- Symbols and Objects of a Bygone Era and How They Relate to the Plot and Themes of Billy Wilder's *Sunset Boulevard*
- An Overview of Contemporary Film Noir: The Same Themes, Moods, and Characterizations but Shot in Color [Select Three Applicable Movies]

Note that some of the topics could also be developed as critical analyses, while others could be better served with a comparative format. Regardless of approach, the research information that you have gathered will be interwoven into your text by means of cited quotations, paraphrases, and summaries supplementing and supporting your own insights and opinions.

The Outline

Once you have arrived at a specific topic for your research essay, you are ready to draw up a working outline. But before you take this step, first convert the topic into a detailed title with the specific movie(s) and/or person(s) as part of it. Once this is undertaken, you are then ready to turn your title into a thesis statement.

Thesis Statement

As stated before, the **complete thesis statement** works in three areas, thus, has three parts: a **subject** (*who* or *what* it is about), a **statement** (the *predicate* statement elaborates on the subject), and **support** (*minor inferences* or *support statements* provide evidence of *support* for the *predicate statement*). Often, in fact, the title of the research paper will reflect the complete thesis statement. Returning to one of the titles just previously listed, we will repeat it and then convert it into a *complete thesis statement* with its three main components: subject, statement, and support.

In many ways, the ***complete thesis statement*** is like a simple algebraic formula, reading:

$$A + B + C_{(multiple)}$$

where:

$$A = \text{subject}, B = \text{statement}, C_{(multiple)} = \text{supports}$$

We can convert the following title about American actress Meryl Streep and her gifts at playing roles of non-American characters to a complete thesis statement.

TITLE:
Meryl Streep: Her Genius for Characterization and Foreign Accents in *Out of Africa*, *Sophie's Choice*, *A Cry in the Dark*, and *The Bridges of Madison County*

SUBJECT:
Meryl Streep

STATEMENT:
has a genius for characterization through her remarkable adoption of foreign accents and mannerisms

SUPPORT:
which is vividly depicted in such films as *Out of Africa*, *Sophie's Choice*, *A Cry in the Dark*, and *The Bridges of Madison County*

There is another way of making and supporting this opinion by employing a *simple thesis statement* = **A** + **B** as a complete sentence followed by another complete sentence consisting of the *support statements* = **C**$_{(multiple)}$

SIMPLE THESIS STATEMENT:
Meryl Streep has a genius for characterization through her remarkable adoption of foreign accents and mannerisms

SUPPORT STATEMENTS:
This is vividly depicted as she plays a Danish writer in *Out of Africa*, a Polish refugee in *Sophie's Choice*, an Australian mother in *A Cry in the Dark*, and an Italian-born Iowa farmwife in *The Bridges of Madison County*.

Let's look at another example which is about contemporary film noir, a sub-genre of the motion picture. This topic is also comparative in nature, discussing certain aspects in common found in the movies discussed.

TITLE:
An Overview of Contemporary Film Noir: The Same Themes, Moods, and Characterizations but Shot in Color as Seen in *Body Heat*, *Se7en*, and *L.A. Confidential*

SUBJECT:
Contemporary film noir

STATEMENT:
has comparable themes, moods, and characterizations (as classic film noir)

SUPPORT:
as evidenced by such relatively recent color productions as *Body Heat*, *Se7en*, and *L.A. Confidential*

Mapping Main Points, Subordinate Points, and Examples

Once the title has been converted into a *complete thesis statement*, the outline can be drawn since it flows out of the thesis statement components.

With the thesis statement reached, building a working outline follows. The term "working" is used because the outline is somewhat incomplete and will be adjusted as research dictates. Initially, there will be certain holes in the outline that will be filled in with the selection of the secondary sources (criticism found in periodicals, books, online, etc.) to be incorporated into the paper.

The typical outline is both *sequential* and *hierarchical*. The outline is *sequential* if it builds in an orderly fashion that emanates from the thesis statement. In some cases, it is chronological and follows a pattern of elapsed time: the first event is analyzed, then the second, the third, and so forth. First let's consider the sequential qualities of the topic which follows and how the pattern develops.

TITLE
Holy Sacraments and Deadly Sins: The Corleones and the Interplay between Religious Ritual and Violent "Business" at Different Times and Places in *The Godfather*

What the topic tries to show is the connection in the plot between a series of sacred or at least ritualistic Corleone family events—a wedding at their home, a church christening, for example—and a number of violent undertakings connected with the family "business" involving illegal undertakings. So to develop the topic sequentially, you would first discuss the wedding and how it was connected with criminal activity (the Corleone family "business") and then discuss the highly religious christening and the separate violent acts coordinated with it.

The outline is *hierarchical* if it denotes that there is a pecking order in the steps of the outline. Thus, the outline is not a multi-step process with each step being of equal weight. Some steps are subordinate to others, or are outgrowths or examples of such steps. Essentially, your paper makes some main points (the major *supportive statements* or *inferences*). These main points are the First Level (using Roman numerals: I, II, etc.) and each would be the topic sentence of its paragraph. Each of these *main points* contains a number of *subordinate points* which elaborate upon them. These comprise the Second Level and are represented by capital letters (A, B, etc.). Finally, *specific examples* or *concrete illustrations* are used to further clarify the subordinate points. These examples to the subordinate points are the Third Level; they are designated by Arabic numerals (1., 2., etc.).

Notice in the following outline that the movement is hierarchical, going from the most important point to the least important and from the most general and abstract point to the most specific. What follows is a conceptual schematic of the outline format:

LEAD-IN/INTRODUCTION
THESIS STATEMENT WITH ITS MAIN SUPPORTIVE POINTS
(INFERENCES)

I. FIRST MAIN SUPPORTIVE POINT
   A. Subordinate Point
      1. Specific example
      2. Specific example
   B. Subordinate Point
      1. Specific example
      2. Specific example

II. SECOND MAIN SUPPORTIVE POINT
   A. Subordinate Point
      1. Specific example
      2. Specific example
   B. Subordinate Point
      1. Specific example
      2. Specific example

III. THIRD MAIN SUPPORTIVE POINT
   A. Subordinate Point
      1. Specific example
      2. Specific example
   B. Subordinate Point
      1. Specific example
      2. Specific example
   C. Subordinate Point
      1. Specific example
      2. Specific example

CONCLUSION

The outline is useful for a number of reasons. The following lists its most important attributes:

- Helps organize your thoughts,
- Enables you to plan and develop logical arguments,
- Points out those areas that are weak or need more data,
- Serves as a guide to keep you focused and not wander off on a tangent,
- Arranges material both sequentially and hierarchically by showing the interconnectedness of its parts, and
- Makes the research phase more efficient.

Now we will look at a working outline with the emphasis on the thesis statement, followed by its main supportive points (inferences), its subordinate points, and its specific examples. Note that the lead-in/ introduction and conclusion sections are indicated but *not* developed; they will be addressed in a later subsection. A typical outline originates from the complete thesis statement and therefore doesn't include previous elements of the Introduction nor any parts of the Conclusion. To illustrate the building of the working outline, we will use the title previously introduced on *The Godfather.*

TITLE
Holy Sacraments and Deadly Sins: The Corleones and the Interplay between Religious Ritual and Violent "Business" at Different Times and Places in *The Godfather*

This title we can easily convert into a complete thesis statement and, subsequently, break that down into its subject, statement, and support.

COMPLETE THESIS STATEMENT:
In *The Godfather,* over the years and in different settings, the lives of the Corleones are marked by the interplay between religious ritual and violent "business."

Subject:	The lives of the Corleone family in *The Godfather*
Statement:	are marked by the interplay between familial or religious ritual and violent "business"
Support:	at different times and places.

LEAD-IN/INTRODUCTION
COMPLETE THESIS STATEMENT: In *The Godfather*, over the years and in different settings, the lives of the Corleones are marked by the interplay between religious ritual and violent "business."

   I. 1945, Long Island, New York
      A. Carlo and Connie's wedding
         1. Eating and drinking by guests and family
         2. Singing by Mama Corleone and guests
         3. Dancing of Vito Corleone and the bride
      B. Don Vito Corleone conducting business
         1. Don Corleone listens to requests
            a. Grants favor to Bonasera, an undertaker
            b. Grants favor to Johnny Fontane, a singer and his godson
            c. Refuses favor to Solazzo, another "capo"

      2. Violent actions soon follow as a consequence
         a. Bonasera's daughter is avenged
         b. Fontane's enemy is threatened and concedes
         c. Don Corleone is seriously wounded by Solazzo's men
         d. This leads to other violent acts

  II. 1948, Corleone, Sicily
      A. Michael and Appolonia's wedding and honeymoon
         1. The newlyweds marching from the church with local brass band
         2. The couple dancing in the square to their music
         3. Appolonia learning to speak English and drive
      B. Assassins try to kill Michael
         1. Appolonia starts car and it blows up
         2. Michael flees back to the United States

 III. 1955, Manhattan and Long Island
      A. The christening of Carlo and Connie's baby
         1. In church Michael takes ritual oaths as the infant's godfather
         2. Makes promises to his wife he has no intention of keeping
      B. Numerous ambushes/assassinations on that very day and night
         1. The killings of Barzini, the Tattaglias, and other enemies from crime families
         2. Murder of Carlo
      C. Michael's lieutenants swear fealty to him, the new Godfather
         1. Michael denies any involvement of Carlo's murder to Kay
         2. Kay, out of view, accidentally witnesses the strange ritual in his office

CONCLUSION

Amassing and Culling Data

After the working outline is completed, it is time to shift gears into the research mode. Using both hard data (books and periodicals) and soft data (computer databases, the Internet, CD ROMs, VHS cassettes, DVDs)—all available at the college library—the writer is ready to amass relevant data pertaining to the paper. Then he or she will speed-read the multiple sources and glean material from them. Only those specific sources that will be used are photocopied or printed out. By having an outline as a guide, those sources that are repetitive or do not address the subject can be discarded, whereas those that will be quoted, para-phrased, or summarized are kept within *documentation packets*, which will be fully discussed later in the chapter.

Hard Data—Books and Periodicals

The bulk of the sources are still probably going to be generated from books, journals, newspapers, and other periodicals. However, as more and more libraries reduce their hardcopy sources available and convert them to digital databases, paper printouts of the articles will be available rather than photocopies. In some instances, newspaper articles are gathered for a given year or series of years and bound in hardcovers. They are made available to students in the Reference section of the library for reading and photocopying purposes on the premises.

Soft Data—Databases, the Internet, CD ROM, VHS, DVD

In many instances, soft data derived from electronic databases also can be converted into paper copies. This is true for local library databases as well as data off of the World Wide Web on the Internet. Data on a computer screen can also be converted by a printer from the screen to a paper copy.

Such paper copies are useful because they offer portability as well as verification of the source. In the system of photocopying and color-coding, which will be discussed in the next subsection, this verification process vouches for the authenticity of the sources and helps prevent plagiarism.

────────── Photocopying and Color-Coding ──────────

The system of photocopying and color-coding was designed to streamline the documentation process of the research paper. It has three main benefits:

- A means of avoiding plagiarism,
- An economical alternative to bibliography cards, and
- An efficient equivalent to note cards.

Avoiding Plagiarism

Plagiarism has many faces. For those who willingly and dishonestly try to pass off another's work or words as their own, little can be done to prevent their deeds. Instructors must be vigilant to discover such actions and then apply harsh measures sanctioned by the department's associate dean and the academic dean to censure the offender. However, too many students commit plagiarism accidentally or out of ignorance. The system described in the ensuing paragraphs was devised to prevent most instances of plagiarism since those pages, paragraphs, sentences, and phrases that are quoted, paraphrased, or summarized are photocopied or printed out for the instructor's perusal and are part of the research paper package.

A folder is used to hold in one pocket the final typed research paper to be submitted. In the other pocket, photocopies or computer printouts of the actual sources are gathered into stapled *secondary source packets* (*documentation packets*) and inserted into the folder. To keep down the expense and waste of paper, only those pages of a chapter or an article or other source that are actually adopted for quoting, paraphrasing, or summarizing are copied. For example, a ten-page article that begins on page 87 and ends on page 96 has material to be used only from pages 87, 88, and 96. Therefore, to create a secondary source packet, just those three pages are photocopied and stapled together with the lowest page number (87) first and the highest number (96) last regardless of what order they are used in the context of the paper. On the top page (87), the title of the article or book and the author must be written in ink if they do not already appear there. The same should be done for the actual page number if it is not already printed. The other pages stapled within the packet should have their page numbers written down if they are not already there.

The process does not stop at this juncture. Color-coding is applied to indicate how the source entry is being used, that is, either as a quote, a paraphrase, or a summary. Any given photocopied page may have one or more entries on it: for example, a quoted phrase, a paraphrased sentence or two, and a summarized paragraph. To indicate the difference between the three, the following color codes and marking conventions should be incorporated:

* paraphrase—yellow highlighting of words, sentence, or passage;
* quote—blue underlining of words, sentence, or passage; and
* summary—red bracketing at the beginning and end of passage or paragraph(s).

Thus, the page with the four entries would have the quoted sentence underlined in blue, the two sentences paraphrased highlighted in yellow, and the small paragraph that is summarized bracketed in red. Sometimes, a paragraph summarized or paraphrased also contains a sentence that is directly quoted within it. If paraphrased, the paragraph would be highlighted in yellow with the specific sentence quoted within also underlined in blue ink; if summarized, the paragraph could be bracketed in red, fore and aft, with the quoted sentence again underlined in blue.

This helps the instructor greatly. When he or she reads the research paper and wants to check the accuracy of the source, it is right there. The photocopy vouches for both. How well the student paraphrases or summarizes can also be judged since the original is available for immediate comparison. The parenthetical (in-text, also known as "internal") citation which follows every paraphrase, quote, or summary easily directs the instructor to the exact source photocopied in a documentation packet in the other pocket of the folder.

Alternatives to Bibliography Cards and Note Cards

Rather than separate index cards for each bibliographic source, a complete alphabetized listing of every source referenced in the research paper should be kept. This will become the works cited section that comprises the last page(s) of the research paper. Note cards are eliminated by the photocopy-color code system. In the old standard method, any sentence or passage used as a source had to be handwritten or typed on index cards, then numbered, with some bibliographic information also entered on these cards. The stack of cards became ever more cumbersome and unwieldy as the separate sources increased and the individual entries accumulated. Instructors dreaded the rubber band suddenly snapping and cards scattering every which way. The photocopy subsystem eliminates much of the drudgery of the old procedure; the color-coding subsystem—when done correctly—clearly indicates how the entries are being employed in the text of the research paper.

———————— Documentation Features ————————

In order to conduct research, one must seek sources—books, articles, and such; then one culls the pieces for those that will contribute to the paper; finally, one must skillfully incorporate those findings into the work. In addition, the research paper will include one final—but major—step: the orderly documentation of the sources used. This is done with *in-text citations* (also known as *parenthetical citations*) and a *work cited* section. Both use the Modern Language Association (MLA) conventions of style.

If writing a paper on film, in the works cited section you must separate the *primary* sources (the films themselves) from the *secondary* sources (criticism from books, magazine articles, newspaper reviews, CD-ROMs, Internet data) when organizing the works. The procedures to be used for creating in-text citations and compiling works cited listings are described in the subsections that immediately follow.

In-Text Citations (MLA)

In writing a research paper about film, you use the same MLA (Modern Language Association) conventions that would be observed for any other type of critical essay on literature. After each quote, paraphrase, or summary from a secondary source, a citation providing minimal information—namely, author and page—is furnished as a quick reference. Author and page alone are sufficient to both direct the reader to the works cited page—which offers the full citation—and guide the reader to the documentation packet, where the appropriate photocopy or computer printout, authenticating that part of the original document, is being discussed.

After a quoted passage, a parenthetical citation (in-text citation) is inserted *after* the closing quotation mark but *before* the period. It contains the name of the author(s) and page number(s). For clarity, it is indicated by **bold print** in the following sentence:

> "'Established' mavericks like Martin Scorsese continued to make audacious movies during the 1980s" **(Giannetti and Eyman 474).**

An extended quotation of four lines or more uses a slightly different convention. The quote is indented by a special margin and justified to the left, quotation marks are discarded since they are understood, and the parenthesized citation *follows* the period.

> Lynch's first aboveground hit was *The Elephant Man* (1980), the story of John Merrick, a nineteenth-century victim of a horribly disfiguring disease. What made the movie remarkable was not so much the narrative as the imagery. Lynch and his cinematographer, the great Freddie Francis, photographed the film in black-and-white CinemaScope, infusing the mise en scene with terrifying shadows. The soundtrack throbs with weird, forbidding, industrial rumblings. Gradually, Lynch enables us to perceive the distorted, tormented, yet oddly poetic creature that was John Merrick, as a human being. **(Giannetti and Eyman 474–75)**

A paraphrase or summary dispenses with the quotation marks since the source, although referred to, is not quoted directly. Although the ideas or opinions are restated in the writer's own language and the sentence structure is altered, the source (shown here in bold print) must still be attributed. The preceding short paragraph about David Lynch's *The Elephant Man* can be restated as follows:

> David Lynch's first mainstream success came with *The Elephant Man* (1980). It tells the story of John Merrick who endured a horribly

disfiguring condition during the nineteenth century. Through imagery rather than narrative, Lynch, together with cinematographer Freddie Francis, uses black-and-white film in CinemaScope to create the terrifying shadows that help drive the plot. This is abetted by the strange, rumbling soundtrack which eventually helps to portray Merrick as a troubled yet sensitive person rather than a freak or monster. **(Giannetti and Eyman 474–75)**

However, if only a sentence is paraphrased, the period moves *outside* the parenthesis. In the example below, the authors are mentioned before the paraphrase; when this occurs, only the page (here in bold print) is given.

In the fourth edition of *Flashback: A Brief History of Film*, Louis Giannetti and Scott Eyman claim that what makes David Lynch's *The Elephant Man* so remarkable is the imagery he uses to drive the story **(474).**

Since none of this should be new to any student who has taken or is taking English Composition (ENC 1101, English 101, or the like), the best source for the intricacies of in-text citations would be the most recent edition of a text such as *Writing Research Papers: A Complete Guide—14th Edition* by James D. Lester and Jim D. Lester, Jr., which contains extensive sections on research paper documentation rules and techniques with an ample portion on MLA writing style. Many "four-in-one" English composition texts, such as *The Longman Writer: Rhetoric, Reader, Research Guide, and Handbook—8th Edition* by Judith Nadell, John Langan, and Eliza A. Comodromos also feature appropriate material on the research paper and documentation process.

Works Cited (MLA)

The works cited section functions in the same manner as a bibliography. It too is arranged alphabetically rather than in the sequential order that the secondary sources appear in the text of the research paper. If a book's sources are cited, entries are listed by initially furnishing the author's last name, then first name and initial for the first part of the citation. The next part provides the title—now preferably in italics—and the edition (unless it is the first edition, where it goes unmentioned). The site (city) of the publisher comes next, with the publishing house following, and then the year of publication. Finally, the type of source is given, such as "Print." You will note that each part of the citation ends with a period. The full citation (in bold for clarity) for the Giannetti and Eyman text is as follows:

Giannetti, Louis, and Scott Eyman. *Flashback: A Brief History of Film.* **4th ed. Upper Saddle River, N.J.: Prentice Hall, 2001. Print.**

For a periodical, such as a journal or newspaper, the full citation has a different format. A daily newspaper citation begins with the author: last name, first name, middle initial; then the title of the article in quotation marks; followed by the name of the publication; the complete date by day, month, and year; the volume (if there is one), and the section and page number. Following is a sample of a daily newspaper citation:

Canby, Vincent. "'The Godfather, Part II': One Godfather Too Many." *New York Times* **22 Dec. 1974, sec. 2: 19+. Print.**

Again, a writer's handbook should be consulted for the exact type of publication and the particular variables that come into play for each individual work to be cited. It is better not to rely on your memory for all the citations since most of them will differ somewhat from each other.

So far, we have been referring to secondary sources. For primary sources you list alphabetically by film title. The components in their proper order are: the film title, the director, the distributor, the year released, and the format (film, videocassette, or DVD). This is the acceptable *short form.* The most common longer form would list the actors (performers) by indicating "Perf." following the title and the director's name; it would be indicated alphabetically and include the leading members of the cast, then the distributor, the year released, and the format which would conclude the citation. Such a citation would look like this:

A Bronx Tale. **Dir. Robert De Niro. Perf. Lillo Brancato, Francis Capra, Robert De Niro, Chazz Palminteri. Savoy Pictures, 1993. Film.**

The following is a works cited listing with eight short form primary sources:

American Beauty. Dir. Sam Mendes. DreamWorks Home Entertainment 2000. DVD.
Ben-Hur. Dir. William Wyler. Metro-Goldwyn-Mayer, 1959. Film.
A Bronx Tale. Dir. Robert De Niro. Home Box Office Home Video, 1995. Videocassette.
Frida. Dir. Julie Taymore. Lions Gate Films/Miramax Films, 2002. Film.
How Green Was My Valley. Dir. John Ford. Twentieth Century-Fox, 1941. Film.
Manhattan. Dir. Woody Allen. United Artists, 1979. Film.
Out of the Past. Dir. Jacques Tourneur. RKO Radio Pictures, 1947. Film.
The Seventh Seal. Dir. Ingmar Bergman. Janus Films, 1958. Film.

Note: Grammatically speaking, although articles (*a, an, the*) are in their normal position of the title, they are not considered alphabetically. See, especially in the previous list *A Bronx Tale* (alphabetized by *B*) and *The Seventh Seal* (by *S*).

The First Draft

The first draft contains all the elements of the final draft except the editing, which includes making corrections, requiring some deletions and/or additions. The first draft includes: the title page; the outline; the lead-in/introduction, which usually culminates in the thesis statement; the body, including the development of the inferences (supporting points) of the thesis statement; the conclusion with its final remarks or posing of questions; and the works cited page(s).

The Title Page

The title should be typed approximately one-third down the page and should be centered (it may or may not be in all capitals). It needs to be double-spaced which makes it more readable. The title must be detailed enough to name the paper's subject and main point(s) to be discussed. If movie titles are included, they should be italicized. The name of the research paper's writer would follow, centered about an inch below. An inch below that appears the title of the course, course number, and section; below that, at the bottom third of the page, is the instructor's name followed below by the date of submission. These last two lines would be centered.

The Lead-in/Introduction

As with any good piece of writing, you need a lead-in statement or a series of lead-ins before establishing the thesis and developing the support statements (inferences). If the paper is eight to ten pages, the reader's interest must be captured and then gradually led to and presented with the main thrust of the paper. The lead-in paragraph or section can use numerous tactics to attract and keep the reader: shock, statistics, facts, an anecdote, sweeping statements, fascinating details, opinions—obviously, the approach varies greatly. Eventually, however, the reader will be smoothly guided to the thesis statement. The thesis statement usually ends the introduction phase or is embedded in a paragraph fairly close to its termination.

If we select the topic on *The Godfather* about the interplay between family's religious rituals and the family's crime business, the lead-in or introduction could first mention other memorable films that feature rituals, such as weddings, that are integral parts of those movies: for example, *Father of the Bride, A Member of the Wedding, The Deer Hunter*, and *Steel Magnolias*. Then there is a segue, a transition to the in-depth descriptive paragraph of *The Godfather's* wedding in the opening scene. Eventually, we would mention how, despite the revelry, hundreds of guests, and opulent setting, business is, nevertheless, being conducted almost throughout the entire nuptial festivities.

The Body

The body is the largest section of the paper and is the natural outgrowth of the complete thesis statement. It develops each inference presented by the thesis and supports each of them by furnishing examples. This is done by adding specific information and providing—when used—documented critical opinions through quotes, paraphrases, and summaries (as in-text citations).

The Conclusion

The concluding remarks are as important as the introduction. They do more than just rehash the thesis statement and voice the obvious. Effective concluding remarks may also raise questions, mention ramifications, or discuss ensuing results of what has been presented and discussed.

Works Cited

The work cited section provides full information on quotes, paraphrases, and summaries that have been cited (by means of the parenthetic or in-text citations). The works cited page validates critical references which have added weight to the insights of the research paper's writer. Specific aspects of this section have already been discussed.

The Final Draft

Following this section highlighting the main aspects of the final draft is an actual final draft of a documented analytical research paper: from its title page through the works cited page, inclusive. However, you will note that the margins are much wider than the other complete reviews and analyses that have previously been presented in this book. Occasional commentary in the right hand margin "analyzes" the analysis, commenting on the motives behind and an insight as to the methods used in preparing this final version of a research paper.

The topic of the specific analytical research paper that follows has been mentioned to previously: namely, the interplay of scenes where sacred rituals are soon followed by those of mob-related violent business. Now you will be presented with the research paper in full on themes within Francis Ford Coppola's *The Godfather*. The research paper begins with a title sheet that approximates MLA style. Note the informative—if somewhat ponderous—title and other necessary information that the title page would contain. What makes this sample analytical research paper so helpful is the incorporation of commentary as marginalia throughout the paper to explain the evidence provided and the views expressed.

HOLY SACRAMENTS AND DEADLY SINS: THE CORLEONES

AND THE INTERPLAY BETWEEN RELIGIOUS RITUAL

AND VIOLENT "BUSINESS" AT DIFFERENT TIMES

AND PLACES IN *THE GODFATHER*

[STUDENT'S NAME]

ENG 2101 - FILM AS LITERATURE

[PROFESSOR'S NAME]

[DATE]

[Student's Last Name] 1

TOPIC OUTLINE

<u>Complete Thesis Statement</u>: In *The Godfather*, over the years and in different settings, the lives of the Corleones are marked by the interplay between religious ritual and violent "business."

    I. 1945, Long Island, New York

      A. Carlo and Connie's wedding

        1. Eating and drinking by guests and family

        2. Singing by Mama Corleone and guests

        3. Dancing of Vito Corleone and the bride

      B. Don Vito Corleone conducting business

        1. Don Corleone listens to requests

          a. Grants favor to Bonasera, an undertaker

          b. Grants favor to Johnny Fontane, a singer and his godson

          c. Refuses favor to Solazzo, another "capo"

        2. Violent actions soon follow as a consequence

          a. Bonasera's daughter is avenged

          b. Fontane's enemy is threatened and concedes

          c. Don Corleone is seriously wounded by Solazzo

          d. This leads to other violent acts, including Sonny's murder and Michael avenging his father's shooting and brother's death

II. 1948, Corleone, Sicily

  A. Michael and Appolonia's wedding and honeymoon

    1. Marching from the church with local brass band

    2. Dancing in the square to their music

    3. She learns to speak English and

  B. Assassins try to kill Michael

    1. Appolonia starts car and it blows up

    2. Michael flees back to the United States

III. 1955, Manhattan and Long Island

  A. The christening of Carlo and Connie's baby

    1. In church Michael takes ritual oaths as the infant's godfather

    2. Makes promises to his wife he has no intention of keeping

  B. Numerous ambushes/assassinations on that very day and night

    1. The killings of Barzini, the Tattaglias, and other enemies from crime families

    2. Murder of Carlo

  C. Michael's lieutenants swear fealty to him, as the new Godfather

    1. Michael denies any involvement of Carlo's murder to Kay

    2. Kay, out of view, accidentally witnesses the strange ritual in his office

[Student's Last Name] 3

[Student's Full Name]

[Professor's Name]

ENG 2101 - Film as Literature

[Date]

Expresses main thrust of the film.

HOLY SACRAMENTS AND DEADLY SINS: THE CORLEONES AND THE INTERPLAY BETWEEN RELIGIOUS RITUAL AND VIOLENT "BUSINESS" AT DIFFERENT TIMES AND PLACES IN *THE GODFATHER*

Lead-in provides "hook" to capture reader's interest by presenting the film's daring concept.

The concept and result were daring: a motion picture three hours long with all the stops pulled out—expenses, cast selection, and locations. Francis Ford Coppola, director and co-screenwriter with Mario Puzo, author of the original book *The Godfather*, ultimately took Puzo's gangster novel and converted it into a sweeping epic of twentieth century America. It fused such interrelated motifs as crime, family, business, wealth, and power, weaving them into a rich cinematic tapestry against which to document the rise and fall of one fictitious Italian-American extended family.

Great success of movie mentioned to spur the reader's interest in the film

The end result is a classic: one of the great achievements in American film. It drew huge audiences, yet also commanded great critical acclaim, including numerous Academy Awards— foremost being the Oscar for Best Picture of 1972.

Introduces one element of the thesis.

Although *The Godfather* may be the apotheosis of the gangster film, it not only raises the standard of the genre but transcends it, thus

[Student's Last Name] 4

helping define the American experience. Its theme
links crime with business, drawing parallels
between them. American organized crime and
American free enterprise mirror each other. Leslie
Taubman perceives *The Godfather* as

> A quintessential gangster film that elevates the
> longstanding popular genre to the highest levels of
> art. [It] portrays a mafia organization [as] a
> malevolent extension of the ethics of capitalism and
> free enterprise. Its Sicilian-American "family"
> serves as a metaphor for corrupt big business and
> government. (638)

Extended quote
by film critic
Leslie Taubman.

    Yet Vincent Canby sees it "[depicting] a
sorrowful American dream as a slambang, sentimental
gangster melodrama (11). In a later piece, he likens
the Corleones to the "'robber barons' of many leading
nineteenth century American industries" (56).

Quote/
paraphrase
N.Y. Times critic
Vincent Canby.

    To Gerald Mast and Bruce Kawin, it is "a
monumental American epic about the conflict
between doing business and living [by] meaningful
values—a conflict built into the very familial and
economic structure of American society" (448).
Coppola believes American enterprises as having
"dark undersides": conflicts between conducting
profitable business with the values necessary to
do so. Rather than a deadly disease on the nation,
the Mafia should be considered as symptomatic of
the way America conducts its economic and
political affairs (448).

Quotes/
paraphrases by
Gerald Mast &
Bruce Kawin

Full thesis of research paper introduced.

The film achieves greatness not solely through thematic strength and accompanying political, historical, economic, sociological, and psychological musings. It also uses several cinematic devices to remarkable effect. These relate to the themes symbolically, while at the same time producing memorable cinematographic sequences and narrative episodes. In the film, the lives of the Corleones are marked by the interplay of religious rite and violent "business." In different times and places in the movie, religious rituals are often performed simultaneously to orgiastic gang violence as retribution, policy

Denotes objectives of paper.

statement, or grab for power. This paper further explores how the movie achieves these ends by discussing its effect narratively and pictorially as it connects its shocking themes and symbols.

Theme announced in the topic sentence and then developed by a narrative example from film. Paraphrase of Taubman's insight into Italian wedding customs.

Juxtaposition of the sacred with the profane commences at once. It is the summer of 1945. In his dark, sinister office, mob kingpin Vito Corleone (Marlon Brando), dressed in a tuxedo, holds court during his daughter's wedding at the family's Long Island estate. Customarily, the bride's father grants favors to those who ask in the midst of the reception (Taubman 639). First seen is the local undertaker Bonasera (Salvatore Corsitto), whose daughter has been raped and mutilated by two men. All attempts to get them arrested by the police and punished by the

[Student's Last Name] 6

judicial system have been fruitless. In desperation,
he beseeches Don Vito Corleone, the godfather, for
the justice that has been denied him.

The sequence is fascinating: despite the
emotional explosiveness of the issue, both
Bonasera and Corleone show verbal restraint as
they go through the ritualistic moves from
explication to supplication to admonition to
ultimate conciliation. Bonasera begins stating "I
believe in America . . ." and then recounts
details of his daughter's assault, disfigurement,
and failure of the American legal system. Don Vito
replies by chiding him for seeking the police
rather than trusting him in the first place.
Bonasera is further berated for never inviting the
don to his home nor "[wanting] my friendship and
to be in my debt. Now you come . . . the day my
daughter is to be married." The irony is strong: a
man asking aid for his daughter rendered
unmarriageable because of facial scars and
internal damage. The aggrieved father, now
penitent, swears friendship and fealty to the don.
Corleone agrees to help him if he would return a
favor, if asked sometime in the future. Bonasera
agrees, they embrace, and terrible justice is to
be meted out to the offenders.

Next, Vito's godson, Johnny Fontane (Al
Martino), a singer trying to break into the
movies, asks the don for help. Again, Don Vito

Lengthy paragraph peppered with snatches of dialogue from the film.

Short quotes/ paraphrases of Canby's views.

accedes. In this and other instances, Corleone employs intimidation, extortion, battery, and even murder to gain loyalty comparable to a feudal knight with his vassals. An "exotic code of honor [set] within a terrible system of rewards and punishment is delineated, provoking violent events in locales as diverse as New York, Hollywood, Las Vegas, and Sicily" (Canby, 12 Mar.1972, 11).

Warmer side of Don Vito Corleone exhibited.

Business completed, Vito leaves his den, emerging into sunlight to dance with his daughter at the lawn party in the spacious family compound in Long Beach, Long Island. The dour, powerful don momentarily becomes the smiling, cavorting clan patriarch, proud of his family.

Lighting used not only to enhance the mood but to furnish symbolic and thematic overtones.

Cinematographer Gordon Willis, in shooting both major scenes of the wedding, uses variation of light and darkness effectively. The irregularly shaped office with its patterned shadows, contrasts with the bright sunlight and dazzling hues of the merry-making outside. The effect, both

Quote by Taubman.

visually and thematically, "reflects the nature of the family and of the man who is warm and generous and is also a murderer" (Taubman 642).

Despite ongoing nuptial festivities, seeds of central conflict of film sown that will grow as movie progresses.

As Mama Corleone (Morgana King) entertains, singing Italian folk songs, Solazzo (Al Lettieri), a high ranking mobster from another crime family suggests that Vito join him in introducing drugs to the business of the five crime families. Corleone refuses—not from any moral scruples—but

[Student's Last Name] 8

because it would threaten his friendly ties with politicians and judges. They could discount gambling pursuits but could not ignore his ventures into the narcotics trade.

Not taking kindly to the rebuff—despite its courteous delivery—Solazzo, soon tries to kill Corleone. Nearly succeeding, his men seriously wound the don. His son Sonny (James Caan) takes over the family and a full-blown gang war results. Sonny is ambushed and murdered at a highway toll booth while enroute to avenge pregnant sister Connie (Talia Shire), who has again been brutally beaten by her husband Carlo (Gianni Russo).

It is now up to Michael (Al Pacino), the Dartmouth-educated and decorated war hero, to assume the mantle of family leadership and run the "business." Kept totally away from criminal activities by his father who had hoped he would someday become a United States senator—it is now up to the youngest son to gain vengeance. He arranges to meet with Solazzo and the corrupt police captain McCluskey (Sterling Hayden) at a small Italian restaurant in the Bronx to talk peace. Instead, using a pistol concealed in the men's room, Michael shoots them point blank, then makes a quick pre-arranged escape to Sicily where he goes into hiding. Meanwhile, the gang war continues back home. Protected by Don Tomassino (Corrado Gaipa), long a friend of Vito, Michael is

Major change of setting from New York to Sicily serves to amplify the thesis.

[Student's Last Name] 9

assigned two bodyguards, who stay with him at all times.

One day, during his customary trek through the countryside, he comes upon a beautiful young woman. Hit at once by the "thunderbolt," all thoughts of Kay Adams (Diane Keaton), his betrothed back home, evaporate as love-smitten Michael soon declares his serious intentions to the girl's father.

Their courtship is very traditional. Everywhere he and Apollonia (Simonetta Stefanelli) go, a horde of her female chaperones and his bodyguard duo follow. After the wedding ceremony, the entourage leaves the church. A procession with a brass band follows the connubial pair, walking through the town's narrow, winding streets to the square where the reception is held. The newlyweds dance to the band's music and offer sweets to those special guests attending.

Life is idyllic for a while. Michael teaches his wife English and how to drive an automobile. Then she is killed by a car bomb—intended for him— when sitting behind the wheel alone about to demonstrate her skill. Michael quickly returns to America, realizing that life is even more

The pattern of sacred and pro-fane continues.

dangerous in Sicily than in the United States. Again we have the juxtaposition of the sacred, a

[Student's Last Name] 10

marriage, intermingled with the profane, a Mafia
feud killing.

Michael becomes the new godfather. Soon after
his return, he resumes the relationship with Kay,
eventually marrying her. The film's climax takes
place in 1955 at a Manhattan cathedral for the
third instance of commingling a religious rite
with mob-related atrocities. Michael and Kay are
at the christening of Connie and Carlo's baby as
godparents. In a series of intercuts we go from
the golden light-suffused ceremony with its organ
music and priest's liturgical drone to several
brutal slayings and back again.

To Joseph M. Boggs, the sequence's irony
builds with each cut, reaching its zenith when
Michael affirms his belief in God, pledging to
"renounce Satan" while a spate of killings he has
ordered occur simultaneously. At ceremony's end,
he makes his final and most cynical decision: to
have the infant's father, his brother-in-law
Carlo—whom he holds responsible for Sonny's death—
killed. His power as both head of his immediate
family and the extended crime family is
underscored. It comes as no surprise that when Kay
later asks if he were responsible for Carlo's
murder, he tells her not to ask about the family's
business, then lies convincingly, "No."

Criticism by
Joseph M. Boggs
highlights terrible
irony of baptism
ritual juxtaposed
with series of
killings occurring
simultaneously

Paraphrase
of Boggs'
statement.

Michael has
become a con-
summate liar.

WORKS CITED

Primary Sources

The Godfather. Dir. Francis Ford Coppola. Perf.
Marlon Brando, James Caan, Robert Duvall, Al
Pacino. Paramount Pictures, 1972. Film.

Secondary Sources

Boggs, Joseph M. *The Art of Watching Films.* 4th
ed. Mountain View, CA: Mayfield, 1996. Print.

Canby Vincent. "The Godfather." Rev, of *The
Godfather* by Francis Ford Coppola. *The New
York Times* 12 Mar. 1972, II, 1. Rpt. *The New
York Times Film Reviews* (1971-1972). 233-34.
Print.

——. "The Godfather." Rev. of The Godfather
by Francis Ford Coppola. *The New York Times*
16 Mar. 1972, 56. Rpt. *The New York Times Film
Reviews* (1971-1972). 235. Print.

Mast, Gerald and Bruce F. Kawin *A Short History of
the Movies.* 5th ed. New York: Macmillan, 1992.
Print.

Taubman, Leslie. "The Godfather." *Magill's Survey
of Cinema: English Language Films Series.* Ed.
Frank N. Magill. 1, Vol. 2, EAS-LON. Englewood
Cliffs, NJ: Salem Press, 1980. 638-43. Print.

A second type of research paper is the documented comparative research paper which we will now discuss. It is presented and developed in a similar fashion as the analytical research paper just read. The comparative research paper that follows centers around a formula that the writer alleges the great director Alfred Hitchcock may have used in casting some of his most popular and critically acclaimed suspense thrillers during the mid-1950s through the early 1960s. Interspersed throughout are quotes, paraphrases, and summaries of secondary sources used to support the contentions of the author or add material relevant to the essay.

The writer, a long-time fan of Hitchcock, noticed that a number of "The Master of Suspense's" films—although they had different plots premises, locations, and actors—seemed to have a similar look. Upon further analysis, it was noticed that in almost all of them, the male lead was tall, slender, and had dark hair. The female lead, on the other hand, was a "cool" blond, beautiful and brainy. This casting formula was especially apparent in three of Hitchcock's most successful films: *Rear Window* (1954), *North by Northwest* (1959), and *The Birds* (1963).

What comes next follows the familiar pattern that you saw in the analytical research paper: Title page, research papers itself with in-text citations, and the works cited page. Note that topic outline is a separate document which is not included *inside* the research paper but is submitted here before it.

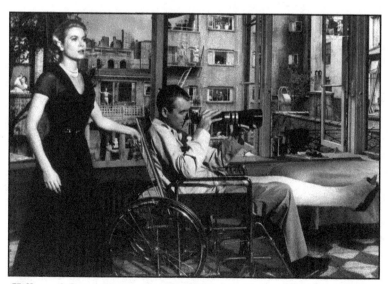

Grace Kelly and James Stewart in Alfred Hitchcock's Rear Window *(1954). Paramount.* Courtesy of Everett Collection.

The development of the comparative research paper is not too different from what has been shown for the analytical research paper. Since you are comparing and/or contrasting two or more things—different films, different actors, different directors, or different period accomplishments in a person's career—the structure would resemble the comparative essay. You choose the format, full block style or point-by-point, and stick to it. The rationale behind the use of secondary sources, to "support and supplement" is the same.

TOPIC OUTLINE

<u>Complete Thesis Statement</u>: Director Alfred Hitchcock's formula for casting male/female lead prototypes, having a series of interior and exterior crises, thus changing their relationship. This can be seen in *Rear Window*, *North by Northwest* and *The Birds*.

   I. *Rear Window*

      A. Casting prototypes and personalities

         1. Male lead (Jeff Jeffries) tall, dark, handsome

            a. Professional photographer in his 40s

            b. Has broken leg; this inactivity leads to voyeuristic behavior

            c. His forced isolation in his two-room studio apartment makes him irritable

            d. Standoffish to girlfriend

         2. Female lead (Lisa Fremont)—beautiful, blond, brainy

            a. Fashion consultant in her 20s

            b. Very stylish

            c. Has a sense for adventure, even danger

            d. Wants a closer, more committed relationship

      B. Interior crisis

         1. Forced inactivity because of broken leg

         2. He looks at people in the other apartments through their picture rear windows to break his boredom

3. From viewing with naked eye, switches to binoculars

4. Becomes obsessed with other people's lives when he views them through telephoto lens

5. More interested in his neighbors' lives than in his own

6. Feels very isolated

C. Exterior crisis

   1. Notices strange couple, the Thorwalds

      a. Thorwald constantly arguing with bed-ridden wife

      b. Thorwald's invalid wife suddenly missing

   2. Jeff suspects foul play

      a. Jeff tells Lisa and his friend, a police detective

      b. He also mentions suspicions to nurse, Stella

   3. He has Lisa act as his surrogate

      a. Lisa breaks into Thorwald's place

      b. Thorwald returns

   4. He suspects Jeff is his antagonist

      a. He breaks into Jeff's apartment

      b. They struggle

D. Ultimate change/move towards intimacy

   1. Jeff's other leg broken fighting for his life

   2. Through Lisa's efforts police arrive and capture Thorwald before he can kill Jeff

3. Jeff realizes his need and love for her

4. They become intimate and committed to each other

II. *North by Northwest*

    A. Casting prototypes and personality

        1. Male lead (Roger O. Thornhill)—tall, dark, handsome

           a. Twice-divorced advertising executive in his 50s

           b. Devoted to his scatterbrained mother

        2. Female lead (Eve Kendall)—beautiful, blond, brainy

           a. Undercover federal agent in her 30s

           b. Posing as mistress to Vandamm, a foreign agent

    B. Exterior crisis

        1. Mistaken identity leads to kidnapping Roger from business luncheon at a downtown hotel

           a. He is mistaken for a "George Kaplan" we later learn doesn't really exist

           b. He is brought to a Long Island estate and meets the owner an alleged U.N. diplomat Vandamm who is really a spy

           c. The foreign agents forcibly get him drunk, place him in a car with the motor running, and put it in gear down a winding cliffside road

    d. In the town of Glen Cove, Roger crashes into a parked car, is unharmed, and then arrested for drunken driving

2. Free on bail, he goes to U.N. to talk to the real diplomat who upon meeting Roger, is killed

    a. Roger pulls out the knife and is blamed for the murder

    b. Is on the lam and goes to Grand Central Station to head to Chicago and find George Kaplan

    c. Meets the beautiful and mysterious Eve Kendall who hides him from detectives looking for him

3. It's arranged: Roger is finally to meet Kaplan at a rural crossroads

    a. No one is there waiting for him

    b. He sees a crop duster; the pilot sees him

    c. The plane flies very low, heads for Roger, and besides dousing him with a cloud of pesticide also shoots a hail of machine gun bullets at him

    d. Plane attacks him again, Roger runs into the road

    e. Is hit by a truck, but unhurt, plane crashes into it

4. Back in Chicago he goes to auction and sees Kendall and Vandamm and smells a rat

   a. Roger causes a ruckus and is arrested by the police before Vandamm's men can get him

   b. He is brought to the Professor who runs the special federal agency and reveals that Eve is a double agent and that Roger has put her in grave danger

   c. Roger agrees to follow her to Vandamm's hideout in Rapid City, SD near Mt. Rushmore

5. Confronts Eve at park restaurant; she "shoots" him

   a. Leaves hospital and gets to Vandamm's compound

   b. Signals Eve

   c. Helicopter arrives; Eve escapes with Roger

   d. Followed by Vandamm's men

   e. Climb down faces of Mt. Rushmore

C. Interior crisis

   1. First has to do with Roger's mistaken identity

   2. Meeting Eve and quick attraction

      a. She saves him from police searching for him

      b. We assume their intimacy that night on the train

3. Meet in Chicago hotel; he has feelings for her

4. Sees her with Vandamm and henchmen at auction

   a. Roger feels betrayed

   b. Acts obnoxiously to humiliate her, get arrested

   c. From the Professor finds out Eve's true situation; feels guilty, and love is rekindled

5. Roger arrives in Rapid City, SD to try to save Eve

   a. As prearranged, she "shoots" him at restaurant

   b. At compound, he signals his presence

   c. They escape and are attacked while climbing down giant presidential faces of Mt. Rushmore

   d. Cut to Roger pulling Eve up to their train car's berth on their honeymoon

D. Ultimate change/move towards intimacy

   1. Physical and emotional attraction between Roger and Eve

   2. It deepens in Chicago; then Roger feels betrayed

   3. Learns real story behind Eve's involvement with him and he feels bound to try and save her

   4. Follows the Professor's elaborate scheme in SD

5. He saves her at Mt. Rushmore and quick cut
   to their honeymoon train ride back east to
   NYC

III. *The Birds*

A. Casting prototypes and personality

   1. Male lead—tall, dark, handsome

      a. Attorney with practice in San Francisco

      b. In his 30s and lives with his widowed
         mother Lydia and 11-year-old sister
         Cathy in Bodega Bay weekends

   2. Female lead—beautiful, blond, brainy

      a. Rich socialite, playgirl

      b. In her early 30s

      c. Likes to play practical jokes

B. Exterior crisis

   1. Lovebirds seems innocent but are
      bellwethers of suspense throughout film

      a. As Melanie rows from Mitch's house, she
         is suddenly attacked by a seagull

      b. Mitch makes sure she gets first aid;
         ultimately she stays for the weekend at
         Annie Hayworth's house

      c. Her attack dismissed as an aberration

2. Visit to poultry farmer's house by Lydia
   a. House in disarray, notices broken china, teacups, dead birds
   b. Farmer dead, eyes plucked out
   c. She drives home in terror
3. Attack on children at party and schoolhouse
   a. During birthday party attack on children
   b. Melanie goes to schoolhouse next day to escort Cathy home
   c. Birds start massing in playground behind her
   d. She notices and warns Annie
   e. They escort children down road to their homes
   f. Birds attack
4. In town tension about strange behavior of birds
   a. Pooh-poohed by ornithologist, Doomsayer puts in his two cents, people blame Melanie
   b. Birds mass and attack service station attendant pumping gas, explosion with fireball
   c. Melanie stuck in phone booth attacked by birds

    5. Assault on the Brenner's home

      a. Birds lay siege to house

      b. Melanie almost succumbs to bird attack
        upstairs

      c. They leave via garage, escaping in
        Mitch's car

  C. Interior crisis

    1. Mitch is surrounded by women: widowed
      mother, kid sister and ex-girlfriend Annie
      Hayworth, a grade school teacher

    2. Initial cold reception to Melanie from
      mother, warm reception from sister,
      grudging friendship from Annie

    3. Will Lydia sabotage Mitch and Melanie the
      way she did Mitch and Annie?

    4. As they abandon Bodega Bay homestead, Lydia
      has finally accepted Melanie. Will they all
      survive the next attack of the birds?

  D. Ultimate change/move towards intimacy

    1. Mitch and Melanie love each other

    2. Her trials and tribulations have matured
      her

    3. Lydia grudgingly accepts Melanie into the
      fold

    4. Cathy considers Melanie her big sister

ALFRED HITCHCOCK'S FORMULA FOR CASTING

MALE/FEMALE LEAD PROTOTYPES, HAVING A SERIES OF

INTERIOR AND EXTERIOR CRISES, THUS CHANGING THEIR

RELATIONSHIP IN *REAR WINDOW*, *NORTH BY NORTHWEST*,

AND *THE BIRDS*

[STUDENT'S NAME]

ENG 2101 - FILM AS LITERATURE

[PROFESSOR'S NAME]

[DATE]

[Student's Full Name]

[Professor's Name]

ENG 2101 – Film as Literature

[Date]

ALFRED HITCHCOCK'S FORMULA FOR CASTING
MALE/FEMALE PROTOTYPES, HAVING A SERIES OF
INTERIOR AND EXTERIOR CRISES THUS CHANGING
THEIR RELATIONSHIP IN *REAR WINDOW*, *NORTH BY
NORTHWEST* AND *THE BIRDS*

> Casting proto-
> types & charac-
> ter development
> in Hitchcock's
> *Rear Window*,
> *North by North-
> west* and *The
> Birds*

Introduction

Alfred Hitchcock was one of the most successful
directors and producers whose career began in the
1920s and continued through the 1970s, first
making movies in England and then the United
States. When Francois Truffaut and other French
New Wave directors and thinkers coined the term
"auteur," they surely had Hitchcock in mind. For
an auteur is multi-faceted and can be omnipotent
as was Hitchcock ultimately.

> Long career
> as director/
> producer,
> admired "auteur"
> in London and
> then Hollywood

In contrast, the "hired gun" director is at
the beck and call of a studio and a project's
bullying producer. His or her role is solely to
direct the film. Such a director can be harassed
by temperamental actors and their interpretations
of a role, by film editors who can snip precious
footage from a reel of celluloid to save a few

> Common direc-
> tors hired for
> particular Proj-
> ect; answerable
> to many others

minutes of running time, and by that ogre, the
producer whose vision of the film driven by the
profit motive overrides the director's concept of
his/her creation.

Auteur not only
multi-talented
but has authority
to decide what
goes into film

The auteur, on the other hand, not only
directs but often is the scenarist or producer or
editor; but even more important than his or her
cinematic abilities, the auteur has the authority
and influence to make the original concept a
reality. This is what Alfred Hitchcock was able to
do for most of his oeuvre. As a result, he
presented to the public such blockbusters as *Dial
M for Murder* (1954), *Rear Window* (1954), *The Man
Who Knew Too Much* (1956), *Vertigo* (1958), *North by
Northwest* (1959), *Psycho* (1960), and *The Birds*
(1963)—all regarded as American classics. Best
known for combining suspense with mysteries and
thrillers, his films of the 1950s and 1960s,
especially, were also known for their instances of
wry humor and visual innovation.

What this comparative research paper will
examine are three Hitchcock suspense thrillers
made during what many consider his Golden Age of
American moviemaking, the ten years from 1954
until 1963. The films selected were released
roughly five years apart—1954, 1959, and 1963. We
will look at *Rear Window* first, then *North by
Northwest* and finally, *The Birds*. In these three
motion pictures, Hitchcock has developed with

[Student's Last Name] 3

varying intricacy a formula most successfully incorporated for casting his acting principals which included physical qualities and personalities. He then involves the two leads in a dangerous external crisis. In addition, the couple have tensions within their relationship which make for an internal crisis. Finally, they undergo a deep change and move closer towards intimacy with each other. With *Rear Window*, the internal crisis is broached first, while in *North by Northwest* and *The Birds*, the external predicaments precede the internal problems.

Hitchcock's casting formula lending character development with external & internal crises and ultimate change in relationship between leading man & lady

Rear Window

As *Rear Window* unfolds, we find L. B. "Jeff" Jeffries, a celebrated photo-journalist, highly frustrated because of his confinement to a wheelchair after suffering a broken leg on his last assignment. To cope with his building frustration with his immobility, he looks out his rear picture window to the courtyard below and then beyond to the line of apartments across it. He soon goes from being mildly interested in the folks living their compartmentalized lives to becoming obsessed with what happens to them and motivates their actions.

Rear Window: Physical & personality qualities of James Stewart. James Berardinelli: "one of his strongest roles"

Jeffries is played by James Stewart who normally would fit the "tall, dark, and handsome"

stereotype often used by Hitchcock in casting his
leading men. But in *Rear Window* he is cast against
type for this role. Critic James Berardinelli
believes this to be one of Stewart's strongest
roles because of the "limitations" imposed by the
part on an actor who cannot utilize many of the
tools of his craft (4). He elaborates by pointing
out

> More than in any of his other films, he must act
> with his eyes, face, and voice. And Jeffries is not
> one of the morally upright, mild-mannered
> protagonists that Stewart became identified with.
> Instead, Jeffries is worldly, impatient, bad-
> tempered, and prone to bursts of anger. (4)

Roger Ebert in
quotes/
paraphrases.
Considers him
"bland,"
"wickedly nosy,"
and "amoral."

Roger Ebert also comments on Stewart's
performance, considering him perfect for the role
because he seems so "normal," but is really
"opaque" and a "total enigma, beneath his Norman
Rockwell exterior. He's so bland, so matter-of-fact
and so wickedly nosy that we're implicated in his
scheme almost without realizing it" (7 Oct. 1983).
Thus, Jeffries is in no way a "typical" hero. In
fact, Roger Ebert considers him "amoral" trampling
on "other people's privacy" (7 Oct. 1983).

Sure we sympathize with his physically
inactive plight, and, at first, see no harm in his
looking out the picture window. But eventually,
his innate voyeuristic and professional tendencies

take over. For doesn't his life normally consist
of capturing moments—often tragic, gruesome, and
private—in other people's lives through the candid
shots of his camera? So from bemusedly looking at
his neighbors through their rear windows with his
naked eyes, he eventually moves to using
binoculars for greater detail to the even more
sinister telephoto camera lens as their lives
totally engross him. And, by the way, he is not
alone in this somewhat sordid activity: we, the
audience, join with him every step of the way.

Jeff's growing
voyeurism
because of
disability.

And what about his lovely, female counterpart,
Lisa Fremont, played by Grace Kelly? She is his
complete opposite. Her professional world is very
public, open, even exhibitionistic as a model. She
constantly deals with people. She follows the
Hitchcockian casting credo of the beautiful,
blond, and brainy heroine, but with additional
qualities that make her more rounded and
individualistic. In her 20s, (as opposed to Jeff's
middle-aged 40s), Lisa is beautiful, accomplished,
and seems to have the world at her feet, but she
wants Jeff and can't really have him. Roger Ebert
brings to light some other insights about their
troubled relationship. She see the problem as his
inability to commit himself and seems more
concerned with the lives of strangers than his own
life and those who are an intimate part of it

(20 Feb. 2000). An excuse he gives is a clash of lifestyles and comfort: she might be used to a runway photo shoot, but dodging bullets in a civil war in some tropical land? He fears a loss of independence but also has great insecurity in measuring up to and keeping up with such a beauty. Along these lines, Ebert sees as Jeff's real reason for keeping her at a distance "is fear of impotence, symbolized by the leg cast" ("Rear Window [1954]").

Plot's second stage: "recreational voyeurism" to suspecting Lars Thorwald of murder

However, when the story reaches the second stage, and Jeff goes from recreational voyeurism to active suspicion of murder having taken place at the Thorwalds' apartment, Lisa is cast in new light as a confidante. And then, with the third stage, she becomes an active collaborator to gather evidence of the crime. Now we can perceive other aspects of her character; she is plucky, resourceful, and courageous. If Jeff is the brain and eyes of the evidence-gathering operation, she is his hands and legs.

Sympathize with Jeff when he sees Lisa in danger and he is powerless to help her.

Perhaps we are most sympathetic with Jeff and his condition at this point in the film. For when he observes Lisa snooping in Thorwald's apartment through one window there and then through another and then sees the killer's entrance into his own domicile, we can relate to the misery of Jefferies' total helplessness in warning and protecting Lisa.

By film's end Jeff & Lisa's relationship strengthened by shared danger.

By the end of the film, a profound change has come in the relationship between Jeff and Lisa.

[Student's Last Name] 7

But they don't discuss it verbally; neither does a
narrator's voice-over nor a screen crawl provide
any expository information. Rather, Hitchcock does
what he has done throughout the film, he provides
visual clues as statements. According to Janey
Place, Lisa wearing blue jeans is quite
significant since they would be more compatible
with his lifestyle. Place goes on to say

> [T]he panning shot from Jeff to Lisa joins them, and
> its manner of discovering first her feet, then her
> leg, and finally her entire body, places her firmly
> in Jeff's apartment. As for her commitment, it would
> seem that the compromise by the blue jeans is a
> necessary movement for her as well. Her life is so
> formally arranged in the beginning of the film that it
> leaves no room for surprise or romance . . . she must
> [leave] her own social isolation through danger to
> reach him . . . Jeff and Lisa each must change . . .
> to come together . . .[I]t is significant that Jeff's
> back is to the window in the last scene as it is that
> Lisa is wearing blue jeans. (1986)

*Janey Place
quote says
this is done
solely through
camerawork and
blocking.*

North by Northwest

We are immediately introduced to urbane, twice-
divorced Roger O. Thornhill (Cary Grant), an
advertising executive, furiously dictating a memo
and barking other orders to his secretary in the
back of a taxicab en route to a business luncheon.

*North by North-
west meet Roger
Thornhill, a twice
divorced adver-
tising executive.*

[Student's Last Name] 8

It is during this mixing of business with dining, that his world is turned upside down.

He is kidnapped from hotel lobby being mistaken for someone else.

In a clear case of mistaken identity, some foreign agents suddenly kidnap Thornhill. They believe he is one "George Kaplan" whom they had paged when, coincidentally, Thornhill left his dining table momentarily. Escorted by two armed thugs, he is hustled into a car that heads for a coastal estate on Long Island.

There, he is questioned by Vandamm (James Mason) and his henchmen. They decide to kill Thornhill but make his death seem accidental. They forcibly get him staggeringly intoxicated, put him behind the wheel of a car with its engine running, and immobilize the brakes. Finally, the car is put in drive, while locking down the accelerator on a steep cliffside road that borders the ocean. Somehow, without injury, he makes it into the town of Glen Cove, where he crashes into a parked vehicle with great damage to his auto and none to himself. He is promptly arrested for drunken driving. The next morning, he is sober, bailed out of jail, and determined to clear his name.

Judith A. Williams identifies two familiar Hitchcock themes here: mistaken identity and normal guy placed in abnormal circumstances.

Before going further, professional critic Judith A. Williams notes that by now Hitchcock has identified two themes that recur in many of his films. One is the theme of mistaken identity and everything that it can entail including great danger. We see it here in *North by Northwest* and

[Student's Last Name] 9

to a lesser extent in *Rear Window.*(since it takes a while to be convinced of Thorwald's guilt). The second theme would be that of an ordinary person being placed in an extraordinary situation and having to deal with it or, possibly die. We see this in not only *North by Northwest* but also *Rear Window* and *The Birds* (1742).

Roger thinks the key is to find the man who owned the Glen Cove estate. The man he asks for is actually the real United Nations delegate and is suddenly murdered while being confronted by Thornhill. As Roger pulls the long deadly blade from the dead man's back, flashbulbs explode and he instantly becomes a man suspected of murder.

Roger, on the lam, wanted by both the police and Vandamm's killers, heads for Grand Central Station, intending to get a train bound for Chicago with hopes of finding George Kaplan. Seemingly by accident, he meets Eve Kendall (Eva Marie Saint) on the train to Chicago. She learns he is fleeing the police and hides him. During the long hours of the nighttime train ride romantic sparks fly and they are both affected. What poor Roger doesn't know is that she is a double agent who gives him information that he is to meet Kaplan at a rural crossroads, miles from the city. George Kaplan doesn't show up but what does appear is a crop duster. It suddenly veers around and then attacks Thornhill, spewing not only noxious

Roger in fleeing to Chicago meets Eve Kendall who helps him. He falls for her. Later, infamous crop duster murder attempt.

pesticide but even more lethal machine gun bullets
at him. He escapes only when the pilot, flying at
ground level, distracted momentarily by Roger's
sudden disappearance, crashes head on into an oil
tanker truck.

Quote by Williams about the "ideal situation for terror."

Judith A. Williams states

It is an ideal situation for terror, combining the
seemingly innocuous setting of open farmland in
broad daylight with the unexpected menace from which
the hero has no place to hide and no way to defend
himself. (1743)

He returns to Chicago and tries to track down
Eve, knowing that she had set him up for harm. He
is even more certain of this when he spies her at
an auction next to Vandamm and notices his
henchmen at the exits. Eve seems indeed "a blond

After auction confrontation between Roger, Eve, and Van-damm., Roger told by the Pro-fessor of Eve's real status as double Agent and that she's in great danger.

Mata Hari" (Weiler 28:1). He disrupts the auction,
hoping to be arrested by the police who once again
can save him from Vandamm and company. He is
successful but this time he is not taken to a
police station but to The Professor (Leo G.
Carroll) who runs the federal agents who are
trying to trap Vandamm and company. He informs
Thornhill that by his rash actions at the auction
he has put Eve's life in peril and is needed to
rescue her. Roger agrees to help save her life.
Soon he is off to Rapid City, South Dakota and
Mount Rushmore National Monument to set Eve free.

[Student's Last Name] 11

Still pretending to be Kaplan, he confronts her in
the dining room at the Mount Rushmore facilities
where she "shoots" him with blanks and then
escapes with Vandamm. Later Roger, unharmed,
leaves the hospital and makes it to the premises
of Vandamm's compound on Mount Rushmore. He
signals his presence, helps her escape from the
house, but they are being chased by Vandamm and
company. They climb across and down the faces of
the Presidents, harassed by the hostile espionage
agents. Roger grabs Eve's hand in an attempt to
save her from falling to her death. In a clever
move by Hitchcock, he cuts at that moment and we
transition to Roger pulling Eve up into their
pullman berth on a train heading for New York City
during their honeymoon (Williams 1744). In a book-
length interview on his theories and practices of
filmmaking, Hitchcock told the great French auteur
Francois Truffaut that

> . . . he is more in emotion and mood than in strict
> logic and plausibility. Also, one can see how
> carefully he withholds or dispenses information so
> that the audience will be caught up in surprises
> rather than in evaluating the believability of each
> action or event. (Williams 1744)

Quote by
Williams on how
Hitchcock
manipulates his
audience's
emotions.

Obviously, throughout the film, Roger Thornhill
undergoes a series of external events that are
highly traumatic and life-threatening. But he also

experiences a number of shocks to his psyche. From

being a fancy-free, doubly divorced man only

occasionally answerable to his mother to someone

whose identity is mistaken and, as a result, is

kidnapped. He then becomes the victim of an

attempted murder who ends up being arrested for

drunken driving. Next, the erstwhile advertising

executive is unofficially accused by the police

and media for murder of a U.N. diplomat and

becomes a fugitive bound for Chicago. He meets a

mysterious woman who aids and abets his escape and

much more (although unseen on the screen). He

emerges from the train finding himself smitten and

hours thereafter almost loses his life again and

is embittered believing he has been set up by the

woman. He returns to Chicago, seeking redress and

sees her with his arch enemy and berates her

morals publicly. When arrested now, he finds out

that she is worthy of his love since she is a

double agent whose ultimate loyalties are with the

U.S.A. He goes through an elaborate charade where

his shooting is faked, "escapes" from the

hospital, and is driven to Vandamm's Mount

Rushmore estate to save Eve. In doing so, they

both almost get killed. And then the next thing he

and we know is that he is pulling her up to lie

down with him on a train heading for New York

during their honeymoon. Quite a roller coaster of

emotions!

Comments on number of traumatic events that Roger experiences.

[Student's Last Name] 13

From being free and easy to becoming smitten then believing himself betrayed, Roger finally learns the truth. Both love and guilt deepen and he gets the will and courage to defy all danger and save her life. Then from them both almost losing everything, including their lives, to getting it all as newlyweds—Quite a roller coaster, indeed!

Comments on the emotional changes that he undergoes.

The Birds

We are in downtown San Francisco and a stylish woman in her early 30s walks into a large, well-appointed pet shop, looking for a mynah bird. She gets into a little mistaken identity tiff with a very attractive man of about the same age after he assumes she is a salesclerk and she plays along. He is actually a successful attorney and she, Melanie Daniels (Tippi Hedren), is the daughter of a wealthy newspaperman and socialite. There are definite sparks between the two and not just of anger or embarrassment. She finds out that he is Mitch Brenner (Rod Taylor) and she plans a practical joke to play on him.

The Birds: Mitch Brenner an attorney meets Melanie Daniels a socialite, in a pet store. Plot begins with practical joke, taking her from San Francisco north to Bodega Bay.

When Melanie finds out that he often spends weekends north of the city in Bodega Bay, she purchases a pair of lovebirds in a beautiful birdcage and jumps in her sports car with her surprise gift heading for the seaside fishing village and wearing her signature mink coat. She gets to Bodega Bay, inquires at a store for his address and how to get there, and then rents an outboard boat to do so. His family's home is visible directly across the bay. When she arrives, Melanie stealthily drops off the lovebirds and a birthday card for Mitch's young sister, Cathy (Veronica Cartwright). Then she jumps into her boat and races back to town. Mitch sees her and hops into his car and heads there overland to intercept her. This race is abruptly ended, when a seagull randomly swoops down and attacks Melanie's head. She receives a gash and is bleeding.

In outboard boat, Melanie is suddenly attacked by seagull; precursor of impending trouble.

Mitch is waiting at the dock and brings her to a nearby restaurant for an antiseptic and bandages. He invites her for dinner and she spends the night at Annie Hayworth's (Suzanne Pleshette), Cathy's teacher and Mitch's ex-girlfriend. A fast but uneasy friendship forms between the two women.

The seagull attack on Melanie, although random, is a precursor of avian violence to come. Lydia Brenner, Mitch's mother (Jessica Tandy), is uneasy about the behavior of her hens and drives off to a nearby poultry farm where she had bought them to inquire. When she gets there, she notices with growing concern that the interior is in shambles. When she discovers the badly mutilated body of the farmer with his eyes plucked out, she flees in horror to her home.

Lydia, Mitch's mother, visits nearby poultry farm, discovers owner's house ransacked and his mutilated body.

[Student's Last Name] 15

Three separate series of massive bird attacks that occur are memorable but in different ways. The first is the assault on the children as they leave the school. The second is the onslaught against the restaurant-gas station. The third are the waves of feathered fury in the siege of the Brenner homestead. Each is cleverly prepared by Hitchcock and then masterfully presented.

Three massive bird attacks are introduced: subsequent paragraphs develop and explain.

Melanie goes to the schoolhouse to pick up fifth grader Cathy and take her home. She sits outside placidly smoking and serenaded by the children singing inside. Behind her are monkey bars. A bird lands and perches on the bars. Then another and another. In a sequence of shots, we see the buildup of the winged phalanx. At first, it seems innocent and natural, but quickly becomes ominous. Finally, Melanie turns around, sees the menacing mass, and enters the school. She warns Annie of the danger outside and they decide hastily on a plan of action. Escort the children quickly but quietly on the road to their homes below. The plan seems to work for a while until the children are halfway downhill, then the birds attack en masse mercilessly. As critic DeWitt Bodeen observes, "[The birds] gather and wait like a satanic army and then swoop in to destroy and kill" (249).

Attack on children as they leave their school. Quote by Bodeen DeWitt.

The genius of this sequence is the mise en scene at the outset to build suspense. Melanie is

quietly smoking unsuspecting in the foreground,
while the birds singly and then in pairs mass
behind her in the playground in clear view.

The second scene takes place initially inside
in the restaurant and then segues outside to the
gas pumps. The bird attacks are heatedly
discussed. An ornithologist discounts them since
they are inconsistent with normal cross species
behavior of birds which can't and thus don't act
in concert to besiege people or engage in another
coordinated activity with flocks of different
species. Then there is a patron who makes
Apocalyptic "doom and gloom-the end is coming"
claims. Finally, some patrons blame it all on
Melanie, the nefarious "Outsider."

Attack on gas attendant and patrons of restaurant as they flee conflagration.

A traveler leaves to go outside and fill his
car's tank with gas. A service attendant does the
actual act. A bird besets him and the young man
drops the fuel hose while the highly flammable
liquid keeps flowing. The traveler, with back
turned and oblivious to the activity taking place
behind him, lights a cigarette, and throws the
match to the ground. It ignites the gasoline,
there is a massive explosion, and the block is on
fire. Ingeniously, a series of long crane shots
from above depict the scene. A swarm of birds then
go after the panicking people escaping from the
restaurant. Melanie seeks refuge in a steel and
glass phone booth while the relentless creatures

fling their feathered bodies into her sanctuary to
do her harm. Mitch saves her and they flee to his
house.

Back at the Brenner residence, Mitch, mother
Lydia, sister Cathy, and Melanie soon are forced
to defend themselves against their antagonists.
Like miniature kamikaze planes, the birds fling
themselves at various parts of the building
without regard for themselves. They hurl
themselves at the doors, impale their torsos in
the midst of window frames, hurtle down the
chimney, and peck away fanatically at the oak
front door. Under Mitch's direction, the human
prey fight back by using heavy furniture to
bolster the doors, by locking the shutters and
battening down the windows by hammering thick
boards across them. The birds attack in waves and
when they do, are unflagging. The family is
barricaded in the living room; its members
uneasily fall asleep during a respite of the
onslaught.

Melanie wakes up and hears some strange noises
upstairs. For some inexplicable reason she decides
to investigate. There's a closed door that leads
to a gable. She opens it. Hundreds of birds are
there, perched or walking about. She backs up
cautiously, hoping to get to the door, then reach
safety downstairs. She doesn't make it and is
engulfed by the harpies. Luckily, she is dragged

Series of coordi-
nated attacks on
Brenner home.

[Student's Last Name] 18

away from further harm by Mitch and the others,
but is injured and in a state of shock. The house
is quiet again. Hundreds of birds are surrounding
the domicile on the ground, in the trees, on the
roof: all waiting.

Escape from the Brenner homestead; they head for San Francisco. Emotional & personality conflicts in the film especially how burgeoning Mitch-Melanie relationship is viewed by Lydia, Annie, and Cathy, Mitch's young sister.

The film ends with Mitch, Melanie (still in a
dazed state), Lydia, and Cathy, quietly entering
the garage and into Mitch's car, the cage of
lovebirds in tow. The car's engine purring softly,
they slowly make it out of the garage and picking
up speed, leave their property, heading south
towards San Francisco and safety. Perhaps. Bodega
Bay—nearly entirely abandoned—has been left to the
birds (Bodeen 251).

There are some internal conflicts that are an
essential element to this film. In fact, some
believe the importance of these supersedes the
mayhem caused by the berserk birds. It is the
conflict caused by a domineering, possessive
mother against the women who would take her son

Bosley Crowther sees symbolic connection between jealousy and possessiveness and attack by the birds.

away from her—first Annie, and now Melanie. Bosley
Crowther isn't sure whether Hitchcock meant for
the birds to "represent the classical Furies . . .
[pursuing] the wicked on this earth" (5:5). But
then he second guesses himself, saying that
Hitchcock rarely would "inject allegorical meaning
or social significance in his films" (5.5). What
Crowther does see is a connection between the

[Student's Last Name] 19

jealousy of a possessive mother who "hovers
anxiously over her son" like a nesting robin.
He continues on this talk by asserting

> There is also this further indication: a young woman
> who is made out to be the vaguely resentful ex-
> sweetheart of the son is killed by the birds in one
> of their onsets before they zero in on the mother's
> house. Evidently, this young woman has been ridden
> with jealousy, too. (5:5)

The movie ends ambiguously with a multiplicity
of questions left unanswered. We know other towns
in the area of Bodega Bay have also been barraged.
How extensively? What is the government doing
about it? Is San Francisco and other large urban
areas in danger? What caused the avian

Movie ends ambiguously. Series of questions about cause of attacks and consequences for principal characters.

aberrations? And finally, in terms of the
characters in this piece, do we know if they ever
get to Mitch's city apartment safely? Regarding
the love triangle (no longer quadrangle since
Annie is dead), we can assume that Melanie has
proven herself in courage and steadfastness and
will be accepted into the fold by a resigned
Lydia. Cathy has already adopted the former
debutante as her big sister. Mitch and Melanie's
love by now has been forged by sharing such danger
and privation. They are all changed—but will their
lives be better? Don't ask me. Ask the birds.

[Student's Last Name] 20

Concluding Remarks

Besides parallel characterization, all three films share thematic motifs of *isolation, alienation, and loss of control*

We've seen that three of Alfred Hitchcock's most popular and critically acclaimed films have qualities in common especially when it comes to characterization, the basic element shared by literature and film. But these motion pictures share other motifs and themes as well. All three movies have their protagonists contending with *isolation* by being cut off from the familiar in activity, environment, or people. In being thusly isolated, they share a sense of *alienation*—not only being alone and on their own but in a hostile environment (as in *North by Northwest*). Sometimes the familiar and the welcoming environment becomes hostile even dangerous, as in *Rear Window* and *The Birds*. A final motif that all three of these movies share is the protagonists' *loss of control* of particular events and their lives.

Themes of a) innocent man wrongly accused; b) ordinary person being put in an extraordinary situation and dealing with it; and c) someone being involved in a murder and the immediate emotions experienced. Janey Place comments on these issues.

Besides shared motifs, a few familiar themes used by Hitchcock in other earlier films make their appearance in the works of our study. The first theme we will consider is that of *the innocent man wrongly accused*. Clearly this is the focus of *North by Northwest*, but to a lesser degree we also see it in *Rear Window* because for a while everyone is skeptical about Thorwald killing his wife given Jeff's somewhat eccentric behavior lately. Another is the theme of an *"ordinary [person] thrust into extraordinary circumstances"*

[Student's Last Name] 21

(Williams 1742). This is experienced by Roger
Thornhill in *North by Northwest*, Jeff Jeffries in
Rear Window, and Melanie Daniels in *The Birds*.
James Berardinelli sees the similar theme of an
"*'everyman' being turned into a detective*" (rev.
of "North by Northwest") which can also be
discerned in *Rear Window*. Then there is the theme
someone *being suddenly involved in a murder and
dealing with the inherent emotions of it*. We find
this theme operating in *Rear Window*, and, of
course, in *North by Northwest*, but also in *The
Birds*, especially when Lydia Brenner discovers the
body of her neighbor, the poultry farmer, pecked
to death in the bedroom of his home. As critic
Janey Place points out in her piece on *Rear
Window*,

> The chaos and danger of the murder and its discovery
> is a device often used by Hitchcock to shake people
> out of their isolated, complacent lives and into
> contact with forces that are alive and volatile.
> (1986)

Finally, all three classics show protagonists
who, to varying degrees, *are initially hesitant of
making a commitment in a relationship; yet because
of their shared mortal danger ultimately move
towards a closer, even permanent status with each
other by films' end.*

All three films
deal with emo-
tional commit-
ment and how
danger can
change it and
bring couples
closer together

WORKS CITED

Berardinelli, James. Rev. of "Rear Window."
    Online. *Reelviews Movie Reviews.*

———. Rev. of "North by Northwest." Online.
    Reelviews Movie Reviews.

Bodeen, DeWitt. "The Birds." *Magill's Survey of
    Cinema—English Language Films.* Second Series.
    Vol. 1 A-CLU. Ed. Frank N. Magill. Englewood,
    NJ: Salem Press, 1981. 249-252. Print.

Crowther, Bosley. Rev. of "The Birds." [N.Y.
    Times] Print.

Ebert, Roger. Rev. of "Rear Window." Online.
    7 Oct. 1983.

———. Rev. of "Rear Window (1954)." Online. 20 Feb.
    2000.

Place, Janey. "Rear Window." *Magill's Survey of
    Cinema—English Language Films.* Second Series.
    Vol. 5 PUT-THE. Ed. Frank N. Magill.
    Englewood, NJ: Salem Press, 1981. 1983-1986.
    Print.

Weiler, A. H. Rev. of "North by Northwest." [N.Y.
    Times] Print.

Williams, Judith A. "North by Northwest." *Magill's
    Survey of Cinema—English Language Films.*
    Second Series. Vol. 4 LUS-PUR. Ed. Frank N.
    Magill. Englewood, NJ: Salem Press, 1981.
    1742-1744. Print.

Rod Taylor, Tippi Hedren, and Jessica Tandy in Alfred Hitchcock's The Birds
(1963). Universal Pictures. Courtesy of Everett Collection.

APPENDIX A

DOCUMENTATION OF PRIMARY AND SECONDARY SOURCES OF WORKS CITED

—— Chapter 1. Preparation for and the Process of Film Criticism ——

Primary: Film

The African Queen. Dir. John Huston. United Artists, 1951.
Double Indemnity. Dir. Billy Wilder. Paramount, 1944.
In the Heat of the Night. Dir. Norman Jewison. United Artists, 1967.
When Harry Met Sally. Dir. Rob Reiner. Columbia Pictures, 1989.

Secondary: Published Film Criticism

(None Used.)

——— Chapter 2. Style and Structure in Film Criticism ———

Primary: Film

The Age of Innocence. Dir. Martin Scorsese. Columbia Pictures, 1993.
  Film.
All the King's Men. Dir. Robert Rossen. Columbia Pictures, Film.
Amadeus. Dir. Milos Foreman. Orion Pictures, 1983. Film.
Avalon. Dir. Barry Levinson. TriStar Pictures/Baltimore Pictures, 1990.
  Film.
Bang the Drum Slowly. Dir. John Hancock. Paramount Pictures, 1974.
  Film.

Barbershop. Dir. Tim Story. MGM Home Entertainment, 2003. DVD.
Best in Show. Dir. Christopher Guest. Warner Brothers, 2000. Film.
Black Orpheus. Dir. Marcel Camus. Lopert Films, 1959. Film.
Body Heat. Dir. Lawrence Kasdan. Warner Brothers, 1992. Film.
Breathless. Dir. Jean-Luc Godard. Films Around the World, Inc. 1961.
   Film.
Cheyenne Autumn. Dir. John Ford. Warner Home Video, 2006. DVD.
Dances with Wolves. Dir. Kevin Costner. Orion Pictures, 1990. Film.
Diner. Dir. Barry Levinson. Metro-Goldwyn-Mayer/United Artists, 1982.
   Film.
Fort Apache. Dir. John Ford. RKO Radio Pictures, 1948. Film.
Glengarry Glen Ross. Dir. James Foley. New Line Cinema, 1992. Film.
Gone with the Wind. Dir. Victor Fleming. Metro-Goldwyn-Mayer, 1939.
   Film.
The Grapes of Wrath. Dir. John Ford. Twentieth Century-Fox, 1940.
   Film.
How Green Was My Valley. Dir. John Ford. Twentieth Century-Fox, 1941.
   Film.
The Informer. Dir. John Ford. Fox Hills Video, 1987. Videocassette.
The Man Who Shot Liberty Valance. Dir. John Ford. Paramount, 1962.
   Film.
Mean Streets. Dir. Martin Scorsese. Warner Brothers, 1973. Film.
Mother and Child. Dir. Rodrigo Garcia. Sony Pictures Classics, 2010.
   Film.
Oklahoma! Dir. Fred Zinnemann. RKO Radio Pictures, 1955. Film.
One Day. Dir. Lone Scherfig. Focus Features, 2011. Film.
On the Waterfront. Dir. Elia Kazan. Columbia Pictures, 1954. Film.
Platoon. Dir. Oliver Stone. Orion Pictures, 1986. Film.
The Quiet Man. Dir. John Ford. Republic Pictures,1952. Film.
Schindler's List. Dir. Steven Spielberg. Universal Pictures, 1993. Film.
The Searchers. Dir. John Ford. Warner Home Video, 1990. Videocassette.
Sergeant Rutledge. Dir. John Ford. Warner Brothers Pictures, 1960.
   Film.
7 Women. Dir. John Ford. MGM, 1966. Film.
Sophie's Choice. Dir. Alan J. Pakula. Universal Pictures, 1982. Film.
Stagecoach. Dir. John Ford. United Artists, 1939. Film.
Taxi Driver. Dir. Martin Scorsese. Columbia Pictures, 1976. Film.
The Ten Commandments. Dir. Cecil B. DeMille. Paramount, 1956. Film.
Thelma and Louise. Dir. Ridley Scott. Metro-Goldwyn-Mayer, 1991.
   Film.
Tin Men. Dir. Barry Levinson. Touchstone Pictures/Buena Vista
   Pictures, 1987. Film.
Zoot Suit. Dir. Luis Valdez. Universal Pictures, 1981. Film.

Secondary: Published Film Criticism

Crowther, Bosley. "Black Orpheus." Rev. of *Black Orpheus* by Marcel Camus. *The New York Times* 22 Dec. 1959, 41+. Rpt. *The New York Times Film Reviews (1959–1968)* 3163–64. Print.

———. "Breathless." Rev. of *Breathless* by Jean-Luc Godard. *The New York Times* 8 Feb. 1961, 26. Rpt. *The New York Times Film Reviews (1959–1968)* 3239. Print.

McAlister, Linda Lopez. "Review of 'Thelma and Louise.'" Rev of *Thelma and Louise* by Ridley Scott. Web. *The Women's Show* WMNF-FM Tampa, Florida 21 Dec. 1998.

——— Chapter 3. Types of Film Criticism: The Review ———

Primary: Film

About Schmidt. Dir. Alexander Payne. New Line Cinema, 2002. Film.

Anything Else. Dir. Woody Allen. DreamWorks Distribution, 2003. Film.

The Artist. Dir. Michel Hazanavicius. The Weinstein Company, 2011. Film.

As Good as It Gets. Dir. James L. Brooks. TriStar Pictures, 1997. Film.

Batman. Dir. Tim Burton. Warner Brothers, 1989. Film.

Batman Begins. Dir. Christopher Nolan. Warner Brothers Pictures, 2005. Film.

The Best Years of Our Lives. Dir. William Wyler. RKO, 1946. Film.

Blow. Dir. Ted Demme. New Line Cinema, 2001. Film.

The Border. Dir. Tony Richardson. Universal Pictures, 1982. Film.

Carnal Knowledge. Dir. Mike Nichols. AVCO Embassy Pictures, 1971. Film.

Catch-22. Dir. Mike Nichols. Paramount, 1970. Film.

Citizen Ruth. Dir. Alexander Payne. Miramax Films, 1996. Film.

The Color Purple. Dir. Steven Spielberg. Warner Brothers, 1985. Film.

Crooklyn. Dir. Spike Lee. Paramount, 1994. Film.

The Crying Game. Dir. Neil Jordan. Miramax Films, 1992. Film.

The Dark Knight. Dir. Christopher Nolan. Warner Home Video, 2008. DVD.

The Dark Knight Rises. Dir. Christopher Nolan. Warner Brothers, 2012. Film.

Death of a Salesman. Dir. Volker Schlondorff. Anchor Bay Entertainment, 2001. Videocassette.

Desperate Living. Dir. John Waters. Saliva Films, 1977. Film.

Do the Right Thing. Dir. Spike Lee. Criterion Collection, 2001. DVD.

Election. Dir. Alexander Payne. Paramount Pictures, 1999. Film.

Fahrenheit 9/11. Dir. Michael Moore. IFC Films/Miramax Films, 2004. Film.

A Few Good Men. Dir. Rob Reiner. Columbia, 1992. Film.

A Fistful of Dollars. Dir. Sergio Leone. United Artists,1964. DVD

For a Few Dollars More. Dir. Sergio Leone. United Artists, 1965. Film.

Frida. Dir. Julie Taymore. Lions Gate Films/Miramax Films, 2002. Film.

The Girl with the Dragon Tattoo. Dir. David Fincher. Sony Pictures Home Entertainment. DVD.

The Good, the Bad, and the Ugly. Dir. Sergio Leone. United Artists, 1966. Film.

The Graduate. Dir. Mike Nichols. Embassy Pictures Corporation, 1967. Film.

Hairspray. Dir. John Waters. RCA/Columbia Pictures Home Video, 1989. Videocassette.

The Hangover. Dir. Todd Phillips. Warner Home Video, 2009. DVD.

The Hangover, Part II. Dir. Todd Phillips. Warner Home Video, 2011. DVD.

How to Make an American Quilt. Dir. Jocelyn Moorhouse. Universal Pictures, 1995. Film.

Il Postino (The Postman). Dir. Michael Radford. Miramax Films, 1994. Film.

Insomnia. Dir. Christopher Nolan. Warner Brothers Pictures, 2002. Film.

In the Bedroom. Dir. Todd Field. Miramax Home Entertainment, 2005. DVD.

In the Company of Men. Dir. Neil LaBute. Sony Pictures Classics, 1997. Film.

Invictus. Dir. Clint Eastwood. Warner Home Video, 2010. DVD.

Jungle Fever. Dir. Spike Lee. Universal Pictures, 1991. Film.

Jurassic Park. Dir. Steven Spielberg. Universal Pictures, 1993. Film.

The Lion King. Dir. Roger Allers and Rob Minkoff. Buena Vista Pictures, 1994. Film.

Mad Hot Ballroom. Dir. Marilyn Agrelo. Nickelodeon Movies/Paramount Classics, 2005. Film.

Malcolm X. Dir. Spike Lee. Warner Brothers Pictures, 1992. Film.

Manhattan. Dir. Woody Allen. United Artists,1979. Film.

Memento. Dir. Christopher Nolan. Newmarket Films, 2000. Film.

Midnight in Paris. Dir. Woody Allen. Sony Picture Classics, 2011. Film.

Mo' Better Blues. Dir. Spike Lee. Universal Pictures, 1990. Film.

Mondo Trasho. Dir. John Waters. Film-Makers' Cooperative, 1969. Film.

Out of the Past. Dir. Jacques Tourneur. RKO Radio Pictures, 1947. Film.

The Pianist. Dir. Roman Polanski. Focus Features, 2002. Film.

Pink Flamingos. Dir. John Waters. Saliva Films, 1973. Film.

The Pledge. Dir. Sean Penn. Warner Brothers, 2001. Film.

Polyester. Dir. John Waters. New Line Cinema, 1981. Film.
Pulp Fiction. Dir. Quentin Tarantino. Miramax Films, 1994. Film.
Reservoir Dogs. Dir. Quentin Tarantino. Miramax Films, 1992. Film.
Sorcerer. Dir. William Friedkin. Paramount Pictures/Universal Pictures, 1977. Film.
Spider Man. Dir. Sam Raimi. Columbia Pictures Films, 2002. Film.
Star Wars. Dir. George Lucas. 20ᵗʰ Century Fox, 1977. Film.
Superman. Dir. Richard Donner. Warner Brothers Pictures, 1978. Film.
A Thousand Acres. Dir. Jocelyn Moorhouse. Touchstone Pictures, 1997. Film.
Tom Jones. Dir. Tony Richardson. Lopert Pictures Corporation, 1963.
Tootsie. Dir. Sydney Pollack. Columbia Pictures, 1982. Film.
Wages of Fear. Dir. Henri-Georges Clouzot. The Criterion Collection, 1999. DVD.
Who's Afraid of Virginia Woolf? Dir. Mike Nichols. Warner Brothers. Film.
Wings. Dir. William A. Wellman. Paramount Home Video, 2012. DVD.
X-Men. Dir. Bryan Singer. Twentieth Century-Fox Home Entertainment, 2000. DVD.
Your Friends and Neighbors. Dir. Neil LaBute. Grammercy, 1998. Film.

Secondary: Published Film Criticism

Adler, Renata. "The Good, the Bad, and the Ugly." Rev of *The Good, the Bad, and the Ugly* by Sergio Leone. *The New York Times* 25 Jan. 1968, 33. Rpt. *The New York Times Film Reviews (1969–1968)* 3731. Print.
Ansen, David. "A Powerful Duet from the Heartland: Pfeiffer and Lange Triumph in *A Thousand Acres.*" Rev. of *A Thousand Acres* by Jocelyn Morehouse. *Newsweek* 22 Sep. 1997, 82. Print.
Barrus, Harrison S. "Invictus." Rev. of *Invictus* by Clint Eastwood. 22 July 2012. Print.
Benatar, Andres. "The Artist." Rev. of *The Artist* by Michel Hazanavicius. 26 Apr. 2012. Print.
———. "Murder within the Bedroom." Rev. of *In the Bedroom* by Todd Field. 19 Apr. 2012. Print.
———. "The Pianist." Rev. of *The Pianist* by Roman Polanski. 15 May 2012. Print.
Copeland, Edward. "From the Vault: *Crooklyn.*" Rev. of *Crooklyn* by Spike Lee. Web. *Edward Copeland's Tangents* 18 Dec. 2005.
Crowther, Bosley. "The Best Years of Our Lives." Rev. of *The Best Years of Our Lives* by William Wyler. *The New York Times* 22 Nov. 1946, 27. Rpt. *The New York Times Film Reviews (1939–1948)* 2146–47. Print.

Ebert, Roger. "About Schmidt." Rev. of *About Schmidt* by Alexander
Payne. Web. *Chicago Sun-Times* 20 Dec. 2002.
———. "The Color Purple." Rev. of *The Color Purple* by Steven Spielberg.
Web. *Chicago Sun-Times* 20 Dec. 1985.
———. "Your Friends and Neighbors." Rev of *Your Friends and
Neighbors* by Neil LaBute. Web. *Chicago Sun-Times* 8 Oct. 1998.
Edelstein, David. "Omaha Lineman: Even Jack Nicholson Can't Save
About Schmidt." Rev. of *About Schmidt* by Alexander Payne. Web.
Slate 12 Dec. 2002.
Englehart, Mark. "(Batman Begins)." Rev. of *Batman Begins* by
Christopher Nolan. Web. *Internet Movie Database* 18 Jul. 2012.
Hofstein, Mary Beth. "Frida." Rev. of *Frida* by Julie Taymore. 23 Nov. 2002.
Print.
Howe, Desson. "Hairspray." Rev. of *Hairspray* by John Waters. Web.
Washington Post 26 Feb. 1988.
LaSalle, Mick. "Not Your Typical 'Friends and Neighbors'/Sex Satire Is
Full of Empty Provocation." Rev. of *Your Friends and Neighbors* by
Neil LaBute. Web. *San Francisco Chronicle,* 21 Aug. 1998.
Longworth, Karina. "'Midnight in Paris': Woody & Owen's Excellent
Adventure." Rev. of *Midnight in Paris* by Woody Allen. Web. *The
Village Voice* 18 May 2011.
Stephens, Bob. "'Out of the Past': Timeless Noir for 50 years It's Been the
Benchmark of the Genre." Rev. of *Out of the Past* by Jacques
Tourneur. Web. *San Francisco Examiner.* 5 Sep. 1997.
Travers, Peter. "Midnight in Paris." Rev. of *Midnight in Paris* by Woody
Allen. Web. *Rolling Stone.* 19 May 2011.
Woolcock, Candice F. Woolcock. "The Girl with the Dragon Tattoo." Rev.
of *The Girl with the Dragon Tattoo* by David Fincher. 25 Apr. 2012.
Print.

—— Chapter 4. Types of Film Criticism: The Analytical Critique ——

Primary: Film

Alien. Dir. Ridley Scott. Twentieth Century-Fox, 1979. Film.
American Beauty. Dir. Sam Mendes. DreamWorks Home Entertainment,
2000. DVD.
Apocalypse, Now. Dir. Francis Ford Coppola. United Artists, 1979. Film.
Auntie Mame. Dir. Morton DaCosta. Warner Brothers Pictures, 1958.
Film.
Bambi. Dir. James Algar et al. RKO Radio Pictures, 1942. Film.

Battleship Potemkin, The. Dir. Sergei Eisenstein. Museum of Art, 1925. Film.

Ben-Hur. Dir. William Wyler. Metro-Goldwyn-Mayer, 1959. Film.

The Bicycle Thief. Dir. Vittorio De Sica. Arthur Mayer and Joseph Burstyn, 1948, Film.

The Birds. Dir. Alfred Hitchcock. Universal Pictures, 1963. Film.

Blazing Saddles. Dir. Mel Brooks. Warner Brothers, 1974. Film.

A Bronx Tale. Dir. Robert De Niro. Savoy Pictures, 1993. Film.

Casablanca. Dir. Michael Curtiz. Warner Brothers, 1942. Film.

Chinatown. Dir. Roman Polanski. Paramount Pictures, 1974. Film.

Citizen Kane. Dir. Orson Welles. RKO Radio Pictures, 1941. Film.

Curse of the Pink Panther. Dir. Blake Edwards. United Artists, 1983. Film.

Dames. Dir. Busby Berkley and Ray Enright. Warner Brothers, 1934. Film.

Death in Venice. Dir. Luchino Visconti. Warner Brothers, 1971. Film.

The English Patient. Dir. Anthony Minghella. Miramax Films, 1996. Film.

Falling Down. Dir. Joel Schumacher. Warner Brothers Pictures, 1993. Film.

Farewell, My Lovely. Dir. Dick Richards. AVCO Embassy Pictures, 1975. Film.

Forrest Gump. Dir. Robert Zemeckis. Paramount Pictures, 1994. Film.

The 400 Blows. Dir. Francois Truffaut. Zenith International Films, 1959. Film.

The Godfather. Dir. Francis Ford Coppola. Paramount Pictures. 1972. Film.

The Gold Rush. Dir. Charles Chaplin. United Artists, 1925. Film.

Goodfellas. Dir. Martin Scorsese. Warner Home Video, 1997. DVD.

The Grapes of Wrath. Dir. John Ford. Twentieth Century-Fox, 1940. Film.

High Noon. Dir. Fred Zinnemann. United Artists, 1952. Film.

The Hours. Dir. Stephen Daldry. Paramount, 2002. Film.

The Ides of March. Dir. George Clooney. Sony Pictures Home Entertainment, 2012. DVD.

It Happened One Night. Dir. Frank Capra. Columbia Pictures, 1934. Film.

Jurassic Park. Dir. Steven Spielberg. MCA/Universal Pictures, 1993. Film.

Knife in the Water. Dir. Roman Polanski. The Criterion Collection, 2003. DVD.

Lawrence of Arabia. Dir. David Lean. Columbia Pictures, 1962. Film.

Little Big Man. Dir. Arthur Penn. National General Pictures, 1970. Film.
Love and Anarchy. Dir. Lina Wertmuller. RCA/Columbia Pictures Home Video, 1982. Videocassette.
Night of the Living Dead. Dir. George A. Romero. Continental Distributing, 1968. Film.
North by Northwest. Dir. Alfred Hitchcock. Metro-Goldwyn-Mayer, 1959. Film.
On the Waterfront. Dir. Elia Kazan. Columbia Pictures, 1954. Film.
The Party. Dir. Blake Edwards. United Artists, 1968. Film.
The Piano. Dir. Jane Campion. Miramax Films, 1993. Film.
The Pink Panther. Dir. Blake Edwards. United Artists, 1963. Film.
Psycho. Dir. Alfred Hitchcock. Paramount Pictures, 1960. Film.
Pulp Fiction. Dir. Quentin Tarantino. Miramax Films, 1994. Film.
Rashomon. Dir. Akira Kurosawa. Museum of Modern Art. 1950. Film.
Ray. Dir. Taylor Hackford. Universal Pictures, 2004. Film.
Rebel Without a Cause. Dir. Nicholas Ray. Warner Brothers, 1955. Film.
Samson and Delilah. Dir. Cecil B. DeMille. Paramount, 1949. Film.
Saturday Night Fever. Dir. John Badham. Paramount Pictures, 1977. Film.
The Seduction of Mimi. Dir. Lina Wertmuller. New Line Cinema, 1974. Film.
The Seventh Seal. Dir. Ingmar Bergman. Janus Films, 1958. Film.
Shadows. Dir. John Cassavetes. Lion International Films, 1961. Film.
The Shining. Dir. Stanley Kubrick. Warner Brothers, 1980. Film.
A Shot in the Dark. Dir. Blake Edwards. United Artists, 1964. Film.
Singin' in the Rain. Dir. Gene Kelly and Stanley Donen. Metro-Goldwyn-Mayer, 1952. Film.
A Soldier's Story. Dir. Norman Jewison. Columbia Pictures, 1984. Film.
Star Wars. Dir. George Lukas. Twentieth Century-Fox, 1977. Film.
Strangers in Good Company. Dir. Cynthia Scott. Castle Hill Productions, 1991. Film.
Swept Away (By an Unusual Destiny in the Blue Sea of August). Dir. Lina Wertmuller. Cinema V, 1975. Film.
The 39 Steps. Dir. Alfred Hitchcock. Gaumont-British, 1935. Film.
The Trail of the Pink Panther. Dir. Blake Edwards. United Artists, 1982. Film.
The Tramp. Dir. Charlie Chaplin. Image Entertainment, 1999. DVD.
Twelve Angry Men. Dir. Sidney Lumet. United Artists, 1957. Film.
2001: A Space Odyssey. Dir. Stanley Kubrick. MGM, 1968. Film.
The Untouchables. Dir. Brian De Palma. Paramount Pictures, 1987. Film.
The Wild Bunch. Dir. Sam Peckinpah. Warner Brothers/Seven Arts, 1969. Film.

Secondary: Published Film Criticism

Barrus, Harrison S. "The Elements of Propaganda, Romance, and the Thriller in the Classic Film *Casablanca*." Analytical Critique. 29 Sept. 2010. Print.

Cook, Casey. "The Use of Sound and Silence in Alfred Hitchcock's *The Birds*." Analytical Critique. 11 Mar. 2004. Print.

Gershuny, Ted. "Alien." *Magill's Survey of Cinema: English Language Series—First Series*. Vol. I A-Eas. Ed. Frank N. Magill. Englewood Cliffs, NJ: Salem Press, 1980. 37–39. Print.

Kempley, Rita. "'Strangers in Good Company' (PG)." Rev. of *Strangers in Good Company* by Cynthia Scott. Web. *The Washington Post* 13 July 1991.

Westerbeck, Colin L., Jr. "Robinson Crusoe." Rev. of *Swept Away (By an Unusual Destiny in the Blue Sea of August)* by Lina Wertmuller *Commonweal* 10 Oct. 1975, 470–71. Print,

—— Chapter 5. Types of Film Criticism: The Comparative Analysis ——

Primary: Film

All Quiet on the Western Front. Dir. Lewis Milestone. Universal Pictures, 1930. Film.

Apocalypse, Now. Dir. Francis Ford Coppola. United Artists, 1979. Film.

Badlands. Dir. Terrence Malick. Warner Brothers, 1973. Film.

Barton Fink. Dir. Joel Coen. 20th Century Fox Home Entertainment, 2003. DVD.

Basic Instinct. Dir. Paul Verhoeven. TriStar, 1992. Film.

Batman. Dir. Tim Burton. Warner Brothers, 1989. Film.

Batman & Robin (Batman 4). Dir. Joel Schumacher. Warner Brothers, 1997. Film.

Batman Begins. Dir. Christopher Nolan. Warner Brothers, 2005. Film.

Batman Forever (Batman 3). Dir. Joel Schumacher. Warner Brothers, 1995. Film.

Batman Returns. Dir. Tim Burton. Warner Brothers, 1992. Film.

Before Sunrise. Dir. Richard Linklater. Columbia TriStar Home Video, 1995. Videocassette.

Before Sunset. Dir. Richard Linklater. Warner Home Video, 2004. DVD.

Before the Devil Knows You're Dead. Dir. Sidney Lumet. Image Entertainment, 2008. DVD.

Best in Show. Dir. Christopher Guest. Warner Brothers Entertainment, 2000. Film.

The Bicycle Thief. Dir. Vittorio De Sica. Arthur Mayer and Joseph
Burstyn, 1948, Film.
The Big Sleep. Dir. Howard Hawks. Warner Brothers, 1946. Film.
The Big Sleep. Dir. Michael Winner. United Artists, 1977. Film.
Bitter Rice. Dir. Giuseppe De Santis. Lux Film Distributing Corporation,
1950. Film.
Boccaccio '70. Dir. Vittorio De Sica et al. Embassy Pictures Corporation,
1962. Film.
Bonfire of the Vanities. Dir. Brian De Palma. Warner Brothers, 1990.
Film.
Breathless. Dir. Jean-Luc Goddard. Films Around the World, 1961. Film.
Breathless. Dir. Jim McBride. Orion Pictures, 1983. Film.
Carmen Jones. Dir. Otto Preminger. 20th Century Fox Film Corporation,
1954. Film.
Chinatown. Dir. Roman Polanski. Paramount Pictures, 1974. Film.
Daisy Miller. Dir. Peter Bogdanovich. Paramount Pictures, 1974. Film.
Dances with Wolves. Dir. Kevin Costner. Orion, 1990. Film.
Das Boot. Dir. Wolfgang Petersen. Embassy Home Entertainment, 1981.
Videocassette.
Death of a Salesman. Dir. Volker Schlondorff. Karl-Lorimar Home Video,
1986. Videocassette.
Deep Blue Sea. Dir. Renny Harlin. Warner Brothers, 1999. Film.
The Deer Hunter. Dir. Michael Cimino. Universal Pictures, 1978. Film.
Dog Day Afternoon. Dir. Sidney Lumet. Warner Brothers, 1075. Film.
Do the Right Thing. Dir. Spike Lee. Universal Pictures, 1989. Film.
8 ½. Dir. Federico Fellini. Embassy Pictures Corporation, 1963. Film.
Exodus. Dir. Otto Preminger. United Artists, 1960. Film.
A Face in the Crowd. Dir. Elia Kazan. Warner Brothers, 1957. Film.
The 400 Blows. Dir. Francois Truffaut. Zenith International Films, 1959.
Film.
The Glass Menagerie. Dir. Paul Newman. Cineplex Odeon Films, 1987.
Film.
The Godfather. Dir. Francis Ford Coppola. Paramount Pictures, 1972.
Film.
The Godfather-Part II. Dir. Francis Ford Coppola. Paramount, 1974.
Film.
Gran Torino. Dir. Clint Eastwood. Warner Home Video, 2009. DVD,
The Grapes of Wrath. Dir. John Ford. Twentieth Century-Fox, 1940.
Film.
Hamlet. Dir. Laurence Olivier. J. Arthur Rank-Two Cities, 1948. Film.
Hamlet. Dir. Kenneth Branagh. Warner Home Video, 2007. DVD.
A Hatful of Rain. Dir. Fred Zinnemann. Twentieth Century Fox Film
Corporation, 1957. Film.

Heaven's Gate. Dir. Michael Cimino. United Artists, 1980. Film.
How Green Was My Valley. Dir. John Ford. Twentieth Century-Fox, 1941. Film.
It Happened One Night. Dir. Frank Capra. Columbia Pictures, 1934. Film.
Jaws. Dir. Steven Spielberg. Universal Pictures, 1975. Film.
The Joy That Kills. Tina Rathborne. Films for the Humanities, 1984. Video cassette.
Jungle Fever. Dir. Spike Lee. Universal Pictures, 1991. Film.
King Solomon's Mines. Dir. Compton Bennett and Andrew Marton. Metro-Goldwyn-Mayer, 1950. Film.
King Solomon's Mines. Dir. J. Lee Thompson. Cannon Group, 1985. Film.
The Last of the Mohicans. Dir. Michael Mann. Twentieth Century-Fox, 1992. Film.
La Dolce Vita. Dir. Federico Fellini. Republic Pictures Home Video, 1985. Videocassette.
L'Amore in Citta. Dir. Federico Fellini. Federico Fellini. I.F.E. Releasing Corporation, 1955. Film.
The Last Picture Show. Dir. Peter Bogdanovich. Columbia Pictures, 1971. Film.
La Strada. Dir. Federico Fellini. Trans-Lux Films, 1956. Film.
The Last Seduction. Dir. Joel Dahl. Bamholtz Entertainment, 2001. DVD.
Little Big Man. Dir. Arthur Penn. National General Pictures, 1970. Film.
The Magnificent Seven. Dir. John Sturges. United Artists, 1960. Film.
A Man Called Horse. Dir. Elliot Silverstein. Paramount Home Video, 2003. DVD.
The Manchurian Candidate. Dir. John Frankenheimer. United Artists, 1962. Film.
The Manchurian Candidate. Dir. Jonathan Demme. Paramount Pictures, 2004. Film.
Manhattan. Dir. Woody Allen. United Artists, 1975. Film.
The Man with the Golden Arm. Dir. Otto Preminger. United Artists, 1955. Film.
Mean Streets. Dir. Martin Scorsese. Warner Bros. Pictures, 1973. Film.
Moulin Rouge. Dir. John Huston. United Artists, 1952. Film.
Moulin Rouge. Dir. Baz Luhrmann. Twentieth Century Fox Film Corporation, 2001. Film.
Mr. Deeds Goes to Town. Dir. Frank Capra. Columbia Pictures, 1936. Film.
Natural Born Killers. Dir. Oliver Stone. Warner Brothers, 1994. Film.
Of Mice and Men. Dir. Gary Sinese. Metro-Goldwyn-Mayer, 1992. Film.
The Old Man and the Sea. Dir. John Sturges. Warner Brothers, 1958. Film.

Network. Dir. Sidney Lumet. Metro-Goldwyn-Mayer/United Artists, 1976. Film.

Paths of Glory. Dir. Stanley Kubrick. United Artists, 1957. Film.

The Pawnbroker. Dir. Sidney Lumet. Allied Artists, 1964. Film.

The Pink Panther. Dir. Blake Edwards. United Artists, 1963. Film.

Play Misty for Me. Dir. Clint Eastwood. Universal Pictures. 1971. Film.

Porgy and Bess. Dir. Otto Preminger. Columbia Pictures, 1959. Film.

Psycho. Dir. Alfred Hitchcock. Paramount Pictures, 1960. Film.

Psycho. Dir. Gus Van Sant. MCA/Universal Pictures, 1998. Film.

The Quiet Man. Dir. John Ford. Republic Pictures,1952. Film.

Richard III. Dir. Richard Loncraine. United Artists. 1995. Film.

Richard III. Dir. Laurence Olivier. Lopert Pictures Corporation, 1955. Film.

Rocky. Dir. John Avildsen. United Artists, 1976. Film.

Rocky II. Dir. Sylvester Stallone. United Artists, 1979. Film.

Rocky III. Dir. Sylvester Stallone. MGM/United Artists, 1982. Film.

Rocky IV. Dir. Sylvester Stallone. Metro-Goldwyn-Mayer, 1985. Film.

Rocky V. Dir. John Avildsen. United Artists, 1990. Film.

Run Silent, Run Deep. Dir. Robert Wise. United Artists, 1958. Film.

Saturday Night Fever. Dir. John Badham. Paramount Pictures, 1977. Film.

Scarface. Dir. Brian De Palma. Universal Pictures, 1983. Film.

Scent of a Woman. Dir. Martin Brest. Universal Pictures, 1992. Film.

Scent of a Woman (Profumo di donna). Dir. Dino Risi. Twentieth Century Fox Film Corporation, 1974. Film.

Se7en. Dir. David Fincher. New Line Cinema, 1995. Film.

Seven Samurai. Dir. Akira Kurosawa. Columbia Pictures, 1956. Film.

Shane. Dir. George Stevens. Paramount, 1953. Film.

A Shot in the Dark. Dir. Blake Edwards. United Artists, 1964. Film.

The Snows of Kilimanjaro. Dir. Henry King. Twentieth Century-Fox, 1952. Film.

Sorcerer. Dir. William Friedkin. Paramount Pictures/Universal Pictures, 1977. Film.

Stagecoach. Dir. John Ford. United Artists, 1939. Film.

Star Wars. Dir. George Lucas. Twentieth Century-Fox, 1977. Film.

Star Wars: Episode V-The Empire Strikes Back. Dir. Irvin Kershner. Twentieth Century-Fox, 1980. Film.

Star Wars: Episode VI-Return of the Jedi. Dir. Richard Marquand. Twentieth Century-Fox, 1983. Film.

Staying Alive. Dir. Sylvester Stallone. Paramount Pictures, 1983. Film.

Stolen Kisses. Dir. Francois Truffaut. United Artists, 1968. Film.

Taxi Driver. Dir. Martin Scorsese. Columbia Pictures, 1976. Film.

Texasville. Dir. Peter Bogdanovich. Columbia Pictures, 1990. Film.

The Thin Red Line. Dir. Andrew Marton. Allied Artists, 1964. Film.
The Thin Red Line. Dir. Terrence Malick. The Criterion Collection, 2010. DVD.
3:10 to Yuma. Dir. James Mangold. Lionsgate Home Entertainment, 2008. DVD.
Unforgiven. Dir. Clint Eastwood. Warner Home Video, 2000. DVD.
Variety Lights. Dir, Federico Fellini and Alberto Lattuada. The Criterion Collection, 2004. DVD.
The Wages of Fear, (Le Salaire de la peur). Dir. Henri-Georges Clouzot. DCA, 1953. Film.
Waiting for Guffman. Dir. Christopher Guest. Sony Pictures Classics, 1996. Film.
Weekend. Dir. Jean-Luc Godard. Grove Press, 1968. Film.
You Can't Take It with You. Dir. Frank Capra. Columbia Films, 1938. Film.

Secondary: Published Film Criticism

Bright, J. David. "The Impact of Modern Special Effects. *Jaws* Versus *Deep Blue Sea.*" Comparative Critique. 8 Dec. 2004. Print.
Griffith, Holly. "Hitchcock's *Psycho* and Van Sant's *Psycho*: Contrasts in Characterization, Detail, and Scene." Comparative Critique. 21 Apr. 1999. Print.

– Chapter 6. Types of Film Criticism: The Documented Research Paper –

Primary: Film

Amadeus. Dir. Milos Foreman. Orion Pictures, 1983. Film.
American Beauty. Dir. Sam Mendes. DreamWorks Home Entertainment, 2000. DVD.
Animal House. Dir. John Landis. Universal Pictures, 1978. Film.
Ben-Hur. Dir. William Wyler. Metro-Goldwyn-Mayer, 1959. Film.
The Birds. Alfred Hitchcock. Universal Pictures, 1963. Film.
Body Heat. Dir. Laurence Kasdan. Warner Brothers, 1992. Film.
The Bridges of Madison County. Dir. Clint Eastwood. Warner Brothers, 1995. Film.
A Bronx Tale. Dir. Robert De Niro. Home Box Office Home Video, 1995. Videocassette.
A Cry in the Dark. Dir. Fred Schepisi. Warner Brothers, 1988. Film.
The Deer Hunter. Dir. Michael Cimino. Universal Pictures, 1978. Film.

Dial M for Murder. Dir. Alfred Hitchcock. Warner Bros. Pictures, 1954. Film.

The Elephant Man. Dir. David Lynch. Paramount Pictures, 1980. Film.

Father of the Bride. Dir. Vincente Minnelli. Metro-Goldwyn-Mayer, 1950. Film.

Father of the Bride. Dir. Charles Shyer. Buena Vista Pictures, 1991. Film.

Frida. Dir. Julie Taymore. Lions Gate Films/Miramax Films, 2002. Film.

The Godfather. Dir. Francis Ford Coppola. Paramount Pictures, 1972. Film.

The Godfather-Part II. Dir. Francis Ford Coppola. Paramount, 1974. Film.

The Graduate. Dir. Mike Nichols. Embassy Pictures Corporation, 1967. Film.

High Noon. Dir. Fred Zinnemann. United Artists, 1952. Film.

How Green Was My Valley. Dir. John Ford. Twentieth Century-Fox, 1941. Film.

L. A. Confidential. Dir. Curtis Hanson. Warner Home Video, 1998. Videocassette.

Manhattan. Dir. Woody Allen. United Artists, 1979. Film.

The Man Who Knew Too Much. Dir. Alfred Hitchcock. Paramount , 1956. Film.

A Member of the Wedding. Dir. Fred Zinnemann, Columbia, 1952. Film

North by Northwest. Dir. Alfred Hitchcock. Metro-Goldwyn-Mayer, 1959. Film.

Out of Africa. Dir. Sydney Pollack. MCA/Universal Pictures, 1985. Film.

Out of the Past. Dir. Jacques Tourneur. RKO Radio Pictures, 1947. Film.

The Piano. Dir. Jane Campion. Miramax Films, 1993. Film.

Psycho. Dir. Alfred Hitchcock. Paramount Pictures, 1960. Film.

Rear Window. Dir. Alfred Hitchcock. Paramount Pictures, 1954. Film.

Se7en. Dir. David Fincher. New Line Cinema, 1995. Film.

The Seventh Seal. Dir. Ingmar Bergman. Janus Films, 1956. Film.

A Soldier's Story. Dir. Norman Jewison. Columbia Pictures, 1984. Film.

Sophie's Choice. Dir. Alan J. Pakula. Universal Pictures, 1982. Film.

Steel Magnolias. Dir. Herbert Ross. TriStar Pictures, 1989. Film.

Sunset Boulevard. Dir. Billy Wilder. Paramount Pictures, 1950. Film.

Vertigo. Dir. Alfred Hitchcock. Paramount Pictures, 1958. Film.

Secondary: Published Film Criticism

Berardinelli, James. "Rear Window." Rev. of *Rear Window* by Alfred Hitchcock. Web. *Reelviews Movie Reviews.* 2012.

————. "North by Northwest." Rev. of *North by Northwest* by Alfred Hitchcock. Web. *Reelviews Movie Reviews.* 2012.

Bodeen, DeWitt. "The Birds." *Magill's Survey of Cinema—English Language Films.* Second Series. Vol. 1 A-CLU. Ed. Frank N. Magill. Englewood, NJ: Salem Press, 1981. 249–252. Print.

Boggs, Joseph W. *The Art of Watching Films.* 4th ed. Mountain View, CA: Mayfield, 1996. Print.

Canby Vincent. "The Godfather." Rev, of *The Godfather* by Francis Ford Coppola. *The New York Times* 12 Mar. 1972, II, 1. Rpt. *The New York Times Film Reviews (1971–1972).* 233–34. Print.

————. "The Godfather." Rev. of *The Godfather* by Francis Ford Coppola. *The New York Times* 16 Mar. 1972, 56. Rpt. *The New York Times Film Reviews (1971–1972).* 235. Print.

Crowther, Bosley. "The Birds." Rev. of *The Birds* by Alfred Hitchcock. *The New York Times.* 1 Apr. 1963. 5:5. Rpt. in *The New York Times Film Reviews (1959–1968).* Vol. 5. New York: The New York Times & Arno Press, 1970. 3378. Print.

Ebert, Roger. "Rear Window." Rev. of *Rear Window* by Alfred Hitchcock. Web. 7 Oct. 1983. *Chicago Sun-Times.*

————. "'Rear Window' (1954)." Rev. of *Rear Window* by Alfred Hitchcock. Web. 20 Feb. 2000. *Chicago Sun-Times.*

Giannetti, Louis and Scott Eyman. *Flashback: A Brief History of Film.* 4th ed. Upper Saddle River, NJ: Prentice-Hall, 2001. Print.

Lester, James D. and Jim D. Lester, Jr. *Writing Research Papers: A Complete Guide.* 14th ed. New York: Pearson Longman, 2011. Print.

Mast, Gerald and Bruce F. Kawin. *A Short History of the Movies.* 5th ed. New York: Macmillan, 1992. Print.

Nadell, Judith et al. *The Longman Writer: Rhetoric, Reader, Research Guide, and Handbook 8th ed.* Boston: Longman, 2011. Print.

Place, Janey. "Rear Window." *Magill's Survey of Cinema—English Language Films* Second Series. Vol. 5 PUT-THE. Ed. Frank N. Magill. Englewood, NJ: Salem Press, 1981. 1983–1986. Print.

Taubman, Leslie. "The Godfather." *Magill's Survey of Cinema: English Language Films series.* Ed. Frank N. Magill. 1, Vol. 2, EAS-LON. Englewood, NJ: Salem Press, 1980. 638–43. Print.

Weiler, A. H. "North by Northwest." Rev. of *North by Northwest* by Alfred Hitchcock. *The New York Times.* 7 Aug. 1959. 28:1. Rpt. in *The New York Times Film Reviews (1959–1968).* Vol. 5. New York: The New York Times & Arno Press, 1970. 3143. Print.

Williams, Judith A. "North by Northwest." *Magill's Survey of Cinema— English Language Films.* Second Series. Vol. 4 LUS-PUR. Ed. Frank N. Magill. Englewood, NJ: Salem Press, 1981. 1742–1744. Print.

—— Appendix C. Film as Literature and the Learning Community ——

Primary: Film

The Snow Walker. Dir. Charles Martin Smith. Lions Gate Films, 2004. Film.

APPENDIX B

GLOSSARY OF CINEMATIC TERMS

This text uses numerous terms that relate to the moving picture. They are common enough, but since assumptions of shared knowledge can be dangerous, the following definitions enable every reader to be familiar with the cinema terminology used in these pages.

angle: The position of the camera in relation to the subject being filmed. If the camera is above the subject, it is at a high angle; beneath, it is at a low angle.

animation: Filmmaking that photographs drawings or inanimate objects frame by frame which is then speeded up and projected to simulate motion.

archetype: Original pattern or model for a character, setting, or theme.

art director: The person who design and supervises set construction who is responsible for the visual look. Also known as the **production designer**.

auteur: The **director** (who often also is the screenwriter) as the primary creator of film art who is involved in every aspect of the filmmaking process and thus giving each work his/her distinctive style.

backlighting: Lighting emanating from behind the actors thus putting them into heavy shadow or even silhouette in the foreground.

biopic: A film based on the life of an actual person or a particular period of it.

blocking: The planning and directing of the actors' movements and positions prior to filming.

cinematographer: The individual who plans a scene (usually with the director) and then shoots it. Also known as **director of photography**.

composition: The arrangement of the actors, three dimensional objects (manufactured and natural), and other visual components that form the image within a frame.

computer-generated imagery (C.G.I.): objects, scenery, characters, special effects, and sound devised by a computer

credits: The onscreen listing of all the personnel who contributed to the making of the film—both in front of the screen and behind it; all names, creative and business, involved.

cut: An abrupt change (break) from one continuous set of images to another.

distribution: After a movie is made, all the practices inherent to its marketing and releasing.

editing: The act of putting together (splicing) images of film that have not been shot sequentially.

exhibition: Following the distribution phase, this third phase of moviemaking, including a films general release into theaters and other venues open to the public.

fade: A transitional effect (also called fade-out/fade-in) where the last image from the previous scene fades to black then gradually, as the light increases, becomes the first image of the next scene.

faithful adaptation: A movie that converts from another medium—such as a short story or novel—and is true to the essence of its literary elements, such as plot, characterization, setting, and theme.

film noir: A genre of mainly American mystery films of the 1940s and 1950's characterized by a pessimistic tone, low-key lighting, and motifs of violence, betrayal, deception, and corrupted passion.

flashback: As part of the plot structure, a sudden leaving of the present by returning to events of the past which add texture to the story and also aids the character development. Eventually returns to the present.

flashforward: Operates like flashback except it suddenly leaves the present and moves to events and settings in the future. Usually, eventually returns to the present.

frame: Like composition in its concern with the elements within a shot; however, here the emphasis is with the borders of that shot.

freeze frame: The reprinting of the same frame a number of times giving the effect of freezing the action into a still photograph on the screen.

genre: A category of motion picture, such as the western, the comedy, the melodrama, the action epic.

mise-en-scene: All the theatrical elements necessary in composing a scene to be filmed: props, sets, lighting, sound effects, costumes, make-up, actors' placement (blocking).

montage: A series of abruptly juxtaposed shots using short, edited sequences and music, often interrelated by theme and/or events, denoting the passage of time.

motif: An image, object, or idea repeated throughout a film usually to lend a thematic effect.

narrative (narrative arc): The **storyline** or sequential plot of a film.

New Wave: A group of young French directors during the 1950s. Among them are Francois Truffaut, Jean-Luc Godard, and Alain Resnais whose films are characterized by shooting scripts written directly for the screen, urban location shooting, improvisation, naturalistic acting, and allusions to earlier films.

oeuvre: A filmmaker's entire collection of work seen as one entity.

period piece: A film that does not use a contemporary setting but rather that of an earlier historical era.

point of view: Either a subjective (first person) or objective vantage from which everything is observed and interpreted. The subjective viewpoint would be from the perspective of one of the characters. The objective would be more neutral and not from any one character's perspective.

postproduction: After a film is shot, all the activity that follows, including: editing, transitions, visual and sound effects, and musical scoring.

preproduction: All the activity before a film is shot, including: script preparation, cast and major crew (such as the director) and creative team selection.

production: First major phase in making a movie involving all aspects of a film's creation up to editing. The other two major phases are distribution and exhibition.

prop: A three-dimensional object used by an actor or present on a set.

scenarist: The person who adapts a literary source for a movie by writing the screenplay, or who writes a script directly for a film; a **screenwriter**.

scene: A series of shots unified in action or established location and time (setting).

screwball comedy: A type of romantic comedy characterized by snappy, witty dialogue between the male and female leads engaged in an ongoing battle-of-the-sexes. With various other eccentricities in the characters and a happy ending.

score: Music—either originally composed for the film or not—used in a motion picture.

sequence: A series of interrelated scenes that establish a certain prolonged effect with a decided beginning, middle, and ending.

set: A soundstage decorated for shooting or any other site prepared for filming to occur.

shooting script: The movie storyline broken down to its individual shots often with technical instructions.

shot: The basic unit of filming which is the unedited, continuously exposed image of any duration made up of any number of frames.

close-up shot: A shot of a character's head or face, for example, that fills the screen.

crane shot: A shot taken from high above the characters and the action by using a mechanical crane.

deep-focus shot: A shot with the visual field in sharp focus: foreground, background, and everything in between.

dissolve: A slow fading out of one shot followed by the slow fading in of another where the images are superimposed at midpoint.

full shot: A medium long shot that shows a complete person from head to foot.

hand-held shot: A shot that follows a character moving—usually through a crowd—using a hand-held camera and characterized by a jumpiness not present in a mounted camera.

long shot: A shot taken at considerable distance from the subject.

medium shot: A shot of a person from the knees or waist up.

pan shot: A shot taken from a mounted camera moving horizontally on a fixed axis.

reaction shot: A shot of a character's reaction to what has been said or done in the previous shot.

tilt shot: A shot taken from a mounted camera moving vertically on a fixed axis.

tracking shot: A shot of a subject filmed by a camera mounted on a moving vehicle.

zoom shot: An ongoing shot through a stationary camera where through the continuous action of the lens, a long shot can very rapidly convert to a close-up as zoom in. A close-up reverting to a long shot is a zoom out.

sound effects: Sounds—neither musical nor dialogue—that are made to realistically approximate a desired noise.

special effects: Various photographic, artistic, animated or computerized effects that are filmed to approximate reality or produce a sense of the surreal. Also known as **visual effects**.

star: An actor, actress, or celebrity having great popular appeal.

star system: Filmmaking that capitalizes on the mass commercial appeal of certain performers to assure maximum box office appeal.

star vehicle: A film produced with maximum publicity to demonstrate the talents or appeal of a specific star.

symbol: As with literature, a device in which an object or event means more than its narrow literal meaning.

voice-over: Narration off-screen while a series of shots unfold onscreen.

APPENDIX C

FILM AS LITERATURE AND THE LEARNING COMMUNITY

Film as Literature is a course with a multiplicity of applications: an introduction to the study of film; a bridge to show corresponding elements and influences between film and literature; a touchstone course for a film studies program; and a Humanities elective offering to fulfill degree requirements.

With the mandate to improve student success outcomes, many campuses are intentionally strengthening classroom engagement strategies across the curriculum by means of Learning Communities (LCs). This construct goes well beyond guest collegial lectures or even team teaching. By pairing or linking two or three courses designated as a Learning Community, collaborating faculty can design several integrated assignments or projects that connect shared course concepts. So in a Learning Community that joins short fiction with a film class, faculty blend elements of the two genres for deeper understanding through class discussions, written responses, and other integrative learning opportunities. The LC views and analyzes films adapted from short stories. Typically in small groups, members of both classes identify commonalities between the film and its literary source.

When this LC experience works successfully, something wonderful happens with the students: a synergistic experience of shared insights, analyses, and reflections. Student panels comprising representatives from both classes parse such questions as the following:

- Is the film plot line faithful to the story's narrative arc?
- What may be the reasons for a change in title of the film from the original story? What slant does the alternate title provide?
- Do the actors' conceptions of character do justice to the original source?

- Is the essence of the story preserved in the film?
- When a filmmaker adapts or embellishes an aspect of the writer's original concept, is the alteration successful?
- What elements appear in the film adaptation that are not present in the original story?

A Learning Community combining film and short fiction might consider the following short stories and films inspired by them:

"The Story of an Hour" Kate Chopin
The Joy That Kills (Tina Rathborne, 1988)

"The Snows of Kilimanjaro" Ernest Hemingway
The Snows of Kilimanjaro (Henry King, 1952)
The Les Neiges du Kilimandjaro (Robert Guédiguian, 2011)

"The Swimmer" John Cheever
The Swimmer (Frank Perry, 1968)

"Who Am I This Time?" Kurt Vonnegut, Jr.
Who Am I This Time? (Jonathan Demme, 1981)

"Harrison Bergeron" Kurt Vonnegut, Jr.
Harrison Bergeron (Patrick Home, 2006)

"Where Are You Going, Where Have You Been?" Joyce Carole Oates
Smooth Talk (Joyce Chopra, 1986)

"The Killings" Andre Dubus II
In the Bedroom (Todd Field, 2002)

"Walk Well, My Brother" Farley Mowat
The Snow Walker (Charles Martin Smith, 2003)

"What Do You Mean When You Say, 'Phoenix, Arizona'?"
   Sherman Alexie
Smoke Signals (Chris Eyre, 1998)

"Million Dollar Baby" F.X. Toole
Million Dollar Baby (Clint Eastwood, 2004)

"Why Don't You Dance?" Raymond Carver
Everything Must Go (Dan Rush, 2011)

In a Learning Community that meets a full term, 12–16 weeks, collaborating faculty may schedule four or five whole-LC-cohort meetings, where students from both classes view a film adapted from a short story. Through the campus procedure of submitting an LC proposal for approval (and gaining support for student recruitment), the collaborating faculty plan learner-centered activities for those times when the entire cohort gathers in a space large enough to accommodate the joint classes.

Valid assessment is a critical piece of co-curricular planning, especially for any new or innovative undertaking. In fact, planning formal and informal assessments for LC activities is one of the building blocks in constructing linked learning activities. Although assessments may generally be formalized, an LC may also incorporate informal assessment activities.

As an example of a linked assignment in such a cohort—and one that may be informally assessed—is Raymond Carver's short story "Why Don't You Dance?" paired with the viewing of Dan Rush's film adaptation, *Everything Must Go*. As learner-centered activity, students could be asked to bring a personal object to class for a hypothetical 'yard or tag sale' to explore the deeper understanding of one of the story's themes, "letting go and moving on." Prior to the film screening, students could display their objects in the classroom and offer their own brief stories about attachment still felt to these ordinary items. This activity, as a result, experientially engages students to relate to the story and the film.

In a more traditional mode of evaluation, a writing and research option would most likely be included in the form of comparative essays in discussing the movie derived from a fictional source; or research papers comparing the two works using full documentation of secondary sources with in-text citations.

As a broader benefit to the college, such an LC may augment campus events, such as film festivals, cinema clubs, literary galas, campus reads, or featured library events.

Along with greater student involvement in a cohort that offers such benefits, faculty engaged in the LC likewise gain from the wider purview of the LC construct. Among the pedagogical joys of faculty participation in a Learning Community is the hard evidence of deep knowledge taking root. This can occur during a mixed panel group discussion when particularly perceptive comments about some aspect of the film or story occur. It is a time to feel proud of the student while simultaneously musing "I wish I had said that" or "How did I miss that before?" When the student puts it all together, not merely in the moment, but through an extended expression such as an insightful comparative paper at the end of the term, the Learning Community has reached its goal.

We have one such paper written by the redoubtable Harrison Sean Barrus, who was part of the linked Learning Community group combining Prof. Trish Joyce's Short Literature class and this author's Film as Literature cohort during 2011. Coming from the Film as Literature side, Mr. Barrus, nevertheless, compared Farley Mowat's "Walk Well, My Brother" and Charles Martin Smith's cinematic adaptation entitled *The Snow Walker*. By the time the reader has completed comparative essay, one will see how both courses impacted the conclusions he has reached in his paper.

Walking Together in Harmony: *The Snow Walker*, a Film Inspired by the Short Story "Walk Well, My Brother"

A great story may not necessarily translate well into an exceptional film adaptation. In the case of the movie *The Snow Walker*, inspired by the short story "Walk Well, My Brother" from legendary Canadian author Farley Mowat, filmmaker Charles Martin Smith has captured the majestic sweep of the Arctic tundra and its desolate beauty. The cinematic landscape, imbued with its singular beauty, flows from Mowat's text to Smith's frames. Seamlessly, what the reader imagines, the viewer witnesses on the screen.

The Arctic tundra of the Northwest Territories is an environment with such a profound and all-consuming presence that it in itself becomes a character in both the film *The Snow Walker* and the short story, "Walk Well, My Brother." The vast land is at once deceptively bland but deadly, yet it hides a mystical beauty with the promise of bounty and nourishment that can be found only when given the respect it is due.

Technically, Charlie (Halliday in the film, Lavery in the story) is of this environment by making his home in Yellowknife, the largest city of the Northwest Territories. However, his culture (Euro-Canadian) with its imagined superiority over this primordial wilderness sees it as a place to either tame or ignore. And the film, especially, shows the same attitude to the native peoples who inhabit it. His reliance on the machines and technology of "civilized man" and his misplaced pride in his own "advanced" skills are put into question by the crisis that drives the story and film's plot.

When his bush plane suddenly crashes hundreds of miles from any mapped settlement, Charlie initially is angered but not frightened. His confidence is based on his belonging to "the new elite who believed that any challenge, whether by man or nature, could be dealt with by good machines in the hands of skilled men" (Mowat 132). In the film, Charlie vainly attempts to repair a vacuum tube in the plane's radio to call for help. It is this knowledge of man-made contraptions and his damning pride in his own competencies that lead him to believe that he can best the silent strength of the boundless terrain. Instead of opening himself to the landscape spread before him and giving it the respect it is due, he sets out to impose his will upon the rugged vastness. As Charlie travels with only a vague idea of where he is headed, the character of the land begins to show itself.

Without truly seeing the trackless expanse as it is, Charlie does not comprehend the hazards and pitfalls that await him. The hidden mire and muck begin to take what little Charlie manages to find and bring with him. In addition, he is besieged relentlessly by indefatigable hordes of mosquitoes that weaken him physically and wreak havoc with his mental state. With his tools breaking and his advanced technology failing him, Charlie presses on, his confidence in his ultimate survival diminishing. After stripping him of the mechanical devices central to his supposed superiority, the land begins to take what little Charlie has left. The hidden rocks and uneven terrain, "a monochromatic wilderness of rock and tundra, snow and ice" (132), begin to consume Charlie's boots and eventually destroy his feet. No longer having a strong body to carry him, he staggers on, all but blinded by the bites of mosquitoes and flies. Now, Charlie, broken and on the verge of death, finally begins to understand the all-consuming trackless barrens surrounding him to the horizon and beyond.

Kanaalaq (Konala, in the story), the young Inuit accompanying Charlie on the plane, has been raised in the unforgiving environment of this Arctic Circle locale; thus, she understands the respect it is due. Her people have taken the time to truly see and appreciate everything the land can take away, yet also comprehend that it can provide for those who have humbled themselves before it. Where Charlie becomes lost in the sludge and slush, his feet never truly able to find purchase, Kanaalaq's footing is sure and steady as she navigates the obstacles of the terrain with ease.

When Charlie treks off for help—in the wrong direction it turns out—Kanaalaq, who has been left behind near the plane wreckage, makes do with her knowledge of the ways of the Arctic. After a few days, she realizes that Charlie is lost and leaves their "camp" to find him. After discovering Charlie unconscious and dying, Kanaalaq nurses him back to health from the natural resources around them. Mowat sets the scene simply yet poignantly as Kanaalaq "uses her curved knife to cut away the useless remnants of his leather boots, then wraps his torn and bloody feet in a compress of wet sphagnum moss" (139). She can see and take from the bounty of the land that is obscured from outsiders like Charlie. Kanaalaq finds food to fill their bellies and skins to clothe their bodies. Her respect for her homeland gives Kanaalaq a strength that Charlie could never hope to match. This devotion to her habitat has taught her compassion and respect for all things. That reverence leads not only to her ability to restore Charlie's health, but then to teach him the ways of the Arctic and "what had seemed to him a lifeless desert was in fact a land generous in its support of those who know its nature" (141).

As their travel together progresses, Kanaalaq's tubercular condition worsens. It is Charlie, armed with a newfound respect and understanding of the land, who begins to support Kanaalaq from what the tundra offers. It is at this point that Kanaalaq imparts upon Charlie the final lesson of the great white wilderness succinctly summed up as the story ends with a heartbreaking parting, "They are not very good boots but they might carry you to the camps of my people. They might help you return to your own land. . . . Walk well in them . . . my brother" (147).

The Arctic tundra is not just a place to walk through; it is a presence which is something so much more. The tundra is a spirit—it is a life giver—yet without due respect, it will rise up to claim the lives of those who seek to traverse it. It is a home and hearth that can give joy and nourishment, yet it is also a place where the dead can go to be at peace.

Through *The Snow Walker* and "Walk Well, My Brother," we see how a place can become something more. A place can become a character in itself, a character with demands and desires which can also give strength and support. By the end, we can also come to see the character of the places which surround them and as both the film and the short story so ably illustrate, teach ourselves to "walk well . . . my brother."

As can be expected, the film puts in clear vision what the mind imagines and after the plane crash, the movie depicts faithfully and most dramatically what is described in print. The main difference between the two would be the opening scenes in Yellowknife and the liberties the film takes with fostering a socio-historical context to the story. The characters that the motion picture creates help establish the typical mindset of the white Canadians in that part of the country: their imagined superiority to the "first peoples," their overconfidence on mid-twentieth century machines and technology, and their ignorance and disrespect for the limitlessness of territory that surrounds their "civilized" enclave. The sinister character of Pierson especially expresses the bigotry and cynicism of such people to an extreme.

Pictorially, the scenes from the bush plane of the tundra below are awe-inspiring. From ground level, the panoramic sweep of the camera shows how daunting the land can appear to the uninitiated. What seems desolate and depressing, just 100 steps later can appear hauntingly beautiful and even reassuring. Such is the magic of the land and the cinematic high technology that brings these images to us. The special effects created for the insect onslaught of Halliday cannot be forgotten as the hellish experience it was meant to depict. The viewer felt his pain from countless stings inflicted all over his body, his extreme frustration in being unable to combat his attackers, and the utter hopelessness of his ever emerging from the situation.

Annabella Piugattuk and Barry Pepper in Charles Martin Smith's The Snow Walker *(2004). Lions Gate Films.* Courtesy of Everett Collection.

This paper by Harrison Barrus, a class member of the "From Text to Screen" Learning Community, embodies the LC's essential learning outcomes to:

- Identify dimensions of the human condition, in particular, approaches to problem-solving
- Analyze the impact of misunderstandings, assumptions, and missed opportunities on causal relationships
- Delineate character development and transformation

It is clear from Barrus' comparative analysis, that he experienced both the power of the text and the sweep of the film. Admittedly, Harrison's work might be an exceptional example; yet the effect on each student experiencing this shared community of interest, preparation, and outcome is not overstated. These distinct media, woven together, allow the LC students to perceive and comprehend far more than either class could, singly, with only one medium. Thus, the LC model in this instance allows students to deepen their understanding and see the aesthetic forms in a new light. The difference between Film as Literature as a stand-alone class and Film as Literature in a Learning Community is that the greater student diversity (in numbers alone and other factors) allows for multiple perspectives on historical, social, economic, cultural, and local-to-global issues.

For the collaborating faculty involved, this result was synergistic and enlightening as well. Speaking of collaboration, I would like to thank Professor Trish Joyce for co-authoring this section of my book.

INDEX

Shang

13
3
30
33

29
32

Abbot

32
29
13
3

attack